The south side of Tiverton Church

THE OLD
PARISH CHURCHES
OF DEVON

Mike Salter

FOLLY PUBLICATIONS

ACKNOWLEDGEMENTS

The photographs and plans in the this book are the product of fieldwork by the author between 1971 and 1999. The author also drew the map and the sketches. The old prints, postcards and brass rubbings are reproduced from originals in his collection. The author would like to thank Lorna Harrison, Andrea Kirkby and John Lowe for their assistance during the the fieldwork and completion of this book.

ABOUT THIS BOOK

As with the other church books in this series (see full list inside back cover) this book concentrates on the period before the Industrial Revolution of the late 18th century necessitated the construction of a fresh series of churches to serve new urban areas. Most furnishings and monuments after 1800 are not mentioned, although additions and alterations to older churches usually are. Churches founded after 1800 are not mentioned in the gazetteer nor do they appear on the map, but are listed at the back.

The book is inevitably very much a catalogue of dates and names, etc. It is intended as a field guide and for reference rather than to be read from cover to cover. Occasionally there are comments about the settings of churches but on the whole lack of space permits few comments about their position or atmosphere. In some cases the most interesting features of a church or graveyard may lie outside the scope of this book as outlined above. The gazetteer features Ordnance Survey grid references (these are the two letters and six digits which appear after each place-name and dedication) and is intended to be used in conjunction with O.S. 1:50,000 scale maps. These are vital for finding buildings in cities or in remote locations.

Plans redrawn from originals in the author's field notes are reproduced to a common scale of 1:400. The buildings were measured in metres and only metric scales are given. For those who feel a need to convert three metres is roughly equal to ten feet. A system of hatching common to all the church plans in the books in this series is used to denote the different periods of work. On some pages there may be insufficient space for a key to the hatching to be shown. Where this is the case refer to another page. The plans should be treated with caution. Some features are difficult to convey on small scale drawings, such as stones of one period being reused in a later period, sometimes in a different location. As is explained in the introduction parts of some buildings are difficult to date so an element of guesswork has been required in these cases. This book contains proportionately less plans to gazetteer entries than in most of the other churches books in the series. As explained on page 9, there is less variety in the planning of parish churches in Devon than in other parts of England, and it was not considered necessary to give a large number of plans of entirely 15th and 16th century churches with very similar layouts.

ABOUT THE AUTHOR

Mike Salter is 46 and has been a professional author-publisher since he went on the Government Enterprise Allowance Scheme for unemployed people in 1988. He is particularly interested in the planning and layout of medieval buildings and has a huge collected of plans of churches and castles he has measured during tours (mostly by bicycle and motorcycle) of all parts of the British Isles since 1968. Wolverhampton born and bred, Mike now lives in an old cottage beside the Malvern Hills. His other interests include walking, maps, railways, board games, morris dancing, playing percussion instruments and calling folk dances with a ceilidh band.

Copyright 1999 by Mike Salter. First published December 1999.
Folly Publications, Folly Cottage, 151 West Malvern Rd, Malvern, Worcs WR14 4AY
Printed by Aspect Design, 89 Newtown Rd, Worccestershire WR14 2PD

Combeinteignhead Church

CONTENTS

Inside the front cover is a map of churches in the gazetteer.

INTRODUCTION

Relics of the Saxon period amongst the parish churches of Devon are very few. There is a small crypt at Sidbury which was probably a mausoleum, but other structural remains are almost non-existent apart from one or two buildings with long and short work probably of the period just before the Norman Conquest of 1066. There are, however, several inscribed stones of the 6th and 7th centuries with names usually in Latin but occasionally in Ogham script. Dedications to Celtic missionaries of this period such as Brannock, Nectan and Petrock are quite common in Devon and give evidence of numerous and widespread ecclesiastical centres by that time, although the churches were probably single-cell drystone huts or timber-framed structures, neither destined for long lives. Of the 9th and 10th centuries are a number of cross-shafts, the best of them at Colyton, Copplestone, Colebrooke, and Exeter St Nicholas, whilst at Dolton two pieces have been converted into a font. Excavations at Exeter have revealed footings of the apsed 11th century minster church which preceded the Norman cathedral.

The system of parishes as we know it today evolved during the 11th and 12th centuries. Almost all of the churches which existed before the 19th century in Devon were founded before the end of the 13th century and the majority must have been founded by year 1200. Although parish churches which are essentially still in their 12th century form are rare in Devon, nearly half of them have some relic of that period. In about a hundred cases a font has survived all the remodelling and enlargement of the original building in the 15th and 16th century. Doorways sometimes remain also, usually on the south side of the nave, commonly with chevrons on the arch and sometimes with a carved tympanum within the arch. Often they have been reset in the outer wall of an added aisle since although the style they represented was out of fashion cut stone was expensive and they were simply too good to throw away. Examples are of Norman doorways in Devon parish churches are at Axminster, Bishopsteignton, Buckland Brewer, Down St Mary, Paignton, Shebbear, and West Woolfardisworthy.

Capitals at Bishopsteignton

Beakheads at Shebbear

Tympanum at Down St Mary

Crediton Church

Some 11th and 12th century churches were single chambers but most were two-celled with a nave for the congregation and a smaller and lower east chancel to contain the altar, with a round arch between the two. Some chancels may have been apsed (round ended), but the surviving examples in Devon are square ended. The main doorway lay in the nave south wall but often there was a second doorway on the north side and there might be a tiny priest's doorway on the south side of the chancel. On each side of each part of the building would be one or two small round-headed windows with deep internal embrasures. These dimly-lit churches lacked furnishings as the congregation stood whilst the priest conducted short services (without the lengthy sermons of later years) in Latin.

As congregations grew so the churches were enlarged by additions or rebuilt on a larger scale. Norman aisles are not common in Devon and are represented mostly by arcades of round arches still remaining after the aisle itself has been enlarged or rebuilt in later centuries. With the main doorway being on the south the obvious place for an added aisle was on the north, as at Farway, Hawkchurch, Salcombe Regis and Sidbury. St Mary Arches at Exeter is the only parish church in Devon with evidence of two aisles before the end of the 12th century.

Tower at Chudleigh

Fremington Church

An alternative way of enlarging a church was to add cross-arms or transepts. In some cases these were only just big enough to contain secondary altars but others could have accommodated part of the congregation. In later years transepts were used to accommodate the owner of the local manor house and his family and servants but it is uncertain whether this was normal in the 12th and 13th centuries. Some churches may have been cruciform as first built but in the majority of cases transepts were added later, often coeval with a larger new chancel. Unfortunately both documentary and structural dating evidence for early transepts in Devon is minimal. Few have any features earlier than the 14th century, but the probability is that most transepts are 13th century, whilst a few could be late 12th century.

As first built Norman churches usually had a single bell in a bellcote set on the west gable of the nave. Gradually towers began to replace bellcotes. As with transepts early towers are difficult to date accurately. Although a 12th century date is claimed for quite a few of them, and especially for many of the 19 towers in Devon which are not at the west end of the nave but in a transeptal position on the north or south side, hardly any have features which can be positively identified as Norman. Again the majority are probably of the 13th century and several have the tall thin lancet windows then in fashion. Only Sidbury has a tower with the sort of features such as pilaster buttresses and twin-arched belfry windows proclaiming without any doubt a 12th century date. This west tower has the quite exceptional feature of a rib-vault at ground level. By the late 13th century we find parapets on corbel tables and the first use of the diagonal corner buttresses common on 14th and 15th century towers. Colyton and Crediton are instances of cruciform churches with central towers of 12th century origin. Rebuilding has seen the replacement of the other early parts of these buildings except for the chancel at Colyton and one transept at Crediton. Central towers of the 13th century exist at Aveton Gifford, Axminster, and Kingsbridge, and of the 14th century at Shute and Tawstock, the last probably a remodelling of a 12th century layout. Branscombe is unique in Devon as having a central tower built without transepts, and when such were added in the 13th century they were placed further west so they open off the nave rather than from the tower.

Transepts and towers of the 13th century in Devon parish churches have already been mentioned as additions to older churches. Over 70 churches have work likely to be of this period but in most cases it is minor and not certainly dated unless original windows remain. The best work now remaining is at Aveton Gifford, Branscombe, Haccombe and Sampford Peverel. It is common for the eastern part of an early chancel to have survived after the rest has been replaced by later extensions. After 1200 the pointed arch was in vogue, giving rise to the long thin pointed-headed windows called lancets. Later in the century they were placed together in pairs, and then with the piercing of the spandrel between the heads with a circle we have the earliest form of tracery, known as plate-tracery, although unrestored examples are rare. Single lancets survive here and there but in Devon there is not even a chancel with a full unrestored set of them, let alone a whole church. Aisles of this period are not common in Devon parish churches. Arcades with double-chamfered arches on octagonal piers appear in the 13th century but as this type was still being built in the 16th century they can be difficult to date unless the pier capitals or bases or the features of the aisle as a whole give a clue to the date or erection.

Work of the 14th century in the parish churches of Devon is common but as with 12th and 14th century work most of it is odd fragments rather than anything like a complete church. Many west towers are likely to be of this period, although a lot of them lack unrestored features allowing a safe dating. In particular there are a small number of spires, notably those at Barnstaple and Ermington. Chancels are more easily dated since the form of sedilia and piscinae gives a good clue even if the windows have been replaced. In transepts piscinae and recesses for the tombs of patrons sometimes suggest a 14th century date. Windows with Y-tracery occur from the 1290s onwards. The ogival arch comes into fashion c1310-20 and is used in the net-like form of tracery known as reticulation. The more complex geometrical patterns of tracery and the forms using floral and star shapes found elsewhere in parish churches are rare in Devon, although there are examples of interest at Bampton, Bere Ferrers and Exbourne. Indeed, the largest building of this period, the collegiate church at Ottery St Mary, which is aisled throughout both the nave and chancel with a Lady chapel at the east end and a pair of transeptal towers, has side windows which are no more advanced than pairs of lancets, then almost a century out of fashion.

Bere Ferrers: window

Cookbury: window

East end of Sampford Peverell c1260

Window at Tawstock

Roof at Cullompton   *Window at Bridstow*

By the late 14th century we have the beginnings of the style of church building that takes us through to the end of the medieval period and well into the 16th century. Instead of having the nave and chancel as separate chambers divided by a stone arch there arose a fashion for building them as a single chamber undivided except by a timber screen. On one or both sides would be an aisle running the full length of the main chamber, and almost all the medieval churches in Devon have at least one aisle of this period. The wealth generated by the cloth trade permitted extensive alterations or a complete rebuilding of almost every church in Devon. Quite often the side facing the approach (more commonly the south side since that was favoured for the main entrance) was rebuilt during this period, whilst the other side retains older masonry, commonly with a transept. The contrast between late medieval work often faced with granite or sandstone ashlar blocks and older walls of rough rubble can be quite dramatic. Clerestories are rare in Devon, occurring only at Crediton, Cullompton, Culmstock, North Molton, Ottery St Mary and Tiverton. In a fully aisled church the three parts would be the same height, covered with wagon roofs with or without ceilings and carved bosses, and having windows of three or four lights in the side-walls but larger, higher windows in the end walls. Sometimes the part of the roof above the screen is a celure with boarding and cross-ribs. The parts of aisles east of the screen were used as chapels containing secondary altars and the tombs of high-ranking patrons. At Combe Martin, Ashburton, South Brent, and a number of other churches in the South Hams district new transepts were erected outside the aisles, accommodating more altars and funerary monuments.

Whilst documentary evidence for dates of construction is rarely available for village churches, rather more exists from the 15th and 16th centuries for the town churches. Where no documents exist heraldry, personal emblems and occasional inscriptions on pier capitals, stained glass, and on associated furnishings such as screens often give clues to the dates of campaigns of work at many places. Particularly fine early 16th century examples of this are the Greenway aisle at Tiverton, the Lane aisle at Cullompton, and the Dorset aisle at Ottery St Mary, all of them richly embellished outer south aisles, the first two built by wealthy merchants.

South Zeal Chapel

St Michael's Chapel, Torquay

Late medieval churches in Devon are much more standardised than in other parts of England, resulting in dozens of churches of basically similar appearance and plan form. However, it is notable that churches with the same plan can vary considerably in size. Features such as tall thin piers, high tower arches and clear glass in the windows can make churches of modest size seem deceptively spacious. The plans in this book illustrate the different sizes and the several standard layouts that occur. The others show some of more of Devon's interesting and unusual churches mostly with work from several periods, rather than presenting numerous plans of mostly late medieval buildings with little variation in layout.

A common form of pier in late medieval Devon has shafts facing the cardinal points and a concave curve in between. Sometimes there are just capitals on the shafts. Granite piers are often monoliths. An alternative form has a wave moulding between the shafts and at Bradninch, Broadhembury and Woodbury several wave mouldings are combined to give the impression of a clustered pier. Capitals with leaves running horizontally are common in Devon. By the 15th century concave and convex curves tend the replace the simple chamfers of 13th and 14th century arches. After the mid 15th century the arches are more likely to take an almost semi-circular form. Some examples have very flat four-centred arcade arches.

Broadhempston Church

Late medieval towers are very common. Many, particularly those of granite, are unbuttressed. When buttresses do occur they are either set diagonally on in pairs slightly set back from the corners, a style peculiar to the south-west of England from the end of the 14th century until the early 17th century. At first such towers were intended to have spires as at South Molton, now destroyed, but the alternative of corner pinnacles soon became the norm. To the west and NW of Dartmoor these pinnacles are large, octagonal, castellated and crocketed as at Buckland Monachorum, Sheepstor, Tavistock, and Walkhampton. Late medieval towers lie at the west end and can be of great height, linking a desire for show with the necessity of being visible and the bells being audible from afar in a deeply incised landscape. Amongst the tallest are those at Chittlehampton, Hartland and South Molton. Few of them are more than 6.5m square externally, excluding the buttresses, making then look very slender. Brixham is an exception, being much broader than that. Another exception worth noting is the octagonal lantern top at Colyton.

In Devon tower staircases are not often accommodated in the thickness of the walls as they are in Cornwall. Most towers have a projection to contain the stair and commonly this is a turret rising above the main roof. A group of churches south of Dartmoor have polygonal turret set in the middle of whichever side was regarded as the show front. The design seems to have originated at Ashburton (where the turret faces north) and in 1449 was chosen as the model for a tower to be built at Totnes. The tower built there has the turret facing south and has image niches.

Late medieval window tracery in Devon parish churches tends to be minimal, especially in the north and south walls. Windows made of granite rarely have cusping of the lights. Four-centred heads were used initially but especially in the 16th century square heads were increasingly used. The only really big spectacular window is one at Colyton with a doorway incorporated into the design. Of the early 15th century are windows at Atherington, Monkleigh and Weare Giffard with intersecting round-headed arches. At Ipplepen, Plympton, Sherford and Staverton a star shape is incorporated into the design, something normally associated with the early 14th century, but in these instances clearly datable to the early or mid 15th century.

Easter Sepulchre at Throwleigh

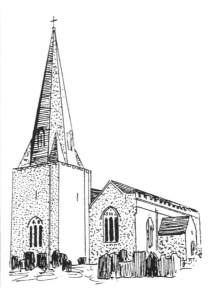

King's Nympton Church

Tower at Lydford   *Tower at Dartington*   *Tower at Winkleigh*

Nearly every church has at least one stone-built porch, usually on the south. A few pre-date 1400, and some of those have resulted in instances of a later aisle on that side being shorter than the aisle on the other side, as at Ermington, but the vast majority are 15th or 16th century and many project in front of an aisle then added. Some porches have upper rooms reached by staircases in polygonal turrets. Those at Brixham and Plympton have liorno-vaults, that at Berry Pomeroy has a tierceron-vault and Holcombe Rogus and Torbryan have fan-vaults. Vaulting in the other parts of churches is rare, although there are fan-vaults over the 16th century outer aisles at Cullompton, Ottery St Mary and Tiverton, and at Buckland Monachorum is a rib-vault of c1600 probably using older material from the nearby Buckland Abbey.

Work on churches between 1600 and the 1820s was mostly confined to minor repairs and the replacement or addition of the odd tower, porch or chapel. Complete churches of this period are mostly found in towns: the large Charles Church of the 1650s in a slightly debased version of the late medieval style at Plymouth, the rebuilding of St Thomas and St Stephen at Exeter in the same period and style, the fine classical style St George of the 1720s at Tiverton and the rebuilding of Stoke Damerell in c1750. A new church was built to serve Devonport docks in the 1770s and of the same period is the small cruciform village church of Teigngrace.

In Devon there are about 100 churches which are 19th or 20th century foundations to serve new suburbs (a fifth of these are in and around Plymouth), and there are a dozen or so instances of where a medieval church has been so completely that no relic of its structure, furnishings or monuments earlier than 1800 now remains on site. Many other churches have suffered such heavy restoration that they have lost much of their medieval character or furnishings, but overall a huge legacy of interesting featurest, particularly 15th and 16th century woodwork, still remains.

Font at Combeinteignhead

Screen at Totnes Church

Font at Dodbrooke

A custom gradually arose of closing off the chancels of churches by a screen with a rood or image of the crucifixion fixed over it. Totnes has a mid 15th century stone screen and amongst a few others one of the early 16th century at Colyton is of note. However the vast majority of the screens in Devon are of wood, date from the period 1450-1560 (those at Bovey Tracey, Halberton, Uffcolme and Welcombe are probably earlier), and most had above them a loft for the use of musicians. Few lofts remain, although stone access stairs in the outer walls are very common, but about a hundred screens remain, making Devon an important county for this particular aspect of church furnishings. Most screens in Devon not only close off the chancel but extend right across the church to close off the aisles east ends as chapels. At Bradninch, Broadhempston, Dunchideock, Harberton, Kenn and Torbryan piers are encased by the screens, whilst at Swimbridge openings are left for altars against the piers. In Devon screens usually have a ribbed coving over arches filled with tracery. Above is a cornice with friezes of foliage, sometimes with birds and human figures within it. The appearance on the coving of medallions, putti and arabesques heralds Italian influence, i.e. the Renaissance, and suggests a date of c1520-40, as at Atherington, Lapford, Morchard Bishop, Warkleigh and Willand. Yet Devon could often be behind the times and a screen of 1547 at East Allington shows no sign of such features.

A small group of screens at St Saviour at Dartmouth, East Portlemouth, Rattery, Sherford, and South Pool have semi-circular heads to the main lights, each pair being linked by a crocketed ogival gable. The earliest of these must surely be the Dartmouth example of the 1490s. The wainscots of screens sometimes have tracery but about forty in South Devon have painted figures of apostles and prophets, or scenes of the life of the Virgin. Renaissance ornamentation here and there confirms these as early to mid 16th century, although the woodwork may be slightly older.

Bench end at Down St Mary

Capital, Stokeinteignhead

Pulpit at Dartmouth

Elizabethan and Jacobean pulpits are common, often with round arches and pilasters, whilst 18th century examples tend to be plain. There are quite a number of late medieval pulpits of stone with figures under projecting canopies or between thickly foliated buttresses as at Chittlehampton and Swimbridge, or within thickly foliated frames as at Dartmouth, Dartington, Dittisham, Harberton and Torbryan. Pilton has an example of a type of late medieval pulpit common throughout England.

Devon churches are noted for their collections of carved bench ends with rectangular tops, the poppy-heads found elsewhere in England only occur at Ilsington. With extended services and a fashion for long sermons in English benches became increasingly important during the 16th century, the need for them being unaffected by the Reformation. Few predate 1500 and many are obviously of the mid to late 16th century, having Renaissance motifs such as heads in roundels. Inscribed dates are quite common and heraldry also often helps with dating them. Examples in South Devon often have just two tiers of tracery and these may be earlier.

Font at Harburton   *Font at Ashton*

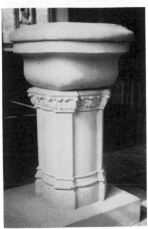

Font at St Mary Steps, Exeter   *Font at Awliscombe*   *Font at Cruwys Morchard*

Late medieval fonts with octagonal bowls adorned with quatrefoils or shields are common and there are several 17th century fonts. Examples from the 13th and 14th centuries are uncommon but there are over 100 Norman fonts varying from simple egg-cup shaped bowls without adornment to circular tubs with palmettes, cable mouldings and chevrons, and square bowls with scallops underneath, and others with faces at the corners and rosettes in circles, trees of life and other motifs on the sides as at Ashwater and Bratton Clovelly. Luppit has a very fine example with decoration on the base as well. Stoke Canon has a font with humans on the corners crouching downwards and caryatid figures on the corner shafts. A common type is a square table top of Purbeck marble with friezes of plain round arches shallowly sunk in.

Haccombe has an interesting range of medieval tiles. Many North Devon churches have embossed tiles of a medieval type but probably of 17th century date made in Barnstaple. Ottery St Mary has an early clock and St Saviour at Dartmouth has a medieval door with fine ironwork. Doddiscombsleigh has a complete aisle of medieval stained glass but only fragments, shields and single figures remain elsewhere.

Medieval effigies carved in stone are not common amongst the parish churches of Devon. There are about twenty single figures or couples from each of the 14th and 15th centuries and and a smaller number of 13th century single figures. Exeter Cathedral has a rich collection of effigies but these do not concern us here. Haccombe has several early effigies still with remains of original paint, Ottery St Mary has two good mid 14th century tombs with effigies, and there are others of note at Atherington, Axminster, Bere Ferrers, Littlehempston and Membury. In the 15th century tomb chests are often set in finely carved niches or under an elaborate canopy set below the arches of an arcade. The effigies of the Kirkham Chantry at Paignton are closed off by stone screens. There are also about a dozen pre-Reformation brasses with the figures engraved and generally cut out and set into an indent either on a tomb chest or on the floor. Whilst the stone effigies tend to be knights and their ladies and ecclesiastics, the brasses include merchants in civilian dress, Stoke Fleming having a fine early example of the 1390s. Medieval incised slabs with effigies are rare in Devon although there is a good early example at Mortehoe with tracery patterns around the figure. There are also a number of slabs with either a plain or floriated cross left in light relief or incised. Sometimes these have an inscription around the edge. Those without can be hard to assign a date to.

Brass at Stoke Fleming

Effigy at Bere Ferrers

Monuments at Crediton Church

The early 16th century saw a fashion for tomb chests set in recesses in the north walls of chancels. They have no effigies other than occasional brasses set on the chest or on the back wall of the recess, allowing these tombs to be used as Easter Sepulchres. Examples are at Bishops's Nympton, Bondleigh, Heanton Punchendon, Holcombe Burnell, South Pool, Throwleigh, West Alvington, and Woodleigh. Brasses of the 16th century number about twenty and tend to have smaller figures in a rectangular plate. Brasses of this period and the early 17th century commonly show a couple kneeling towards each other, sometimes with prayer desks, with numerous kneeling children either below or beyond the main figures. Some late 16th century and early 17th century stone monuments in the form of wall tablets have a similar layout and a monument at Musbury has three generations of couples of almost life-size figures set one behind the other. In total there are about forty stone monuments of the 16th century, whilst there are nearly two hundred of the 17th century. The earliest tomb chest with Renaissance details is one of the 1520s adorned with wreaths at Bere Ferrers. Many tombs mix late medieval and classical motifs freely. Devon tended to be a conservative backwater and there is a tomb chest of c1580 at Tiverton still medieval in style. The earliest example of a common type of imposing monument with columns and a coffered vault over the tomb is one of c1590 at Tawstock. There are 17th century examples at Cadeleigh, Colyton, Marystow and Wembury. At Crediton, Holcombe Rogus, Tavistock and Torquay are more modest monuments of this type with the vault reduced to an arch set upon pilasters.

In the 17th century effigies are sometimes shown reclining rather than recumbent. There are standing figures at Tamerton Foliot, Eggesford, Newton St Cyres, Ottery St Mary and Tawstock, the first of these being clothed in a burial shroud. Busts either on pedestals or in medallions are also common. Gradually, however, the emphasis on effigies decreased and the most common form of monument in the 18th century is a tablet with a lengthy inscription. Often there is an architectural surround, and there may be urns, cherubs, or symbols of death or of a profession or a claim to fame.

Altar-tomb at Ermington   *Tomb at Totnes*

FURTHER READING

Devon, Buildings of England series, Bridget Cherry & Nikolaus Pevsner, 1989.
Around the churches of Exeter, Walter Jacobson, 1998
The Churches of Devon, J.M.Slader, 1968.
Ecclesiastical Antiquities of Devon (3 vols), G.Oliver, 1840-2.
Picturesque Sketches of the Churches of Devon, W.Spreat, 1832.
Some Old Devon Churches (3 vols), J.Stabb, 1909-16.
Rood Screens and Rood Lofts, vol 2, F.Bligh Bond & F.Camm, 1909.
The Ancient Sepulchral Effigies of Devon, W.H.H.Rogers, 1877.
The Victoria County History of Devon.
Transactions of the Devonshire Association.
Proceedings of the Devon Archaelogical Society.
Devon & Cornwall Notes and Queries.
See also articles in The Archelological Journal and Archeologia.
Many churches, too numerous to be listed here, have pamphlets available.

GAZETTEER OF PARISH CHURCHES IN DEVON

ABBOTS BICKINGTON   *St James*   SS 385134

This is one of the smallest churches in Devon, a chamber just 11.6m long by 3.2m wide with a south transept, a tiny west tower and a north porch. The earliest features are 14th century, but three windows are Victorian and the joint in the north wall suggests the chancel with its trefoiled pointed north lancet is an addition to a 12th or 13th century nave. There is old glass in the east window. That end has old tiles made at Barnstaple and a diagonally-placed monument to Thomas Pollard, d1710.

ABBOTSHAM   *St Helen*   SS 424265

This is a 13th century church comprised of a nave with one north lancet, a narrower and lower chancel with one south lancet and triple Victorian east lancets, a south transept with Victorian south and west windows, and a north transeptal tower with low buttresses slightly set back from the corners. There are plain mullioned windows high over the chancel arch. The 16th century bench ends show the Crucifixion, Christ carrying the cross, saints, a tumbler, a kneeling figure, tracery, medallions, and leaves. Slightly earlier are the wagon roofs, that over the nave having moulded ribs and angels with shields, whilst that over the chancel has large bosses. The round Norman font has a fluted bowl and a cable moulding round the waist. There is a monument with Corinthian columns and putti to John Willett, d1736.

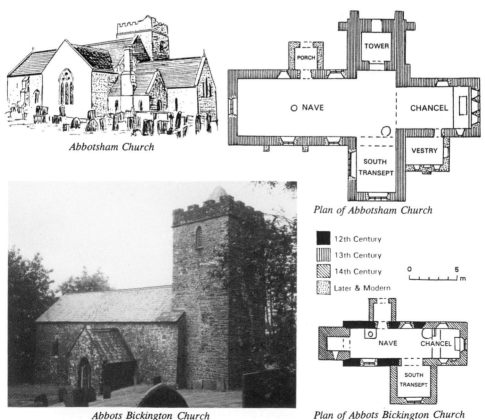

Abbotsham Church

Plan of Abbotsham Church

■ 12th Century
▥ 13th Century
▧ 14th Century
▨ Later & Modern

0   5
⌐—┴—┴—┴—┴—┐ m

Abbots Bickington Church

Plan of Abbots Bickington Church

ABBOTSKERSWELL   *St Mary*   SX 856687

The chancel has one 13th century north lancet. Of the 15th century are the north aisle with a leaf frieze on the arcade capitals, and the diagonally buttressed west tower with a stair-turret in the middle of one side. The lower parts of the screen are old and there is an old parclose screen. There is a large but fragmentary statue thought to be of the Virgin and Child.

ALPHINGTON   *St Michael*   SX 918899

This red sandstone church is mostly 15th century but was restored in 1876 by Hayward and Son, when the east end was lengthened, widening the fifth bay of the arcades and adding a sixth bay. The piers have four major shafts, four minor shafts and deep hollows in between, and there are shield-holding angels. The arms of the Courtenays of Powderham appear on the two storey north porch with a niche over the outer entrance. The diagonally buttressed west tower has pinnacles and a higher NE stair-turret. The circular Norman font has a band of scroll roundels carved with St Michael, a dragon, and an archer above a set of intersecting arches. The screen has painted wainscot panels of c1520, and there is a restored parclose screen.

ALVERDISCOTT   *All Saints*   SS 520252

The west tower has small pinnacles and a high SE stair-turret. The south doorway looks Norman although only the imposts seem unrestored. Certainly Norman is the block-capital shaped font carved with a small rosette, a fleur-de-lys, and other motifs. The north aisle is of 1579 but the north arcade is early 19th century with a straight timber entablature instead of arches. There are late medieval tiles in the porch and the pulpit contains 16th century panels. There is an effigy on a tomb chest of the ten-year-old Thomas Welshe, d1639.

ALWINGTON   *St Andrew*   SS 405232

The church lies alone except for a farm. It has a tall west tower with set-back buttresses, gargoyles and large pinnacles. The north side has a transept possibly of early date. The south aisle has late 16th century ashlar work with plain mullioned windows of three lights and an arcade of granite monolith piers with capitals only on the shafts. At the east end of the aisle is a family pew with Jacobean carving brought over from the hall at Portledge. The pulpit has Renaissance medallions and the Coffin arms and was made up in 1792 from bench ends and wall-plates from the wagon-roofs. The reredos was created from bench ends from Parkham church in 1806. The octagonal granite font has elementary patterns. The bench ends are carved with motifs such as tracery, Renaissance heads and monsters and one is dated 1580. The monument with half-figures of Richard Coffin, d1617, and his wife was not erected until 1651. There are also tablets to the Morrisons of Yeo Vale.

Alwington Church

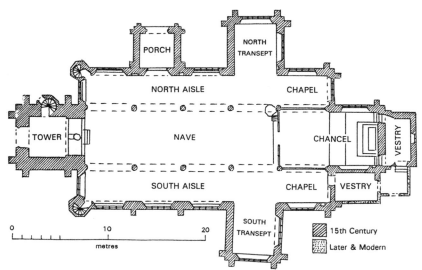

Plan of Ashburton Church

ARLINGTON   *St James*   SS 613406

The church lies in the landscaped grounds of the house and was rebuilt in 1846 by R.D.Gould. The west tower survived until a faithful copy was built in 1899. The many monuments include a worn 14th century effigy of a lady, and memorials to Gascoigne Canham, d1667, Edward Bampfield, 1720, John Meadows, d1791, and Mary Ann Chichester, d1791, plus several 19th century Chichesters.

ASHBURTON   *St Andrew*   SX 755698

The church is entirely 15th century, only the choir vestry being later. It has arcades of five wide bays of double-chamfered arches on tall octagonal piers with concave sides. One pier on the south side is a monolith. The western corners of the aisles have polygonal stair turrets. Set-back buttresses occur on the west tower, the north porch, the north and south transepts projecting from the fourth bay, the eastern corners of the chancel chapels occupying the fifth bay and the chancel, east of which lies a low vestry, the only part not embattled. Originally there was a south porch also. The windows are mostly of four lights but are of five lights in the transept end walls. The letter L appearing on the south aisle ceiling is thought to refer to Bishop Lacy (1420-56). Both transepts and both chancel chapels have re-used trefoil-headed piscinae from the preceding church, which was probably cruciform and of some size. The tower has a polygonal stair-turret in the middle of the north side and is 28m high. It must have existed by 1449 when it was chosen as the prototype for the tower at Totnes. Two fine 18th century candelabra are the only pre-Victorian furnishings.

ASHBURTON   *St Lawrence*   SX 756699

In St Lawrence's Lane is a early 16th century tower with set-back buttresses from a chapel given to the town in 1314 by Bishop Stapleton to accommodate a new guild. The body of the church was rebuilt c1700 as a schoolroom-cum-courtroom and was extended at the east end in 1911.

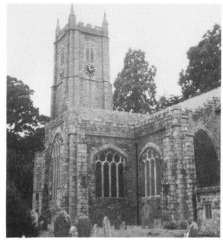

Ashcombe Church

Ashburton Church

ASHBURY *St Mary* SX 508980

Except for the diagonally buttressed west tower the church was rebuilt by J.F.Gould in 1871-3 for Henry Woollcombe, Archdeacon of Barnstaple, using some of the old materials. Declared redundant in 1977, it has been preserved by the Woollcombes.

ASHCOMBE *St Nectan* SX 912796

The dedication is rare but also occurs at Hartland and in Cornwall. Much of the cruciform church consecrated in 1259 remains, with lancets preserved in the chancel and south transept. The tapering west tower is perhaps 14th century and the north aisle with a three bay arcade and the arch into the south transept are 15th century. Except for the tower all the parts now have windows and set-back buttresses of the 1820s and also of the period are the SW porch and the panelling flanking the tower arch. The east window contains some old glass and there are old bench ends.

ASHFORD *St Peter* SS 534354

The 13th century north tower has a spire of the 1790s. The rest was rebuilt by R.D.Gould in 1864 but the chancel may retain 13th or 14th century masonry, old bench ends survive in the pulpit, and in the vestry there is Elizabethan panelling in some bench ends and a small damaged 14th century relief showing St John.

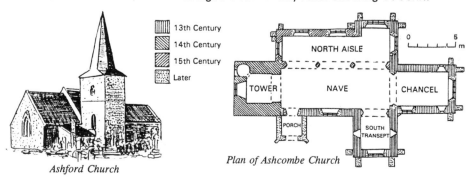

	13th Century
	14th Century
	15th Century
	Later

Ashford Church

Plan of Ashcombe Church

ASHPRINGTON   *St David*   SX 808572

The tall slim tower with a low NE stair-turret is probably 14th century. The aisles are both embattled and have arcades with tall piers but all the windows are of 1845. There is a rood-loft stair-turret on the north side and a porch which has lost its upper floor on the south. The nave and chancel have ceiled wagon roofs. There is an old screen with painted saints on the wainscoting, and there is a circular Norman font with a palmette frieze and a strip of cable moulding. The memorials include a brass with an inscription and shields to William Sumaster, d1589, tablets to Sir John Kelland of Painsford, d1679, and Henry Blackhaller of Sharpham, d1684, plus a standing figure bent over an urn to Jane Pownall of Sharpham, d1778.

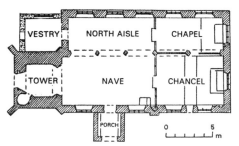

Plan of Ashton Church

15th Century

Later & Modern

Ashreigny Church

Arcade in Ashton Church

Screen wainscot panel at Ashton

ASHREIGNY   *St James*   SS 629136

The north transeptal tower has set-back buttresses. The four bay south arcade has piers with capitals on the main shafts only. The capitals are octagonal with concave sides. The inner south doorway has an outer moulding on angel corbels. Above this doorway inside are Royal Arms of Queen Anne dated 1713. There are wagon roofs in both nave and aisle, those of the aisle with angel corbels. During the restoration by Samuel Hooper in 1889 the west end was rebuilt, the east end given a new window and buttresses, the windows are renewed and new arches provided to divide off the chancel and the east end of the aisle as a south chapel.

Ashton Church

ASHTON   *St Michael*   SX 856846

Except for a modern NW vestry, the church is all late-medieval and has a nave and chancel divided only by a screen which extends also across a north aisle with a fine bay arcade and renewed three-light windows. There is a west tower with diagonal buttresses, a west doorway with quatrefoils in the spandrels, obelisk pinnacles and a multi-shafted tower arch built of huge sections of granite. The south side has a porch, a projection for the rood-loft staircase and a priest's doorway. The arcade of five bays has piers of an unusually complex section, and there are unceiled wagon roofs. The screen wainscoting has thirty-two painted figures of saints and doctors of the church. Further figures appear on the back and on the parclose screen of the north chapel. The chapel also has a wall painting of Christ with the Emblems of the Passion and stained glass with the arms of the Chudleigh family and bishops Lacy (1422-55) and Courtenay (1478-86). The bench ends have two-tier tracery and there is an original studded south door. Above it are Royal Arms of George II dated 1735. The monuments include a medieval Purbeck marble slab with a cross, a brass to William Honnywell showing bones and a skull, and a painted monument to George Chudleigh, d1657 with heraldry and death symbols but no effigy.

ASHWATER   *St Peter*   SX 387953

The oldest parts are Norman, a head over the priest's doorway and the font with corner faces, tendrils, scrolls and on the west a running animal in a frame with two symmetrical animal heads. By the late 13th century the church seems to have been cruciform with an unusually wide nave. The wide south aisle has a six bay arcade with piers alternately octagonal and of a variety of the usual late medieval type with the east and west shafts duplicated. Probably the octagonal piers originally formed part of a 14th century arcade only extending as far east as the former south transept. The north transept still survives but has no ancient features. Both nave and aisle have old wagon roofs. The chancel was rebuilt in the 1880s and was then given a wooden chancel arch. The west tower has obelisk pinnacles and a lofty NE turret curved towards the west. Some of the bench ends are old. There are plaster Royal Arms of Charles I dated 1638. On a tomb chest is a recumbent effigy, probably Thomas Carminow, d1442. The monument has a canopy with a leaf band and quatrefoils.

ATHERINGTON   *St Mary*   SS 591231

The west tower is of exceptional hight, and the stair-turret near the SE corner rises still higher. There are diagonal buttresses lower down. Restoration by J.L.Pearson in 1882-4 has removed most of the old features of the nave, lower chancel, south transept and north aisle with a four bay arcade, although the unusual window tracery is said to replicate what was there before. The screen is though to have come from a manorial chapel at Umberleigh demolished c1800. Between the aisle and chapel is a finer screen still complete with a rood-loft. Behind the loft are painted boards with post-Reformation inscriptions and heraldry. There are old bench ends and one window in the chapel contains 15th century stained glass fragments reassembled in 1883. The effigy of a cross-legged knight may be Sir William de Champernowne, c1240. The late 14th century effigies of a knight and lady are thought to be Sir Ralph Wylmington and his wife. On a tomb chest are brasses of Sir John Basset, c1530 and his two wives and twelve children brought here from Umberleigh.

AVETON GIFFORD   *St Andrew*   SX 696479

The church was rebuilt in 1948-57 after being bombed in the war. It is a cruciform structure of the late 13th century with a rebuilt central tower with a large circular SW stair-turret. The crossing arches rest on three big shafts with moulded capitals. In the nave north wall are lancets high up with nook-shafts. The other windows are Victorian but may represent what was there before. The fine 14th century north porch has a stair-turret on the west side. Only foundations now remain of wide 15th century chapels on either side of the chancel but their windows have been reset into the walls blocking the pairs of arches between each chapel and the chancel.

Aveton Gifford Church

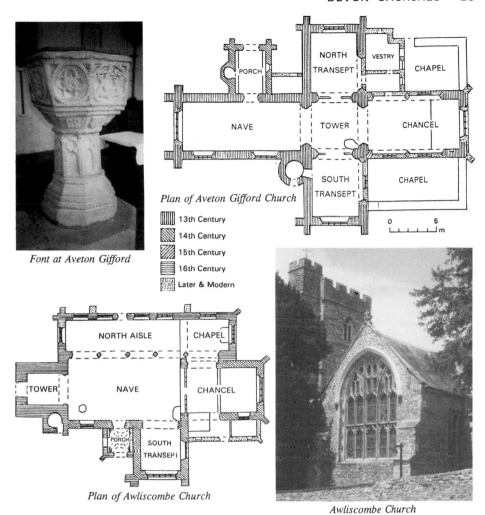

Font at Aveton Gifford

Plan of Aveton Gifford Church

13th Century
14th Century
15th Century
16th Century
Later & Modern

Plan of Awliscombe Church

Awliscombe Church

AWLISCOMBE *St Michael* ST 134018

Relics of a 14th century cruciform church are the chancel, the south transept and the nave south wall. The vaulted porch with openings to the south and west with fleurons is tucked into the angle between nave and south transept. It was built by Thomas Charde, last abbot of Forde Abbey. Of his period are the panelled arches into the west tower with a square SE stair turret, into the south transept and from the chancel into the north chapel, plus the north aisle with a four bay arcade and the five-light south transept south window. There are ceiled wagon roofs although that in the chancel was mostly renewed in a restoration of 1886-7 by Palfrey when an organ chamber was added on the south. The 15th century font has four-petalled flowers in the panels. The stone screen may originally have had another one parallel to it with a vault between the two to support the rood-loft. The south transept east window contains a few fragments of old glass. There are Royal Arms of George III dated 1820 and of Queen Elizabeth II.

Axminster Church

AXMINSTER   *St Mary*   SY 296985

The piers of the crossing tower are 13th century, those on the east being pierced by squints into the narrower chancel. The east end of the chancel is early 14th century with typical sedilia and piscina. This part contains effigies thought to be Alice de Mohun, c1257, and the 13th century priest Gervase de Prestaler. The Younge family added a chapel on the south side of the chancel c1480. The arch to the chancel from the chapel contains an original screen. A north aisle and chapel and a porch were erected in the 1520s, sweeping away the north transept. The south transept (used as the Drake family chapel) and south wall of the Norman nave survived until a south aisle was added c1800. Two windows on the north side are of about that time when also the Norman south doorway of two orders with chevrons was reset in the south chapel east wall. The west window was renewed and the clerestory windows added in 1834 and there was a restoration by Edward Ashworth in 1870, from which date all the pier capitals. The pulpit and reading desk are of 1633. There are Royal Arms of 1767 and a brass candelabra of c1750.

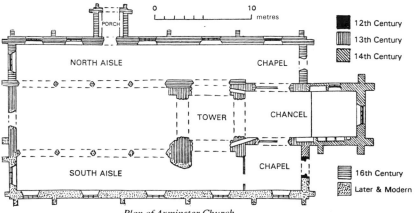

Plan of Axminster Church

AXMOUTH   *St Michael*   SY 256910

The nave and the narrower chancel are both Norman and have a north doorway with one order of columns and chevrons and crenellations on the voussoirs. Of the 13th century are the south aisle with a three bay arcade with round piers and the chancel south window with two pointed trefoil-headed lights. The 15th century additions are the north porch, the west tower with diagonal buttresses and a higher NE stair-turret and the south chapel (unless it has older masonry). A chancel arch then inserted lacks capitals just like the chapel and tower arches and the tower west doorway. The buttresses against the arcade piers and against the south aisle wall in line with them, and the paintings of Christ showing his wounds and St Peter are also of that period. A recess in the chancel north wall contains an effigy of a 14th century priest.

AYLESBEARE   *St Mary*   SY 038920

The west tower has a south doorway because it was rather close to the churchyard boundary for a west doorway to function properly. The north aisle and chapel, the octagonal font with an 18th century domed cover and the panelled chancel arch are also 15th century work. The church was restored in 1896-9 by E.H.Harbottle.

BAMPTON   *St Michael*   SS 957222

The tower with diagonal buttresses low down and the chancel with an ogival headed piscina and renewed Decorated style windows are early 14th century. The 15th century nave is higher than the chancel and has a north aisle, both parts having restored wagon roofs and four-light windows. The mid 16th century pulpit has a green man carved upon it. The Bourchier family emblem of a knot appears on the screen, which was restored in 1938 and the cresting renewed in 1965. The fragments of panels with figures in niches may have come from a medieval stone pulpit. In the chancel north wall are fragments of a tomb chest, possibly that of Lady Thomasine Bourchier, d1453.

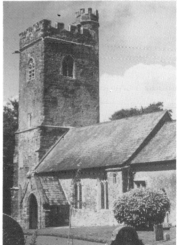

Aylesbeare Church

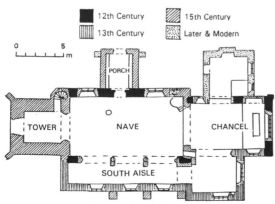

Plan of Axmouth Church

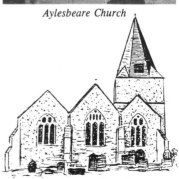

Beaford Church

BARNSTAPLE   *St Peter & St Paul*

SS 560334

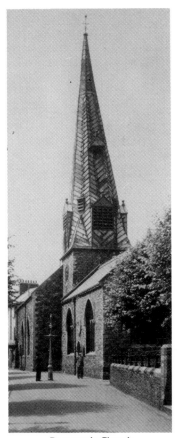

Barnstaple Church

The three altars consecrated in 1318 lay in the chancel, north transept and in the base of the 13th century south transeptal tower with a lead-covered broach-spire of 1388-9. Despite frequent repair, particularly in 1636 (as recorded on a pediment) the spire is now badly twisted. A south chapel was later added to the chancel and the nave given wide aisles. New arcades inserted in 1810 were replaced by Gilbert Scott in 1866 and the window tracery, south porch, and NE organ chamber date from then. The work continued under his son until the 1880s. North of the east end of the chancel is the two storey Bibliotheca Doddridgiana added in 1667 with wooden mullioned windows. The straight-headed mullioned windows of the north aisle are probably also of that period. There are a few locally made old tiles around the pulpit. The other furnishings are Victorian. Outside the south chapel is a sundial of 1732 in the form of an elongated octagon.

In the south aisle are kneeling figures of Elizabeth Delbridge, d1624, and Raleigh Clapham, d1636, and his wife. There is a frontal bust of George Peard, d1644, and a semi-reclining effigy in relief of Richard Ferris, d1649. There is also a figure of Walter Tucker with his daughter and her baby below. In the south chapel is a bust of Nicholas Blake, d1634, a half-figure of Richard Beaple, d1643, and an allegorical monument to Richard Harris, d1688. In the north transept is a half-figure of Thomas Horwood, d1658. Other monuments were lost in the Victorian restorations.

Just to the east lies the early 14th century chantry chapel of St Anne. It has a fine east window and an arch-braced roof. It contains 16th century desks from when it became a grammar school. The chapel lies over an undercroft with timber piers with braces supporting a longitudinal beam, and has a later two storey south porch.

BEAFORD   *All Saints & St George*   SS 552150

The short tower with a broach-spire in a north transeptal position is probably 13th century. The nave has two 16th century windows west of the tower. A four bay arcade divides off a south aisle running the length of the building. The aisle has a wagon roof with cross-ribbed panels. The goblet-shaped font is Norman. The bowl is fluted and there are cable mouldings at the rim and between bowl and shaft.

BEAWORTHY   *St Alban*   SX 461995

The south doorway has two Norman capitals with heads, so the single chamber probably has masonry of that period. The low west tower with a plain pointed tower arch is probably 13th century. The church was restored in 1871 by Samuel Hooper.

BELSTONE   *St Mary*   SX 619936

A restoration of 1881-2 by Hayward removed most features of interest. Medieval are the granite ashlar west tower and the south arcade with low granite piers.

BERE FERRERS   *St Andrew*   SX 459634

The nave is probably Norman, although its earliest feature is a window with intersecting tracery of c1300, whilst the thin west tower could be 13th century. The chancel has late 13th century north windows, double sedilia and a piscina of that date on the south side, and a five-light east window with intersecting tracery containing some contemporary glass including images of the de Ferrers donor and his wife. The long transepts were probably added after 1333, when William de Ferrers found an archpresbytery here with four priests under an arch priest. In the north transept the east windows have reticulation whilst the west window has a big circle above various small cusped lights. This transept has a squint towards the chancel. The two bay south chapel and the south aisle with an arcade of three normal bays plus a wider one for the transept are late 15th or early 16th century and so is the south porch with a ribbed ceiling. A font has been formed out of two Norman capitals, the top one having volutes. There are many old benches with blank traceried arches. One at the front has the arms of the Willoughby de Broke family. Between the north chapel of c1300 and the chancel is a tomb recess with effigies of that period thought to be Sir William de Ferrers and his wife Matilda. The north transept has an early 14th century effigy of a knight in a recess in the north wall and a freestanding tomb chest thought to be that of Lord Willoughby de Broke, d1522.

Plan of Bere Ferrers Church

Window at Bere Ferrers

Tomb chest at Bere Ferrers Church

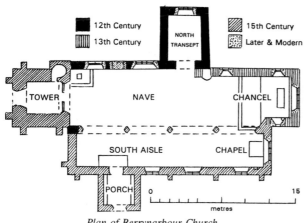

Plan of Berrynarbour Church

Berry Pomeroy Church

BERRYNARBOUR　*St Peter*　SS 560468

The north transept looks Norman, with a battered base on the west side and a round arch on simple imposts to the nave. The 13th century chancel has a trefoil-headed piscina and several renewed lancets. Of the 15th century are the blocked north doorway, the south aisle with a porch and an arcade of four wide arches with niches on the easternmost pier, and the 29m high west tower with set-back buttresses and a square NE stair-turret. The tower has a tall tower arch and a west doorway with fleurons below a large four-light window with a transom. There are large niches high up on all sides and projected pinnacles. The square Norman font has scallops under the bowl. On the chancel north wall is a kneeling early 17th century effigy, and there are other kneeling figures on the monument of Richard Berry, d1645 and family.

BERRY POMEROY　*St Mary*　SX 829610

The church is mostly of the late 15th century and has a west tower with set-back buttresses and wide aisles with battlements. There is a rood-loft staircase on the north side and a porch vaulted in two bays on the south side. The piers on the south have inscriptions on the capitals commemorating benefactors of the church and their wives. The screen is unusually well preserved with its original coving, a cornice with one band of decoration and its cresting. The painted figures on the wainscoting are cut short at the knees. The altar table and the altar rails now at the north aisle west end are early 18th century. In the south chapel east window are bits of reset stained glass including three shields. There is a tomb chest with two tiers of quatrefoils to Sir Richard Pomeroy, d1496, and his wife. A large tomb of 1613 has tiered reclining effigies of Lord Edward Seymour, d1593, and his son Sir Edward with his wife.

BICKINGTON　*St Mary*　SX 799727

The principal features of interest left after R.M.Fulford's restoration of 1882-4 are the early 16th century priest's doorway in the chancel, the four bay north arcade of double-chamfered arches on octagonal piers, the west tower with a centrally-placed stair-turret and low pinnacles, and a plain font with an early 17th century cover.

BICKLEIGH   *St Mary*   SX 521623

The old parts are the west tower with set-back buttresses and projecting polygonal pinnacles, two fonts, one octagonal with crenellations and a flat leaf pattern and the other with incised chevrons, and the base of a quatrefoil pier lying loose. The church was rebuilt by Charles Fowler in 1838 and altered by J.D.Sedding in 1882, and contains various 19th century monuments to the Lopes family of Maristow.

BICKLEIGH   *St Mary*   SS 943072

The west tower with a stair turret may be 13th century and there is a late medieval south arcade. The rest was rebuilt in 1847-8. There are old bench ends with tracery and one with a man with a bundle of tools. The pulpit is 18th century. In the south chapel is a kneeling figure of John Carew, d1588, and a reclining effigy of Elizabeth Eriseys, who died in 1618 bearing a baby to one of the Carews. There are busts of Peter Carew, d1654, and his wife in niches, and effigies of Sir Henry Carew, d1681, and his wife and family.

BICTON   *St Mary*   SY 073857

In 1850 Lady Rolle commissioned Hayward to design a new church in memory of her husband. It stands east of the remains of the old church comprising a small 13th century west tower and the 13th century south wall of the nave with two 15th century windows. This joins up to a mausoleum designed by Pugin and containing not only the tomb of Lord Rolle, d1842, but also a Baroque tomb with the reclining figure of Denys Rolle, d1638, and a recumbent figure of his wife, plus a baby on the floor.

Bicton Old Church   *Bickington Church*

BIDEFORD   *St Mary*   SS 454264

Old features which survived the rebuilding of the large church in 1862-5 by Edward Ashworth are the diagonally buttressed west tower with a polygonal NE stair-turret, some 16th century woodwork in the tower screen, a large circular Norman font with thick rope mouldings separating panels, one of which has a Maltese cross, monuments to Sir Thomas Grenville, d1513, and John Strange, d1646, mayor of Bideford when the plague struck the town that year, and a few other tablets.

BIGBURY   *St Lawrence*   SX 668867

From Ashburton have come the pulpit and the wooden eagle lectern donated by Bishop Oldham (1505-19). The church was rebuilt in 1868-72 by E. and J.D.Sedding but there remain a diagonally-buttressed 14th century tower with a short spire, sedilia, piscina and a tomb recess of the same period in the chancel, and the arches of the south transept and north aisle, together with some fragments of old glass, 15th century brasses of two sisters of the de Bikebury family, and a slate with incised figures of John and Jane Pearse, d1612 and 1589.

Burgh Island, 3km SW of Bigbury Church, has slight remains of a medieval chapel.

BISHOP'S NYMPTON   *St Mary*   SS 758238

The only pre-15th century parts are the square Norman font with four shallow arches on each side and perhaps some masonry of the chancel, since it is narrower than the nave. The lofty south arcade is of six bays. Both the nave and aisle have ceiled wagon roofs with fine bosses. The windows are mostly of three lights, those to the east and south being renewed. The lofty west tower has large set-back buttresses and gargoyles below the battlements. The pinnacles were rebuilt shorter in 1959. In the wall above the Victorian NE vestry is a wooden effigy of St James the Less from the tower. The chancel north wall has an ornate monument which also served as an Easter Sepulchre, probably to the lawyer Sir Lewis Pollard, d1540. There are charity boards with a painted wooden tablet to John Blackmore, d1733, one of the donors.

Tympanum at Bishopsteignton

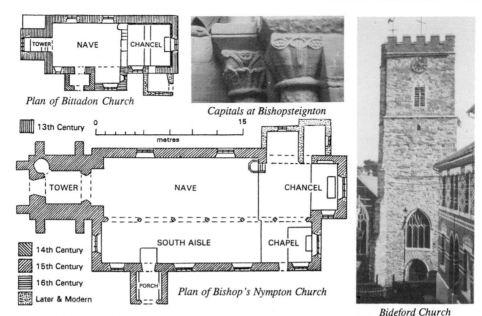

Plan of Bittadon Church

Capitals at Bishopsteignton

13th Century

0   15
metres

14th Century

15th Century

16th Century

Later & Modern

TOWER

NAVE

CHANCEL

CHAPEL

SOUTH AISLE

PORCH

Plan of Bishop's Nympton Church

Bideford Church

BISHOP'S TAWTON   *St John Baptist*   SS 565301

There is a crocketed octagonal stone spire, the only medieval one in Devon, upon the north transeptal tower with buttresses low down only. It has an early 14th century east window now looking into the vestry. On the other side is a window looking into a 15th century aisle rebuilt except for the arcade of three and a half bays in 1878. The nave has an original ceiled wagon roof. The chancel was rebuilt in 1864-6 by Gould. Part of an old screen remains in the tower arch. On the spandrels are the arms of Thomasine Hall and Richard Chichester, d1502. The Chichester memorials include a kneeling figure of Lady Ursula, d1635, a tablets to John, d1669, and Francis, d1698, and a tablet to the baby daughter of Charles Dart, d1662. There are also several 19th century memorials to the Law family.

BISHOPSTEIGNTON   *St John Baptist*   SX 911735

The fine Norman west doorway has two orders of colonettes with chevrons and scale patterns and voussoirs with more chevrons, fleur-de-lis, beakheads and a large bird. In the south wall is a reset Norman tympanum from a south doorway. It shows the Three Magi marching along below arcades and what is perhaps the warning angel set frontal in a pleated skirt. The circular font is also Norman but of less interest. The north arcade is late medieval but the rest is much restored and the tower in front of the aisle is of 1815.

BITTADON   *St Peter*   SS 545415

This is a small single chamber with windows of 1883 and a tiny 16th or 17th century south transept adjoining a shallow porch with a sundial dated 1764 over what looks like a 14th century outer entrance. The square font on four round shafts lies under the tiny west tower with a pyramidal roof. On the north wall are monuments to Henry Ackland, d1675, and Edward Pointz, d1691.

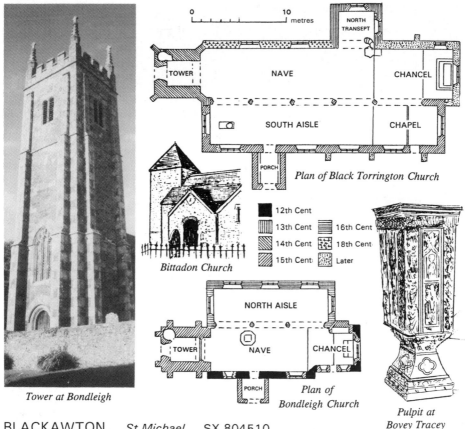

Tower at Bondleigh

Plan of Black Torrington Church

12th Cent	
13th Cent	16th Cent
14th Cent	18th Cent
15th Cent	Later

Bittadon Church

Plan of Bondleigh Church

Pulpit at Bovey Tracey

BLACKAWTON   *St Michael*   SX 804510

The low west tower has diagonal buttresses, a polygonal stair turret in the middle of one side and battlements on a corbel table. The chancel with its sedilia and double piscina was part of the church dedicated in 1333. The chancel arch has been modified and the north windows blocked. The aisles and arcades are late medieval, the windows having four-centred arches and no tracery. The circular Norman font has a cable-moulding above a palmette frieze. The screen has panels painted with the cyphers of Henry VIII and Katherine of Aragon. There is a brass depicting Nicholas Forde, d1582, and his wife, and a tomb chest of Richard Sparkes, d1700.

BLACK TORRINGTON   *St Mary*   SS 464057

The north transept with a plain pointed arch to the nave is 13th century. It has late medieval east and north windows. The nave north wall of 1798 has two large plain mullioned windows of three lights. The diagonally buttressed west tower may be late 14th or early 15th century. The wide south aisle has an arcade of five wide arches set upon piers with capitals on the shafts only. The former Jacobean communion rail now screens off the 15th century granite font. There are a few old tiles with motifs such as a rose and fleur-de-lis, and slate plates to Benoni Bamopfylde, d1721, Mary, d1722, wife of Lewis Coham, and Mary, d1725, wife of Stephen Coham.

Norman capitals at Bondleigh

BONDLEIGH *St James* SS 652048

Of the Norman church there remain the nave south wall with a doorway having a tympanum with birds set either side of a lamb in a circle, also the east and south walls of a small chancel, and a square font with blank arcading, chevrons and other motifs. The nave SE corner has long and short work. Set into the east wall of the 16th century north aisle lighted by square headed windows with transoms are two very finely carved Norman capitals with volutes and squares with diagonals and dots. They must have formed part of a chancel arch removed to make way for the third eastern bay of the arcade. Of the 15th century are the tall window with a transom in the nave south wall and the west tower with set-back buttresses. Also of that period are the fragments of stained glass in the chancel, the east window flanked internally by niches and the effigy of a priest on a tomb with quatrefoils in a recess in the chancel north wall. There are late 16th century bench ends and the tower screen incorporates fragments from the former rood screen.

Bondleigh Church

Bovey Tracey Church

Tomb in Bovey Tracey Church

BOVEY TRACEY   *St Peter, St Paul, & St Thomas Becket*   SX 821787

The dedication is of interest since the manor was held by the Tracy family, one of whom, William, was involved in the murder of Thomas Becket, Archbishop of Canterbury, in 1170. The structure of the present church at the east end of the town, plus the font with quatrefoil panels, the stone pulpit with panelling, the brass lectern made in East Anglia, three chancel stalls with misericord seats, and the fine screen are all essentially 15th century work, but with much restoration in 1858 when an outer north aisle was added and the galleries and original pews removed, and again in 1887-8. The blocked-up priest's doorway is the only part likely to be earlier. The church benefitted from patronage by Henry VII's mother Lady Margaret Beaufort, Countess of Richmond and Derby, who founded a college nearby. The ashlar pinnacles of the unbuttressed tower were re-used when the top stage was added. There are arcades of five bays with the screen dividing off the east bay, and an aisleless sanctuary beyond. The embattled south aisle is impressive, with four light windows and a fine porch with a ribbed vault with four heads with meeting chins on the central boss. The screen has a fine frieze in the cornice and early 16th century paintings of apostles and prophets on the wainscot. The colouring on the screen is Victorian and the fan-coving is quite recent. There are Royal Arms of Charles II dated 1662 and a font cover of that period, when the lectern was returned to the church after being thrown out by Puritans. It was preserved by the ejected Royalist vicar James Forbes. The curious little shrine-like tomb outside the chancel south wall is to his wife Maria, d1655. Other monuments include an effigy propped on one elbow of Nicholas Eveleigh, d1618, and a similar monument to Elizeus Hele, d1636.

Forbes monument at Bovey Tracey

Bow Church

BOW   *St Bartholomew*   SS 728007

The church lies at Nymet Tracey, 1km SE of Bow, and is said to have been built by Sir William de Tracey as part of his penance for his part in the murder of Thomas Becket, Archbishop of Canterbury in 1170. The head of a knight over the south doorway is a possible relic of that period. The windows were mostly renewed and provided with stained glass as a result of rebuilding in 1859-62 and 1889 but two on the south side may reproduce 14th century originals, the west tower and south porch may also be of that period, and there are medieval wagon roofs to the nave and north aisle. The knots appearing on some of the bosses are emblems of the Bourchier family. The arcade has granite piers with shafts and hollows. The 15th century octagonal font has fleurons above traceried panels. The screen retains some original colouring and there is a later screen in the aisle with linenfold panels on the wainscot. The communion rail with alternate plain and twisted balusters is 17th century and there is a plain 18th pulpit. The oak chest is probably that purchased in 1634.

BRADFORD   *All Saints*   SS 422073

The Norman south doorway has one order of colonettes and there is a font of that period with a circular fluted bowl. The low 14th century tower was repaired and heightened in 1550. The chancel has early 14th century features on the south side but was rebuilt by Hooper in 1871. The north aisle is said to be of 1438 and has a variety of window types all with straight heads. There are some old bench ends and medieval tiles. On the aisle west wall is an incised slate to the Maynards of Bovacott, 1666-8, and there is a tablet to William Bickford, d1689.

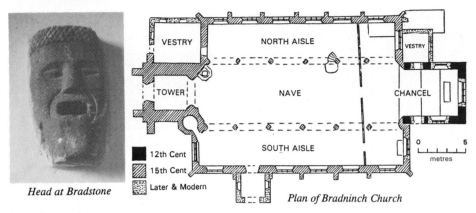

Head at Bradstone

Plan of Bradninch Church:
- VESTRY
- NORTH AISLE
- VESTRY
- TOWER
- NAVE
- CHANCEL
- SOUTH AISLE
- ■ 12th Cent
- ▨ 15th Cent
- ▦ Later & Modern
- 0 — 5 metres

Plan of Bradninch Church

BRADNINCH   *St Disen*   SS 999042

The oldest part is the chancel, narrower than the nave and with eastern quoins which look Norman. It contains a white marble monument of 1679 to the Sainthill family. In 1437 a two-year indulgence was offered to those who contributed funds for the building of the tower. Of pink sandstone, it has set-back buttresses and a polygonal SE stair turret. The aisles are of about the same period and have three-light windows with buttresses between them. The piers of the five bay arcades have two waves in the diagonals between the main shafts. They were re-erected in 1841 with the roof was heightened, although the existing arch-braced nave roof is of 1889. The fine screen of c1500-20 with fan-vaulted coving to both east and west runs across the whole width of the church. It is crookedly set in relation to the east-west axis and two of the uprights are very crooked also. There are original wainscot paintings of prophets and apostles, the four Latin doctors, sibyls and scenes including the Annunciation, the Visitation, Adam and Eve, and the Expulsion from Paradise. The colouring and the figures in the northern wainscot panels date from 1853. Also Victorian are the south porch and the NE and NW vestries.

Bradstone Church

BRADSTONE   *St Nonna*   SX 381809

The diagonally buttressed west tower with castellated pinnacles and the south porch with a green man ceiling boss are late 15th or early 16th century. One south window and the north aisle with several original windows, blocked up doorway and rood-loft stair, and a four bay arcade are of the same period. The nave has a Norman south doorway with one order of columns into which a later doorway is set, whilst the chancel is late 13th century with a pair of trefoil-headed lancets in the south wall. There is a ceiled wagon roof with bosses. Just inside the doorway is a triangular water stoup. The octagonal font is the only ancient furnishing to survive. Since 1996 the church was been cared for by the Redundant Churches Fund.

BRADWORTHY   *St John Baptist*   SS 325140

Unmoulded arches probably of 13th century lead off the wide nave into a south transept and a very shallow north transept. The chancel has one south window of that date. The north window is thought to have been in the east wall until this part was extended c1400 and given a new doorway. The nave windows are also of that date. The early 16th century west tower with a square-headed label on the west doorway was rebuilt in 1884 after being struck by lightning. There are old wagon roofs, that in the chancel being ceiled. The plain square font is probably Norman. The pulpit of c1700 has open baluster-work at the bottom. The tripartite reredos with pokerwork decoration is 18th century. There are old tiles from Barnstaple. The best memorial tablets are those of Ann Nichols, d1694, and Thomas Cholwill, d1714.

BRAMPFORD SPEKE   *St Peter*

SX 928982

Only the diagonally buttressed late medieval tower with obelisk shaped pinnacles and a tomb recess with a cusped arch in the south transept survived the rebuilding of 1853 by Butcher with windows in the Decorated style. The interior was later whitewashed and given new fittings.

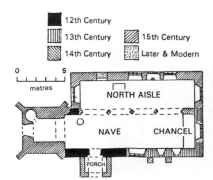

- ■ 12th Century
- ▥ 13th Century
- ▨ 15th Century
- ▨ 14th Century
- ▧ Later & Modern

Plan: NORTH AISLE / NAVE / CHANCEL / PORCH

Plan of Bradstone Church   *Interior of Bradstone Church*

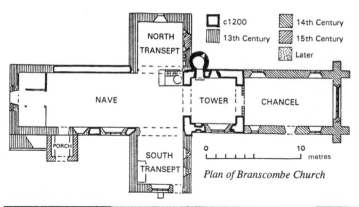

c1200 14th Century
13th Century 15th Century
Later

NORTH TRANSEPT

NAVE TOWER CHANCEL

PORCH

SOUTH TRANSEPT

0   10
metres

Plan of Branscombe Church

Pulpit at Branscombe

BRANSCOMBE   *St Winfred*   SY 196885

The central tower dates from the end of the 12th century and has a circular stair turret on the north side. It has unmoulded pointed arches to west and east, the latter containing a screen of c1660 on a medieval stone base. It was probably during the episcopacy of Bishop Branscombe in the 1250s that the nave was lengthened and transepts added west of the tower, an unusual layout. One lancet remains in the north transept and traces of two others in the south transept east wall. The nave retains its Norman corbel table and has one south lancet. The 14th century chancel has original side windows and stepped sedilia and a piscina in the south wall. The five-light east window was inserted by Bishop Neville (1458-64), and the west doorway is probably of the same period. The only other 15th century work in the church (apart from a painting of the Seven Deadly Sins on the north wall) is a large octagonal font with quatrefoil panels brought here from East Teignmouth during W.D.Caroe's restoration of 1911. There are medieval open roofs throughout the church, those in the nave having bosses. The fine three decker pulpit is 18th century. There are box pews in the north transept and there is a 16th century west gallery in the nave reached by an open stair west of the porch. The altar rails are of c1660. The monuments include parts of a 14th century arcaded tomb chest, cartouches to Ann Bartlett dated 1608, and kneeling effigies of John Kellaway and Sir John Wadham, successive husbands of Joan Wadham of Edge Barton, d1583.

BRATTON CLOVELLY   *St Mary*   SS 463919

The tower superficially looks of c1500, with a lofty NW stair-turret but has arches to the north and south of early type so it may have been a crossing tower with a nave beyond it in the 13th century. The north arch is blocked. The south arch has double chamfered arches and looks into a western extension of the south aisle. The arcade piers rest on square blocks which may be remnants of earlier arcades. The aisles have ceiled lean-to roofs and the south side has battlements reached by a stair turret on the SW corner. Certainly the church has had its present layout since the early 14th century, the date of the chancel. Chapels were added to it in the 15th century. The circular Norman font has faces at the corners and rosettes and other motifs in between. Part of the wainscoting of the old screen survives. The aisles have a series of 17th century wall paintings discovered and conserved in 1986. The subjects include Christ and the Apostles, prophets, many scrolls, a military encampment with David and Goliath, and a figure in armour. In the vestry is some 15th century heraldic glass, and there are two angels in one of the south windows.

BRATTON FLEMING   *St Peter*   SS 644377

A collapse of the tower resulted in it and the nave and north aisle being rebuilt in 1702-3. The arcade and windows are of 1855-61.The 14th century arcade of the north chapel now only has two bays instead of three. There is a monument to the 97-year old rector Bartholomew Wortley, d1749.

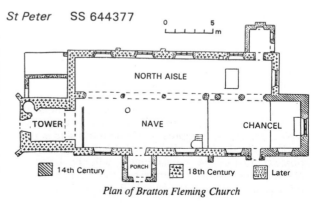

Plan of Bratton Fleming Church

Interior of Braunton Church

BRAUNTON   *St Brannock*   SS 489271

The south transeptal tower is claimed to be Norman but it has lancet belfry windows, a pointed arch towards the nave and a broach-spire, so it may be no older than the wide nave and modest chancel with three north lancets which are 13th century. Of that period are the west doorway and the angle buttresses on the west corners. A lancet in the nave east wall north of the chancel arch suggests that originally the 10m wide nave had arcades dividing off narrow aisles. If such a scheme ever existed it must have gone by the late 13th century for there is a north transept with an east window with Y-tracery. The unmoulded arch to this transept is now filled by the organ. The south doorway and porch are 14th century, and the renewed nave windows may have also have been of that date. The Victorian north porch now serves as a vestry. The 15th century south chapel has a two bay arcade towards the chancel and an arch towards the nave. Heavy buttresses were added to take the thrust of the 16th century wagon roof of the nave. On a roof boss above the square Norman font with faces at the corners and tracery of c1300 are a sow and pigs. The reading desk is dated 1636 and the pulpit, communion rail and north transept gallery are of about that period. There is an old screen below the chancel arch. The nave is filled with old benches, the parish records noting additions to them in 1560, 1568, 1578, 1579, 1583 and 1593. There are carvings of the instruments of the Passion, shields, initials, and figures. A Saxon tomb slab is re-used as a lintel on a tower west window. On the back of the brass depicting Lady Elizabeth Bourchier, d1548, in a kneeling posture, is a palimpsest with the head of an earlier knight. There is a splendid monument to members of the Incledon family who died in 1736 and 1746, and also a monument to Frances Baker, d1782.

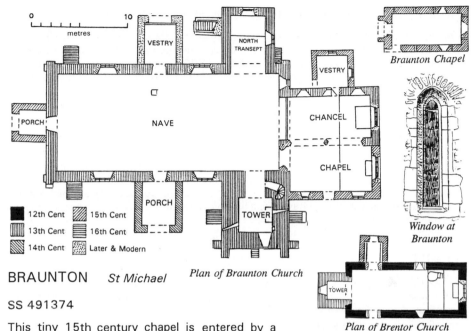

Braunton Chapel

Window at Braunton

Plan of Braunton Church

Plan of Brentor Church

BRAUNTON   *St Michael*

SS 491374

This tiny 15th century chapel is entered by a west doorway set in a shallow porch and had a single lancet in each of the north and south walls and a small two-light east window. The ruin stands on a commanding hill.

BRENDON   *St Brendon*   SS 750477

This remote Exmoor church was rebuilt in 1738, but the tower is a rebuild of 1828 and the arcade and windows are of 1873. Norman are the square font with curved lines towards the bottom of the bowl and the circular stoup or pillar piscina with chevrons, foliage, birds, a beaded wavy band and animals in lozenges.

BRENTOR   *St Michael de Rupe*

SX 471804

This is a small single chamber with an embattled parapet upon a corbel table and a tiny west tower which stands close to the edge of the volcanic rock upon which the building is spectacularly placed. The south doorway and a north window are 13th century but the south window may be part of the church which existed by 1150. The north porch is 15th century. The Duke of Bedford had the church restored in 1889-90.

Bench end at Braunton

BRIDESTOWE   *St Bridget*   SX 513895

Remains of a Norman arch have been set up in the churchyard. The church was rebuilt in 1450-1 but little work of that period remains since the tower was rebuilt in 1828-30 and the rest is mostly of 1866-8 and 1890. A few fragments remain of the wainscoting of the old screen, and there is a monument to Honor Calmady, d1665.

BRIDFORD   *St Thomas-a-Becket*   SX 816864

The church is entirely of granite. The windows of the 14th century chancel are renewed. Of the 15th century are the west tower, the nave and north aisle with wagon roofs and remains of a celure over the screen, and a porch with fine windows in the nave wall on either side of it. The screen has lost its coving but retains carved figures on the wainscoting and a ring probably for a chained bible. It once had a board with initials of Walter Southcote, rector here 1508-50. Both the screen and the parclose screen of the chapel have grisaille paintings, the latter with what appear to be alternate wise and foolish men. With the screen goes a three sided pulpit. There are bench ends with two-tier tracery. The north windows have bits of old glass.

BRIDGERULE   *St Bridget*   SX 281032

The church lies alone above the village. The north transept has a plain 13th century arch towards the nave. The nave and the south aisle have good wagon roofs and are divided by a five bay arcade. The 13th century chancel has an original piscina. The south porch has a square-headed doorway flanked by quatrefoils. The granite ashlar west tower has large cusped pinnacles. Norman are the pillar piscina used as a stoup in the porch and the font with an egg-cup shaped bowl. There are 19th century memorials to the Kingdon family.

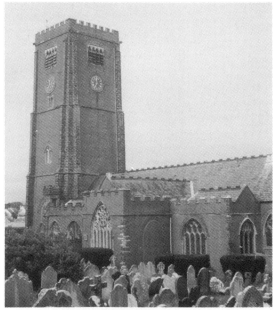

Brixham Church

Window at Bridford

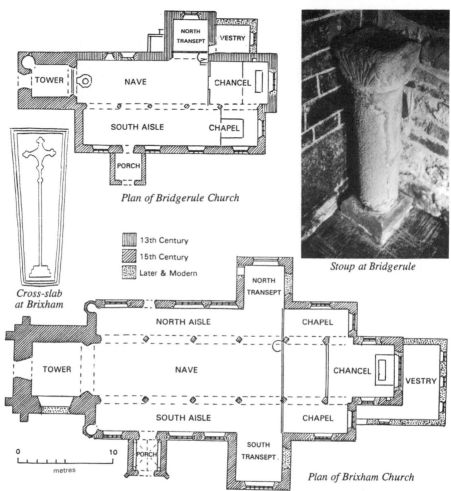

Plan of Bridgerule Church

13th Century
15th Century
Later & Modern

Cross-slab
at Brixham

Stoup at Bridgerule

Plan of Brixham Church

BRIXHAM   *St Mary*   SX 921552

The church has a similar layout to Ashburton, the aisles having polygonal western stair-turrets, and transepts projecting from the fourth bays, the fifth bays being chancel chapels with arched recesses for tombs between them and the chancel, that on the south side being 16th century and having a little vault. Here set-back corner buttresses only appear on the very large west tower, and rest of the building is unbuttressed apart from diagonal buttresses on the south porch. This side is all-embattled and the porch has a lierne star vault with the central boss carved with the Virgin and angels. The shell piscina in the sanctuary has the arms of Bishop Courtenay (1478-87). The north transept, formerly the Churston family pew, has a screen made up from part of the south gallery built in 1792. The early 14th century font has a square base with dogs at the corners, and an octagonal pillar supporting the bowl by nodding-ogee canopies on angel brackets. Also in the church are a clock of 1740, a coffin lid with a foliated cross, a monument to Anne Stucley, c1720, and several minor monuments to members of the Upton family of Lupton House.

Broadhembury Church

Brixton Church

BRIXTON   *St Mary*   SX 554522

The 14th century west tower has diagonal buttresses and battlements upon a corbel table. There are aisles and chancel chapels, the latter with squints. A two light window in the vestry is said to be from the Fortescue mansion at Spriddlestone. The other exterior features are of the restorations of 1887 and 1894 by Charles King.

BROADCLYST   *St John*   SX 982973

The north aisle, and the chancel with sedilia with tall crocketed gables and a fine east window are 14th century. The south aisle and the arcades with arches with fleurons springing from angels are 15th century, one capital having the Stafford knot, probably a reference to Bishop Stafford, d1419. Both aisles are embattled and have stair turrets at the end ends and there is a south porch. The fine west tower begun in the 15th century was not completed until the 16th century. It has gargoyles under the buttress pinnacles and elaborately decorated battlements and west doorway. The ribbed paster vault is of 1832-3. Under the sedila is an effigy of a mid 14th century knight thought to be Sir Roger de Nonant. There is a sumptuous monument with a reclining effigy of Sir John Acland erected some years before his death in 1620. There are kneeling effigies of Henry Burrough, d1605, and his wife, and there are also recumbent effigies of Edward Drew, d1622, and his family.

BROADHEMBURY   *St Andrew*   ST 102046

The two storey porch partly obscures one of the 14th century windows of the nave. The porch has a panelled vault, a 17th century wooden gate and an elaborately decorated doorway with a niche above it. Further east is a fine 15th century window with at the springing of the tracery figures of a man and woman projecing outside and angels projecting inside towards the pulpit. The south arcade has four arches to the nave and a fifth arch towards the chancel. The chancel was otherwise rebuilt in 1843 by Hayward, although the east window may reproduce the original. The priest's door in the south chapel was reopened in 1974. The 15th century west tower has set-back buttresses, a stair-turret, and three-light bell-openings. The wagon roofs were heavily restored in 1930. The octagonal font has primitive tracery and figures. One of the Drewe family has a monument with his kneeling effigy between double columns, and there is a monument to Francis Drewe, d1675.

BROADHEMPSTON   *St Peter & St Paul*   SX 801663

The thin west tower with lancets and a marked batter and the chancel with remains of plate-tracery in the windows are 13th century. An indulgence for rebuilding the nave was granted in 1402, but the present arcades of five bays are probably late 15th century. The south porch has a wagon roof. Some of the four-light windows have survived restorations of 1777, 1842, 1853-4, 1876-7, and 1896-8. There is a plain octagonal font. The top parts of the screen were renewed in 1903. One south window has old heraldic glass referring to the Rowe family. A monument of 1654 commemorated Robert Warrying and his wife and daughter.

Interior of Broadhemston Church

BROADWOOD KELLY   *All Hallows*   SS 618059

The south aisle with straight-headed uncusped windows is 16th century and the octagonal font with simple decoration goes with it. It and the nave and south porch have original wagon roofs and the south door is dated 1695. The west tower has set-back buttresses. The chancel was restored in 1868-9 by Gould. One north window has glass dated 1523 with a Virgin, a praying cleric in a roundel and a man and woman, probably donors, shown kneeling. There are old tiles and also a wooden monument of 1754 to the Webber family.

BROADWOODWIDGER   *St Nicholas*   SX 411892

The church is very irregularly laid out. The 13th century chancel inclines to the north and is considerably narrower than the nave, yet its featureless north wall lies further north than that of the nave. The north transept and the plain pointed chancel arch are also 13th century. The nave seems to have been rebuilt wider in the late 13th century and was then given a west tower with a NE stair-turret. The south chapel with a two bay arcade is probably 14th century. In the 15th century a south aisle was added with a porch. The arcade has three full bays plus a half arch abutting against what was originally an arch between the south chapel and south transept. The piers have capitals to the shafts only. Other relics of the late medieval period are the wagon roofs, the octagonal granite font with rosettes, the screen, and the damaged effigy of a knight of the Upcott family. The bench ends are of c1530-50 and have instruments of the Passion, initials and human heads.

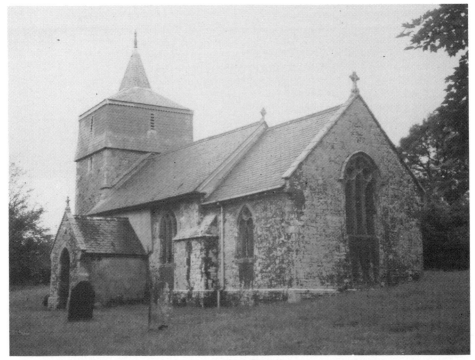

Brushford Church

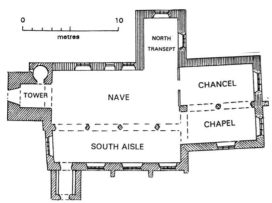

Plan of Broadwoodwidger Church

▥	13th Century
▧	14th Century
▨	15th Century
▦	Later & Modern

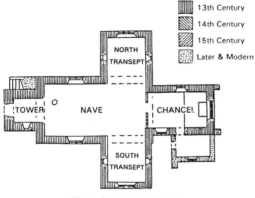

Plan of Buckerell Church

Tower at Broadwoodkelly

BRUSHFORD   *St Mary*   SS 676077

This small church lies alone except for a farm. The nave and chancel are both Norman, with a plain south doorway and one small north window, and the low west tower with a shingled top and low slated spire is perhaps 13th century. The screen with Flamboyant tracery is of some interest and there is an early 17th century hexagonal pulpit, whilst two bells cast in London c1400 lie on the nave floor.

BUCKERELL   *St Mary & St Giles*   ST 123004

The plan form of a nave with a narrower tower and narrower chancel and transepts suggests an early date for the walling, probably 13th century, but the outside is all rendered, the windows are Victorian and the only early internal feature is the chancel piscina. A stone bears the date 1403 but it is unclear what it refers to, although the wagon roof could be of that period. The restored screen has come in from elsewhere. The west gallery and box pews are 18th century. The best of the monuments to the Grave family of Hembury Fort are those of Elizabeth, d1767, and Admiral Samuel, d1787. There are also minor tablets to the Smythe family of Deer Park.

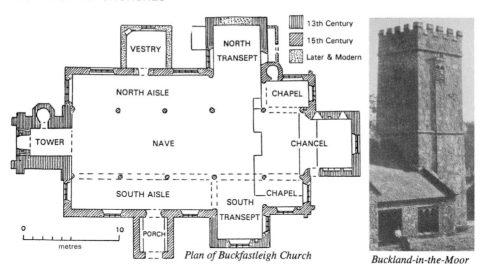

13th Century
15th Century
Later & Modern

VESTRY

NORTH TRANSEPT

NORTH AISLE

CHAPEL

TOWER

NAVE

CHANCEL

SOUTH AISLE

CHAPEL

SOUTH TRANSEPT

PORCH

0   10
metres

Plan of Buckfastleigh Church

Buckland-in-the-Moor

BUCKFASTLEIGH   *Holy Trinity*   SX 743666

The church lies isolated on a hill above the town and has been a ruin since being the victim of an arson attack in July 1992, only the tower upper levels remaining in use. It had arcades of five bays with the fourth bays opening into transepts and the fifth bays forming chancel chapels of later medieval date, beyond which the est end of the 13th century chancel survives with north lancets and a three light east window, plus sedilia and a piscina on the south. The west tower with angle buttresses, a west doorway with a drawbar-slot, and a polygonal stair turret on the north may also be 13th century, although the spire within the parapet upon a corbel table is later. The south doorway and the still-roofed porch are 15th century, and there is a 19th century vestry, also still roofed, on the north side. The outer walls are roughcasted and contain 19th century windows, the result of John Hayward's restoration in 1844-5 which left a Norman font as the only ancient furnishing. Not far to the east is the ruinous east end of a late 13th century chantry chapel.

Buckfastleigh Church

BUCKLAND BREWER *St Mary & St Benedict* SS 419209

The Norman south doorway has one order of colonettes with volute capitals. The north chapel has an arcade of two bays with double-chamfered arches and an octagonal pier. The west tower with set-back buttresses and pinnacles and a few 15th century windows have survived the rebuilding of 1879-80 by Hooper. An elaborate SE doorway leads to a room thought to be a rebuilding of the chapel of the Fraternity of St Michael which is mentioned in 1547. The font is of 1771. There are kneeling effigies of Anthony Dennis, d1643, and his wife, and a small half figure of Philip Venning, d1656. There is also a monument to John and Mary Davie, d1710.

BUCKLAND FILLEIGH *St Mary* SS 466092

The church lies close to the house and is an embattled building with a north aisle, a west tower with low pinnacles and a plain Norman south doorway. The windows were renewed in 1886-7. The pulpit contains 16th century panels with Renaissance motifs. There are old bench ends, some of which have initials. The monuments include those of Henry Fortescue, d1691, and Mary Spooner, d1752.

BUCKLAND-IN-THE-MOOR *St Peter* SX 720731

The 14th century west tower has a stair-turret in the middle of one side. The 15th century north aisle has a three bay arcade. There are old wagon roofs in the nave, chancel and south porch. Under the tower are old tiles and there is a goblet-shaped Norman font with cable ornamentation and palmettes and rosettes. The screen has crudely painted 16th century figures on the wainscoting.

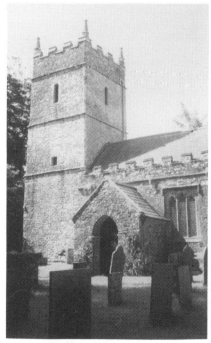
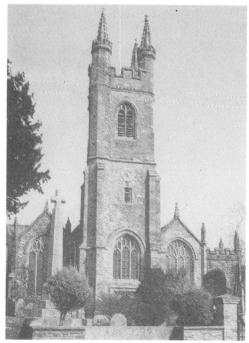

Buckland Filleigh Church   *Buckland Monachorum Church*

BUCKLAND MONACHORUM   *St Andrew*   SX 491683

This is a substantial 15th century church erected under the patronage of Buckland Abbey. It has an aisled nave of five bays with transepts corresponding to two bays, and at the east end two further lower bays of arches into chancel chapels thought to be Elizabethan, i.e. of post-monastic date. The south chapel or Drake Aisle has a ribbed tunnel vault of granite, probably re-used from the abbey and contains monuments of the 1790s to Admiral Lord Heathfield and Sir Francis Henry Drake, plus other memorials of that family. The west tower has set-back buttresses replaced at the top by polygonal projections on which sit large pinnacles. The nave has a much renewed hammerbeam roof with music-playing angels. There are two fonts, one Norman and eggcup-shaped, the other octagonal. Part of the screen from Sheeptor church lies under the tower arch and near it is an incised slate slab to Joseph Rowe, 1708. There are old bench ends with two tiers of arches. See photo on page 51.

BUCKLAND-TOUT-SAINTS   *St Peter*   SX 757461

This is a small, isolated cruciform church of 1799 with a modest west tower. The reredos contains work of the 15th and 17th centuries.

BULKWORTHY   *St Michael*   SS 395142

According to a lost inscription the church was built by Sir William Hankford, Chief Justice of the King's Bench under Henry V (1414-22). He probably added the south porch and the two bay aisle east of it to a small 13th century single chamber with one renewed lancet on the north side. An external stair leads to the porch upper room. A bellcote of 1874 is perched on two buttresses flanking the west window. The octagonal font is a later remodelling of a Norman one.

Bulkworthy Church

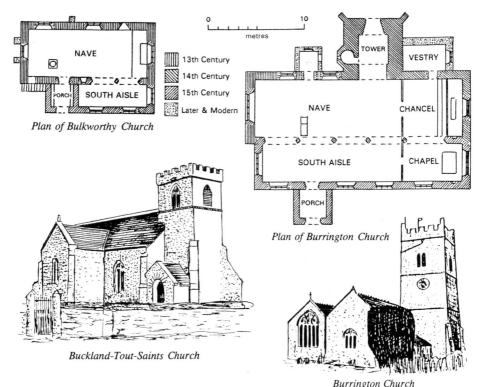

Plan of Bulkworthy Church

13th Century
14th Century
15th Century
Later & Modern

Plan of Burrington Church

Buckland-Tout-Saints Church

Burrington Church

BURLESCOMBE   *St Mary*   ST 076166

According to a tablet upon it, the diagonally buttressed west tower was rebuilt in 1637-8. The arcades differ slightly, for the south aisle piers only have capitals on the shafts whereas the northern ones have leaf capitals covering the whole pier. The windows on this side also have richer cusping and fragments of heraldic glass. The nave and both aisles have original wagon roofs. The Ayshford Chapel at the east end of the north aisle has a roof with angels with shields and a carved wall-plate. The octagonal font has quatrefoils, a moulded underside and an unusual base with square shafts. The top parts of the screen are renewed. There are tombs of Nicholas Ashford, d1557, and Henry Ayshford. d1660, and also monuments with kneeling figures of Roger Ayshford, d1610, and his wife Elizabeth, d1630.

BURRINGTON   *Holy Trinity*   SS 638167

The oldest part is the diagonally buttressed north transeptal tower with a polygonal stair turret on the west side. The rest is 15th century work restored in 1869 by Hayward. It comprises a nave and chancel in one with a five bay arcade to a south aisle with granite windows of three lights to the south and four light windows at each end. A screen with ribbed coving and a crested cornice divides off the east bay of each part. There is a south porch and the inner south doorway has an original door with tracery. The wagon roofs are also original. The square Norman font has four scallops underneath each side. There are communion rails of c1700 with alternating straight and twisted balusters.

BUTTERLEIGH   *St Matthew*   SS 974082

The church was mostly rebuilt by John Hayward in 1861 but the nave and west tower probably have 13th century masonry. There is a 17th century poor box.

CADBURY   *St Michael*   SS 911050

In 1856-8 William White heavily restored the nave, chancel and north aisle, the nave east bay being raised to form a longer chancel. The west tower with a square stair-turret rising higher on the north side is 15th century. Two old bench ends have been made into a prayer-desk. The square Norman font has four big scallops on each side. There is an Elizabethan double lectern with a richly carved bulbous foot. The aisle east window has 15th century glass of Christ showing his wounds. There are several tablets to the Fursdon family of Fursdon.

CADELEIGH   *St Bartholomew*   SS 914080

The diagonally buttressed west tower has a NE stair-turret and two ogival-headed recesses with small images of St Bartholomew and St Anthony. The box pews and the white plaster panelling in the nave and north aisle are of 1766. The windows are all of 1902-10. There are 13th century tiles in the aisle floor. The communion rail is of c1700. The tomb with recumbent effigies of Sir Simon Leach, his second wife and his son and daughter-in-law made c1630 is the largest of its type in any Devon parish church. There is also a monument to Lady Bridget Leach, d1691.

CALVERLEIGH   *St Mary*   SS 923144

A three bay arcade divides the nave and south aisle and there is a west tower with a polygonal NE stair turret and an old screen. The 14th century south doorway may be reset. The chancel and north wall were rebuilt in 1883-7. There is a kneeling effigy of Mary Coleman, d1636, with three faces in medallions behind.

Chagford Church

Challacombe Church

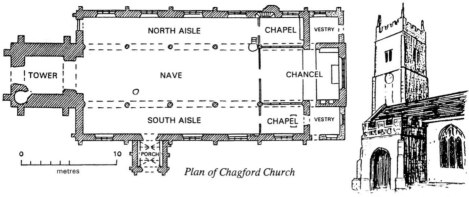

Plan of Chagford Church

Chawleigh Church

CHAGFORD *St Michael* SX 701875

Apart from the 19th century vestries flanking each side of the sanctuary, the whole church is probably of c1400 with a lofty west tower with set-back buttresses, and aisles with five bay arcades of double-chamfered arches on octagonal granite octagonal columns. The two storey porch is vaulted in two bays on blank wall arcades and has three foliated bosses. The chapel screens are medieval. There is a tomb chest to Sir John Whiddon, d1575 and a tablet to John Prouz, d1664.

CHALLACOMBE *Holy Trinity* SS 680406

Rebuilding in 1850 and restoration in 1874-5 have left only a 15th century tower with diagonal buttresses. The church lies by a farm on the edge of Exmoor.

CHARDSTOCK *St Andrew* ST 309045

Only the embattled 15th century south aisle and porch survived rebuilding in 1863-4.

CHARLES *St John Baptist* SS 688330

The west tower has a square NE stair-turret but no west doorway. The nave has an old coved wagon roof and traces of a former wide north doorway. The 15th century porch has a plaster ceiling. The four windows in the nave and most of the chancel dates from rebuildings of 1875 and 1890. There are monuments to several Gregorys.

CHARLETON *St Mary* SX 750426

The church was mostly rebuilt in 1849-50 except for the four bay north arcade, the south transept and the diagonally buttressed west tower with an octagonal NE stair-turret. In 1891 the medieval sedilia were moved to the north side of the chancel. There is a monument to Thomas Whinyates, d1783, and his family.

CHAWLEIGH *St James* SS 712127

The church is mostly 15th century. The south porch has quatrefoils on the base and battlements. There is an arcade of four bays, plus a fifth bay east of the old screen. The ceiled wagon roofs have cross-ribbed panels, the scale being reduced in the chancel. The west tower has diagonal buttresses and pinnacles. There are fine tablets to George Radford, d1667, and Ambrose Radford, d1703.

Cheldon Church   *Tower at Chilvelstone*

CHELDON   *St Mary*   SS 734134

This is a tiny church composed of a nave with one three light window on each side, a narrower chancel rebuilt or refaced in the 19th century, plus a west tower with set-back buttresses and a 17th century top stage. A screen is formed from mace rests of 1737 and 1743. There are bench ends with tracery patterns. From a monument of 1711 have come the busts of Mary Connell and Alice Eliston.

CHERITON BISHOP   *St Mary*   SX 773936

The late 13th century chancel has lancets in the side walls and more ambitious east window. The rest is 15th century, except that the south side and porch are a rebuilding of 1884. The arcades are of five bays and there are ceiled wagon roofs, that in the chancel having bosses. The north aisle of granite has three-light windows with tracery. The west tower has diagonal buttresses and is now roughcast. The circular Norman font has four bands of ornamentation. The pulpit has 16th century panels. The screen between the north aisle and north chapel still remains with painted saints of c1520 on the wainscoting. Parts of the chancel screen now lie on the south wall. There are old bench ends with two-tier tracery. Over the south door are Elizabethan Royal Arms. There is a small 15th century sculptured alabaster panel.

CHERITON FITZPAINE   *St Matthew*   SS 866062

The tower has set-back buttresses and a central polygonal stair-turret, and the upper part is roughcast. Much of the rest was restored in 1883-5 by James Crocker except for the 15th century three bay arcades with piers of an unusually complex section modelled on those of Exeter Cathedral, and the two storey porch with stepped up battlements on the front and a fan-vault with angel corbels and bosses with emblems of the Passion. There are monuments to John Moore of Upcott Barton, d1691, and Nicholas Hickes, d1704, and his wife.

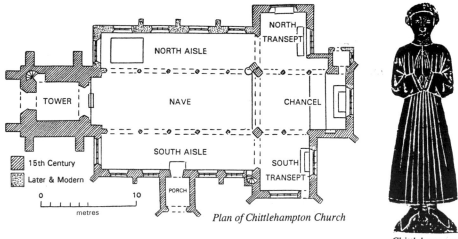

Plan of Chittlehampton Church

Chittlehampton Brass

CHITTLEHAMPTON *St Hieritha* SS 636256

The 35m high west tower has set-back buttresses and ornamented double two-light bell-openings of a Somerset rather than Devon type. The buttresses have pinnacles on their set-offs and friezes of quatrefoils. The rest of the church is also 15th century except for the north aisle of 1872 by Hayward and the rebuilt chancel east wall. There are arcades of five bays, then bigger piers to carry a chancel arch, after which are two more bays of narrower arches opening into transepts, then the north side has one further arch into a small chamber which contained the shrine of St Hieritha, who was murdered by local heathens with scythes in the 6th century. The south side is all embattled with a porch in the middle of the aisle and a staircase turret in the angle between it and the transept, all the corners having diagonal buttresses. The porch entrance has fleurons and a niche above and the ceiling has cusped wooden panels and bosses. The inner doorway also has fleurons and a foliage bracket above. It contains an original door with tracery, pinnacles and ironwork.

The octagonal font has a panelled base and sides. The stone pulpit has figures under nodding ogival canopies with leaf frames. There is a medieval chest with three locks. In the north transept or Giffard Chapel are small brasses depicting John Cobleigh and his two wives. There is a semi-reclining effigy of Grace Giffard, d1667. Another monument erected in the 1620s has a recumbent effigy of John Giffard and kneeling figures of his son (d1622) and grandson. In the south transept is a marble monument with mourning putti to Samuel Rolle, d1746.

CHIVELSTONE *St Silvester* SX 784388

The church is mostly 15th century with arcades of five bays with granite piers and a west tower with set-back buttresses and a central polygonal stair-turret. More important are the nicely decorated pulpit carved out of a single piece of wood and the screen with painted 16th century figures on the wainscoting. There are also parclose screens of the 1530s with the panels painted with imitation brocade, and a set of late 17th century altar rails.

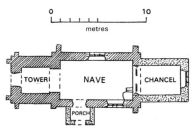

Plan of Cheldon Church

CHRISTOW   *St James*   SX 836850

The granite tower with set-back buttresses and obelisk pinnacles is of 1630 and the
arcades are also of granite. The nave and aisles have ceiled wagon roofs. In 1862
Edward Ashworth rebuilt the chancel and added the south porch and NE vestry.
There are carved stone Royal Arms of Charles II. Some of the south windows have
fragments of old glass. The square Norman font has three scallops under each side.
There are bench ends with two-tier tracery and leaf patterns, an old screen, and the
pulpit incorporates one 16th century Renaissance style panel.

CHUDLEIGH   *St Martin & St Mary*   SX 867794

The west tower with low buttresses, small windows and battlements on a corbel
table could be part of the church consecrated in 1259. The chancel has 14th century
north windows and there is a 16th century south arcade of seven bays. Other
features are mostly of the restorations of 1847-9 by David Mackintosh and 1868-9
by Woodyer. Old furnishings include a circular granite font, old screens with apostles
and prophets painted on the wainscoting, bench ends with two-tier tracery, and a mid
18th century clock. There are kneeling effigies of 1607 of Sir Piers Courtenay and his
wife and a relief of the mourning husband of Elizabeth Powney, d1782.

Chulmleigh Church

Christow Church

CHULMLEIGH *St Mary Magdalene* SS 688142

A college existed here by the 13th century but the only pre-15th century feature is a Norman roundel carved with a Crucifixion flanked by dragons in the porch. The arcades of five wide bays, the ceiled wagon roofs, the screen with ribbed coving and a cornice, the panelled octagonal font, the embattled south porch and the fine west tower with boldly projecting set-back buttresses are all medieval but the chancel east end and the outer walls of the aisles were mostly rebuilt during a restoration by J.F.Gould in 1879-81 and many of the furnishings are Victorian. The four evangelist figures on the screen are later foreign-made imports.

CHURCHSTOW *St Mary* SX 712459

This is the original mother church of Kingsbridge. The north transept is perhaps 14th century and the west tower with a higher stair-turret and the south aisle with a six bay arcade of almost semicircular moulded arches and a two storey porch are probably 15th century. There are ceiled wagon roofs and the pulpit and screen incorporate old parts.

CHURSTON FERRERS *St Mary* SX 904564

The whole church appears 15th century except for the vestries at either end of the north aisle. The aisles partly engage the diagonally buttressed west tower but stop short of the sanctuary. The arcades are of five bays with animals and the arms of the Yarde family on the capitals. Fixed on the two storey SW porch is a Crucifixion originally probably from the head of a cross. The upper room has a squint through a quatrefoil opening in the jamb of an adjacent aisle window. Parts of the rood screen are reused in the tower screen. One south aisle window has old heraldic glass.

Chudleigh Church

Clannaborough Church

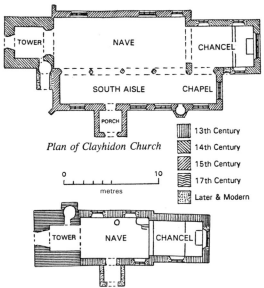

Plan of Clayhidon Church

13th Century
14th Century
15th Century
17th Century
Later & Modern

Plan of Clannaborough Church

CLANNABOROUGH   *St Petrock*   SS 937067

This is a small church composed of a west tower with a NE stair turret and a 16th century west doorway, a nave with a south porch and a narrower chancel inclined to the south. The chancel arch and windows are of the restoration of 1858-9 except for one 15th century south window. There are memorials to Grace Freke, d1783, Richard Freke, d1800 and later members of the Wreford and Hardman families.

CLAWTON   *St Leonard*   SX 349993

The chancel has one Norman north window but is otherwise mostly Victorian. The 14th century west tower has a polygonal stair turret in the middle of the south side. The four bay arcades may also be 14th century, with double chamfered arches on octagonal piers with castellated abaci. The east bays with piers with eight shafts were probably intended as transepts, and on the south side there is a squint into the chancel. The north aisle has a fine wagon roof. The porch outer entrance has a sunk quadrant moulding decorated with balls carved with crosses with end roundels. Medieval tiles surround the circular Norman font with a band of cable moulding and a base with four faces and half-rosettes. There are Royal Arms under the tower. There is a slate plate and a relief effigy of 1631 to Christopher Osmond.

CLAYHANGER   *St Peter*   ST 022230

The 14th century west tower has diagonal buttresses at the lowest stage. The east window with reticulated tracery is also 14th century although the rest of the chancel and the chancel arch are of the restoration of 1879-81 by Hine and Odgers. The small font of c1200 has a fluted bowl. The reredos incorporates fragments of a Jacobean gallery and cresting from the medieval rood screen. The double lectern is Jacobean and there are many 16th century bench ends with figures and motifs.

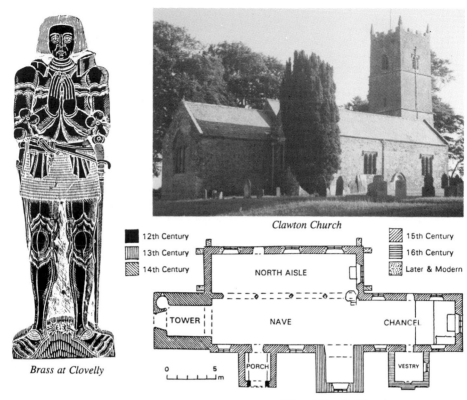

Clawton Church

12th Century
13th Century
14th Century

NORTH AISLE

15th Century
16th Century
Later & Modern

TOWER   NAVE   CHANCEL

PORCH   VESTRY

0   5   m

Brass at Clovelly

Plan of Clovelly Church

CLAYHIDON *St Andrew* ST 162156

The west tower and the chancel may be 14th century although the chancel features are all renewed. The nave north wall is 15th century and so is the south aisle with a porch and an arcade of four bays to the nave and a fifth beyond a rood-loft stair-turret to the chancel. The 19th century west gallery is the oldest of the fittings.

CLOVELLY *All Saints* SS 309252

The church lies by Clovelly Court, some way from the village. The plain block-capital shaped font and the reset outer arch with chevrons on the porch outer entrance are Norman. The massively built south transept may have been intended to be carried up as a tower, and if so an early one for the present west tower probably goes back to the 14th century. The undivided nave and chancel are 15th century and so are the north aisle with a four bay arcade and the south porch, whilst the south vestry is perhaps 16th century. There are open wagon roofs, plain medieval benches, fragments of old heraldic glass in a chancel north window and a pulpit dated 1634.

There are many memorials to the Carys, two of them having mid 16th century brasses, and another having a monument with six columns. A group of similar wall tablets have dates 1652, 1675, 1677, 1680, 1685, 1686, with one later one of 1728. They were succeeded by the Hamlyns, monuments to whom include that of Zachary, d1759, a noted lawyer at Lincoln's Inn, and Lady Hamyln, d1797.

Interior of Clovelly Church

CLYST HONITON   *St Michael*   SX 981935

Features surviving the rebuilding by William White in 1876 are the west tower with set-back buttresses and a circular stair turret, the low north arcade with capitals only on the shafts, the square Norman font with blank arches on one side, fluted chevrons on another and the others recut later, and a monument to John Yarde, d1575.

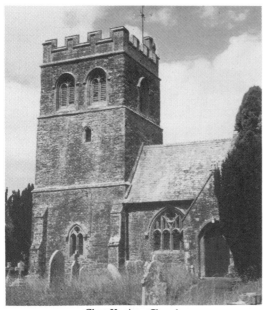

Clyst Honiton Church

Clyst St Lawrence Church

CLYSTHYDON   *St Andrew*   ST 035056

The west tower with set-back buttresses and classical pinnacles is dated 1658, probably referring to a rebuilding of an earlier structure. The south aisle of c1500 has an embattled rood-loft stair-turret and a porch with a fan vault and the arms of the St Clere family supported by an angel over the outer portal. The north aisle is of 1856. The plaster wagon roofs and furnishings are of that period except for some 18th century box pews and the 15th century font.

CLYST ST GEORGE   *St George*   SX 984889

The slender sandstone west tower with a stair turret has a panelled tower arch. The rest was heavily restored in 1854-5 by the Reverend H.T.Ellacombe, and was rebuilt again after being gutted during World War II.

CLYST ST LAWRENCE   *St Lawrence*   SY 027999

The rubble chancel is probably older than the 15th century ashlar nave, porch and diagonally buttressed west tower with a figure of the Virgin in a niche on the stair-turret and two more figures higher up. The tower arch is panelled and the west doorway has fleurons on the jambs. The nave has original windows and wagon roof and there is an old screen. The font is Norman. In the churchyard is a medieval cross.

CLYST ST MARY   *St Mary*   SX 978904

The transepts of the original small cruciform 13th century church with a west tower were enlarged in 1818 to such a degree that in c1869 Ashworth re-orientated the church, the north transept then becoming the chancel.

Clyst St Mary Church

Coffinswell Church

Font at Cockington

COCKINGTON   *St George & St Mary*   SX 891639

This is a mostly 15th century church, only the porch of the priest's doorway on the north and the SW vestry with its stair turret being obviously Victorian. Entrance is through the base of the west tower with diagonal buttresses and a polygonal stair turret on the north side. There are old bench ends there. The aisles are of five bays with decorated capitals on the south side. A sanctuary projects one further bay to the east. The octagonal font has quatrefoils and heraldry. The screen has been much restored. There is a very fine 16th century early Renaissance style pulpit transferred here from Torre church. One south window contains 15th century stained glass figures of apostles, and there is a 14th century figure of St Paul in a north window.

Interior of Cockington Church

COFFINSWELL

St Bartholomew

SX 891685

The battered and roughcast west tower is 13th or 14th century. The western piers of the north arcade have heraldry relating to John Holbeame, d1473, and foliage on the capitals. Other features of note are traces of a wall painting and a circular Norman font with palmettes, crosses saltire and a cable moulding.

COFTON   *St Mary*

SX 968803

In 1838-9 a small 13th century church recorded as ruinous in the 18th century was mostly rebuilt by Charles Fowler for the 10th Earl of Devon. A north aisle was added in 1863. The features and fittings are all Victorian.

COLATON RALEIGH

St John Baptist

SY 082872

Rebuilding by Fulford in 1873-5 left only the early 16th century west tower with a polygonal south stair-turret, a Norman font with cable moulding, a reset piscina and the north arcade of c1200 with round columns. The Victorian east end is elaborately decorated with sgraffito work.

Cockington Church

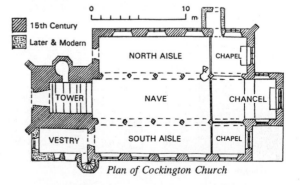

Plan of Cockington Church

Font at Colebrooke Church

Pulpit at Coldridge Church

COLDRIDGE *St Matthew* SS 699077

The chancel has a Norman window with voussoirs of alternate red and yellow stone. Probably of c1200 is the plain pointed arch towards the west end of the nave north aisle. It may have led to a former NW tower. A 15th century north aisle starts east of it, with two bays up to the screen, beyond which there is a narrow bay and then a wider bay for an early 16th century north chapel containing the monument of John Evans, keeper of the Marquess of Dorset's deer park at Coldridge. He is assumed to have donated the rood screen, the chapel screen, the stained glass in the chapel east window, the fine pulpit with nodding ogival canopies and tracery, and the bench ends, one of which has linenfold panelling and an inscription referring to the year 1511. The aisle of four bays on the south side also stops short of meeting up with the west tower, which has a polygonal NE stair turret and diagonal buttresses on the other three corners. The aisles have ceiled wagon roofs with fine bosses. The chancel east end was rebuilt in 1877. The square Norman font has seven shallow arches on each side. There are old tiles in front of the altar and there is a slab with a foliated cross in the south aisle.

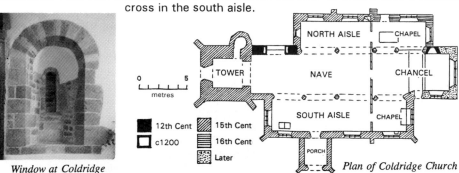

Window at Coldridge

0 5
metres

■ 12th Cent
☐ c1200
▨ 15th Cent
▤ 16th Cent
▦ Later

Plan of Coldridge Church

Blocked arch at Coldridge   *Colebrooke Church*

COLEBROOKE   *St Andrew*   SS 770001

The nave south wall has two blocked round-headed arches of a former Norman south aisle. There seems to have been a Late Norman south transept also but the present one is 14th century, like the chancel to which it is connected by a squint, and has windows of that date and two low ogival-headed tomb recesses. It contains two heads from the Norman nave. The north chapel is thought to have been built to house a chantry to John Copplestone and has a window with Flamboyant tracery and a screen with linenfold panelling probably by a Belgian carver, since the decorative forms are Franco-Flemish. The blocked fireplace was inserted when the chapel became a family pew in the 16th century. From this chapel has come the prayer desk with the Copplestone and Gorges arms (the families intermarried in 1472) and carvings of a fool and a wild man now in the chancel. The north aisle is of about the same date, and perhaps also the diagonally buttressed west tower with three light straight-headed bell-openings. The octagonal font has quatrefoil panels and shields and tracery on the pillar. The cover is Jacobean. Outside the chancel doorway is a medieval foliated cross slab. There is a wall monument to Elizabeth Coryton, d1667.

COLYTON   *St Andrew*   ST 246941

Norman are the chancel, the nave west corners, and the lower parts of the central tower with plain pointed arches on all four sides. The transept arches are of different width and so were the transepts, although both are now effectively swallowed up into the wide 15th century aisles with four bay arcades west of the tower. The west end has four-light windows in the aisles and a nine-light window in the nave. The upper parts of the nave and aisles were rebuilt in 1769 and the diagonally-placed capitals and round arcade arches are of 1818. The rare octagonal top stage of the tower is 15th century. The chancel has a five-light early 14th century window and two bay arcades to a pair of 15th century chapels. The stone screen in the south chapel was part of the chantry of Thomas Brerewood, vicar 1522 to 1544. The north chapel has a Jacobean stone screen. During repairs after a fire in 1933 fragments of a 10th century cross came to light. The shaft has scrolls with a bird and a lion on the front and interlacing on the sides. There is a brass candelabra of 1796.

On a tomb chest is a small recumbent effigy of Margaret Beaufort, Countess of Devon, d1449. Under one of the arches to the south chapel is a monument with reclining effigies of Sir John Pole, d1658, and his wife, d1628. There is a monument to William Pole, d1587, and his wife. The chapel contains various other monuments to the Poles of Colcombe and Shute. There are also kneeling effigies of William Westover, d1617, and his wife.

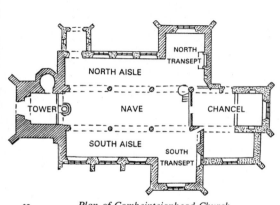

Plan of Combeinteignhead Church

| 12th Century |
| 14th Century |
| 15th Century |
| Later & Modern |

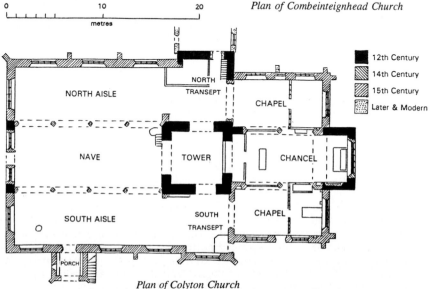

Plan of Colyton Church

COMBEINTEIGNHEAD   *All Saints*

SX 902716

The church has quite an ambitious plan with an aisled nave, transepts, and a west tower with a polygonal stair turret on the north side, but the scale is modest, the nave and chancel being only 3.6m wide. Most of the exterior dates from the restorations of 1851 (that date appears on the NW porch) and 1887, with diagonal corner buttresses on all parts except the aisles, and a SE vestry. The wide spacing of the piers inside (just three bays) creates a deceptive spaciousness. The transepts have squints into the chancel. In the north transept east wall is a ogival-arched recess for the tomb chest of Alice Hockmore, d1633. Under the tower arch is a circular Norman font with palmettes and bands of saltire crosses and cable moulding. There are bench ends carved with single saints, and pairs of saints with below them two wild men and a fool and an archer. The screen was restored c1905.

Monument at Combeinteignhead Church

Colyton Church

Combe Martin Church

COMBE MARTIN   *St Peter ad Vincula*   SS 586464

The 13th century chancel has a triple east lancet, and renewed lancets flanking a priest's doorway on the south side. Another lancet has been reused in a shorter form in the NE vestry east wall. The south transept is also of that period and may have been intended to be carried up as a tower. The south doorway is 14th century and is entered through a porch of 1726 bearing a sundial dated 1753. In the 15th century a show front on the north was created by adding to the nave an aisle with a lofty three bay arcade with leaf capitals to the piers, and also adding a north chapel with a single wide arch to the chancel. Projecting from them are a porch and north transept, both with diagonal buttresses. The square pier at the junction of the nave and chancel has two niches facing west which visually form part of the screen, which is the only example in North Devon to retain original painted figures on the wainscoting. The 30m high west tower has set-back buttresses, niches for images, two tiers of gargoyles, battlements and tall crocketed pinnacles. There are fleurons on the west doorway and the three-light bell openings are unusually big for Devon.

The octagonal font has slightly recessed blank arches. There and many old bench ends and under the tower are undated Royal Arms. The chapel parclose screen has a cornice frieze. There is a frontal demi-figure of Judith Hancock, d1634, and there is also a monument to George Ley, d1716.

COMBE RALEIGH   *St Nicholas*   ST 158024

The nave south wall probably is the same age as the 14th century tower with a SE stair-turret. The south porch, the chancel and north chapel with a two bay arcade between them and the north aisle with a four bay arcade and a rood-loft staircase projection are all 15th century. There are no furnishings of interest.

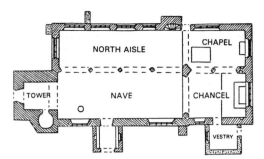

Plan of Combe Raleigh Church

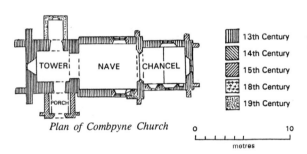

▉	13th Century
▩	14th Century
▨	15th Century
▥	18th Century
▦	19th Century

Plan of Combpyne Church

0   10

metres

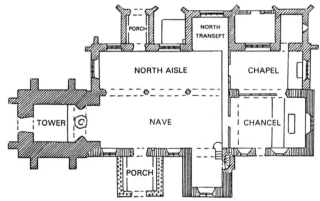

Plan of Combe Martin Church

Combe Raleigh Church

Combe Martin Church

COMBPYNE *St Mary* SY 290924

The small church is mostly 13th century, the low west tower with large angle buttresses and the triple east lancets of the saddle-back roofed chancel being of that date. The chancel side windows look late 13th century and two south windows and rood-loft staircase are 15th century. Because of the road being immediately to the west the tower has a doorway on the south side and this has a porch in front of it, balanced on the other side by a Victorian vestry. The church was much restored in 1878 by Jones and Willis.

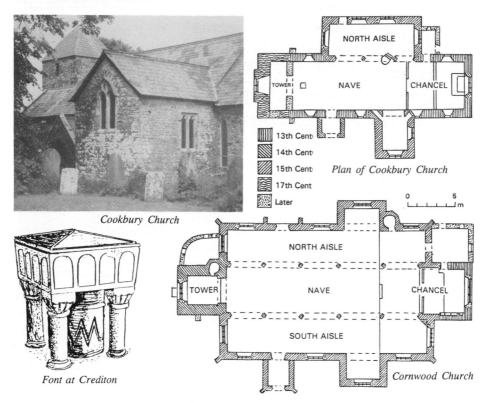

Cookbury Church

Plan of Cookbury Church

13th Cent
14th Cent
15th Cent
17th Cent
Later

NORTH AISLE

TOWER   NAVE   CHANCEL

NORTH AISLE

TOWER   NAVE   CHANCEL

SOUTH AISLE

Font at Crediton

Cornwood Church

COOKBURY   *St John & the Seven Maccabees*   SS 407061

The Norman nave and the 13th century chancel form a single chamber. The south transept is later since it partly obscures a chancel lancet window. It has 15th century windows and squints without any cut stone to both east and west. The short aisle on the north is also 15th century. It had wooden windows in the early 19th century but now has plain mullioned windows. The south porch may be 13th century and there is an east window of three cusped lights of c1300. In the 17th or 18th century a small tower was raised over the nave west end, a cross-wall being built to support it. The font with corner shafts is 13th century, there is a Jacobean font from Launceston, there are several plain medieval bench ends and some medieval tiles, plus some medieval panels, perhaps from a screen, reused in the altar.

CORNWOOD   *St Michael*   SX 606594

The low west tower with a NE stair-turret is late 13th or 14th century. Except for a Victorian vestry and the 13th century sanctuary with sedilia and piscina and traces of lancets, the rest is all late 15th century with arcades of five bays using monolithic granite columns, a south porch, transepts projecting from the fourth bays and the fifth bays forming chapels. There is a polygonal rood-loft stair-turret in the angle between the north transept and north chapel. There is a patterned Jacobean pulpit. There are kneeling effigies of Robert Bellemaine, d1627 and his wife, and Philip Cole, d1596, and his wife Joan, and also an effigy of the child John Savery, d1696.

Cornwood Church

CORNWORTHY *St Peter* SX 829556

The west tower has set-back buttresses and a central polygonal stair-turret. The rest was remodelled c1820 and the wooden intersecting tracery dates from then. The arcades have limestone arches set upon granite piers. A porch with an image bracket is located at the west end of the south aisle, with its outer portal facing west. There is a two storey vestry on the north side. The circular Norman font has friezes of palmettes and crosses saltire. The pulpit with an ogee-roofed tester and trumpeting angel was given in 1757 by John Seale, d1777, of Mount Boone, Dartmouth, to whom there is a monument. The screen has been much renewed. There is a brass candelabra of the 18th century. There are recumbent effigies of 1610 of Sir Thomas Harris and his wife on a tomb chest with a tester above.

CORYTON *St Andrew* SX 457836

The chancel has one original 13th century south lancet. Two south windows of the nave and the diagonally buttressed west tower are 15th century. In 1885 the church was restored by Alfred Norman for the Newmans of Mamhead and a two bay north aisle then replaced the original north transept. The porch could be 18th century.

COTLEIGH *St Michael* ST 206022

The diagonally buttressed west tower, the north aisle and nave with ceiled wagon roofs and square-headed windows and the octagonal font with quatrefoil panels are all 15th century. The chancel was mostly rebuilt in 1867.

COUNTISBURY *St John the Baptist* SS 747498

One bench end with a crowned swan and arms is the only medieval relic. The screen with a broken pediment is of c1700. The nave was rebuilt in 1796, the tower in 1835, and the north aisle and its arcade are of 1846.

CREACOMBE *St Michael* SS 818194

The plain circular font is the only ancient feature. The church, comprising a nave, chancel, south porch and bellcote, was entirely rebuilt in 1857.

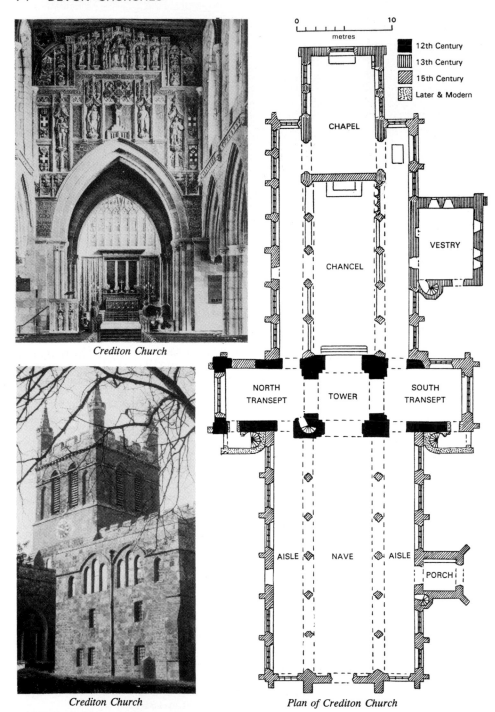

Crediton Church

Crediton Church

Plan of Crediton Church

Legend:
- 12th Century
- 13th Century
- 15th Century
- Later & Modern

metres 0 — 10

CHAPEL

CHANCEL

VESTRY

NORTH TRANSEPT

TOWER

SOUTH TRANSEPT

AISLE   NAVE   AISLE

PORCH

CREDITON   *Holy Cross*   SS 836003

Nothing remains of a Saxon cathedral here, Credition being the seat of a bishop from 909 to 1050. The church was collegiate from the early 12th century until the Reformation and is a cruciform building 66m long. The massive crossing piers, the lower part of the tower above and the north transept are Norman, and originally the transepts had eastern chapels. The Lady Chapel at the east end and the rectangular chapter house raised over what was once a chapel with two arches towards the south choir aisle are 13th century. Probably of just after 1413, when the church was described as almost ruinous, are the nave and aisles with arcades of six bays and the chancel with five bay arcades but with the aisles extending further to flank the west end of the Lady Chapel, a necessary arrangement as there is a solid wall behind the chancel high altar. On the south side the fifth arch contains contemporary sedilia with lierne-vaulting, backing onto which is a tomb chest with a vaulted recess above. Above is a frieze of figures showing the Annunciation, the Nativity, the Resurrection, two views of the Ascension and a soul carried by flying angels. The Lady Chapel has an original double piscina, windows of c1420, and a blocked 16th century south doorway put in to serve the grammar school which occupied this part of the building from the Reformation period until 1860.

The nave and chancel arcades have wave mouldings and capitals only on the pier shafts. There are clerestories, with three light windows on the nave, and four light windows on the chancel. Of the 16th century are most of the south transept, the eight-light west window and the diagonally buttressed south porch with a NE staircase to an upper room. Much of the exterior was refaced between 1848 and 1877 and further work was done in 1887-9 and 1913. The only old furnishings are a Norman font and an oak chest of 1500. There are three foliated cross-slabs and effigies of Sir John Sully, d1387, and his wife on a tomb chest. There is a reclining effigy of Sir William Perrian, d1605, with his family kneeling below. There is a bust of John Tuckfield beside a full length effigy of his wife Elizabeth erected in 1630.

CREDITON   *St Lawrence*   SS 825004

This chapel is perhaps of 13th century origin but its features are modern. It was used as a cottage until restored as a chapel in 1920-1 by Sir Charles Nicholson.

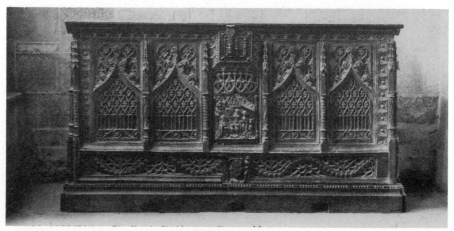

Chest at Crediton

CRUWYS MORCHARD   *Holy Cross*   SS 874122

In the 1520s a south aisle with a five bay arcade with piers with leaf capitals was added to a 14th century single chamber with intersecting tracery in the east window. Similar tracery lies in the west window of the diagonally buttressed west tower. The top stage was rebuilt in brick in 1689 after a fire. Of the 18th century are the white plaster panelling, the plastering of the wagon roofs, the fine screen with Corinthian capitals and a central pediment, the altar rails with twisted balusters, the box pews, the pulpit and the font cover with a dove. The oldest monument is that of John Avery, d1695, with Corinthian columns and angels flanking an achievement.

CULLOMPTON   *St Andrew*   ST 022072

The main body of the church is 15th century work with arcades of six bays with figures and leaves on the pier capitals, north windows of four lights and the rare feature in Devon of a clerestory. The boarded wagon roof has angel brackets and cross-ribs to all the panels. An outer south aisle flanking the five bays west of the screen was added by the wealthy cloth merchant John Lane a few years before his death in 1529. An inscription about the donor runs along the west wall. The south side has large windows probably re-used from the former south wall on the site of which is now an arcade with piers having towards the aisle buttresses with two tiers of saints. The windows are separated by buttresses with symbols such as ships, cloth shears and teasel frames plus monograms. Below the ornate battlements is a frieze with worn scenes of the Life of Christ. The position of the springers suggests the fan-vault over the aisle was not part of the original design. The pendants have emblems of the Passion of Christ and cloth shears, teasel frames and Lane's merchant's mark. The brass on John Lane's tombstone is now lost.

Cullompton Church

The 30m high west tower of red sandstone was added in the 1540s and bears the arms of Bishop Veysey. The buttresses have three orders of gargoyles under pinnacles and there are pierced battlements with clusters of five pinnacles at each corner and threes in the middle of each side. Over the west window are large panels with the Crucifixion, the Virgin and St John. There is a stair turret on the north side. On the south side a porch overlaps the junction of the tower and nave south wall. This porch contains the only surviving medieval monument, a foliated cross-slab.

The fine screen has coving to the east and west and an original cornice. Higher up is the rood beam, recorded as lying in the churchyard in 1834 but evidently later reinstated. In the south aisle is the Golgotha carved with rocks, skulls and bones with mortices for figures. There are also parclose screens to the chapels, that on the north being probably late 16th century. The sanctuary was rebuilt in 1848-50 by Edward Ashworth with a large east window and a vestry provided south of it. The Jacobean west gallery has Ionic columns. The other furnishings are of 1849.

CULMSTOCK   *All Saints*   ST 103135

A yew tree now grows on top of the diagonally buttressed tower with a stair turret in place of the spire removed in 1776. The south aisle has a squint towards the chancel and an original piscina. The nave ceiling dates from 1825 when the north aisle was added. The medieval stone screen was adapted as a reredos in 1835. There is a sculptured fragment of a 15th century figure found in a cottage at Prescott.

DALWOOD   *St Peter*   ST 248025

The chancel arch was inserted by Benjamin Ferrey in 1876-8. The rest is 15th or 16th century, comprising a nave and north aisle with a low three bay arcade, a chancel with a single arch to a north chapel continuing the aisle, a south porch. and a diagonally buttressed west tower with a polygonal SE stair-turret. The south windows are square headed with three arched lights. The north doorway is blocked.

DARTINGTON   *St Mary*   SX 798627

Hidden away behind the west side of the late 14th century Dartington Hall stands the modest tower of the medieval church. Probably of the same period as the hall, it has a NE stair-turret and contains a wall monument to Sir Arthur Champernowne, d1578, who purchased the estate in 1559. Other monuments to his descendants include that of Henry, d1656, and Rawlin, d1774.

In the 1870s the rest of the medieval church was dismantled and a new church designed by J.L.Pearson on a similar plan was erected on a new site 1km to the west by the main road. Late medieval parts re-used from the old church are the south porch with a fine vault, the arcades (which are higher than they were in the original building), the south door, the pulpit, and the font stem.

Porch vault at Dartington new church

St Clement's Church, Dartmouth

DARTMOUTH   *St Clement*   SX 869516

This church lies high above the town, 1km west of the shore. Much of it dates from c1300-30, including the north arcade with piers which are octagonal with concave sides with shafts in the diagonals, the north and south transepts and the south doorway with one order of colonettes. In 1983 the south transept was divided off by a glazed screen. The chancel north wall has an unusual eye-shaped squint. The diagonally buttressed west tower with a stair-turret and pinnacles is late 14th or 15th century. There is a Jacobean communion table with the top supported by heraldic beasts. The octagonal Norman font has two shallow blank arches on each side. There is a brass to Robert Holland, d1611 and other monuments include those of William Roope, d1666, Thomas Boone, erected 1681, and Mary Roope, d1739.

Interior of St Petrox Church, Dartmouth

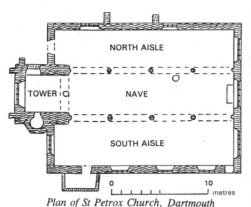

Plan of St Petrox Church, Dartmouth

St Petrox Church, Dartmouth

DARTMOUTH   *St Petrox*   SX 887504

The church is of early foundation and contains a circular Norman font with a palmette frieze, but the present building lying within the area of the late 14th century castle, and adjacent to the late 15th century artillery blockhouse, some way south of the town, seems to be entirely of 1641, the same date as the pulpit. It has aisles of four bays as wide as the central nave and extending further west to partly engage a west tower with set-back buttresses and a polygonal stair-turret on the south side. The windows are mostly of four lights, but those on the south only have three lights with the mullions rising through a transom, below which are arched lights, to steeply pointed heads. The War memorial contains woodwork from a former 17th century west gallery. There are boards with texts from a former reredos. There are several good 17th and 18th century ledger stones, plus a brass depicting John Roope, d1609, and an undated 17th century memorial to Elizabeth Roope.

Interior of St Saviour's Church, Dartmouth

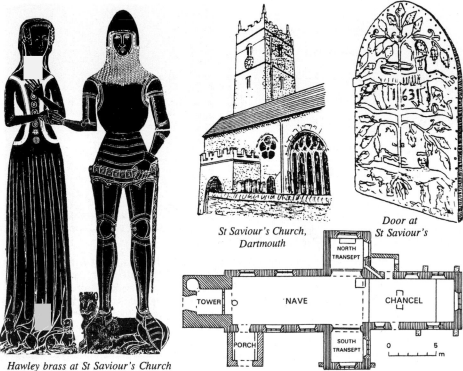

Hawley brass at St Saviour's Church

St Saviour's Church, Dartmouth

Door at St Saviour's

Plan of Denbury Church

DARTMOUTH   *St Saviour*   SX 869516

Permission for the construction of a chapel by the harbour was granted by Edward I in 1286. The west bays of the arcades with double-chamfered arches on octagonal piers with shafts on the diagonals may be older than the "honesta capella de novo constructa" consecrated in 1372. The tall west tower clasped by the aisle may be of that period. The town corporation took over the advowson from 1586 and had the building largely rebuilt in 1633-7, the tower top and west gallery being of that period, although the porch was added earlier, in 1620. Beside the entrance is an old door with fine ironwork depicting lions striding across a tree. The date 1631 must refer to a repair. Of the late 15th or early 16th century are the eastern parts of the arcades, but the transepts projecting from the fourth bay contain 14th century work. East of this bay is a screen known to have been under construction in 1496. The parclose screens are later, having arms and initials of James Pelliton, mayor in 1567-8.

There is a medieval stone pulpit. The communion table of 1588 has four carved figures of evangelists, since 1893 fixed to the front, but originally forming the legs. The chancel was restored by E.H.Sedding in 1887 but retains 14th century sedilia and piscina with crocketed ogival tops. The brass candelabra in the nave is of 1708. In the chancel is a fine brass showing the shipping magnate and three times mayor John Hawley, d1408, with his two wives under cusped ogival canopies. In the south chapel is a brass of a 15th century lady. By the pulpit is the lower part of an incised slab of a priest in Eucharistic vestments discovered in 1983. There are other monuments to Nicholas Hayman, d1606, and Roger Vavasour, d1696, & son d1727.

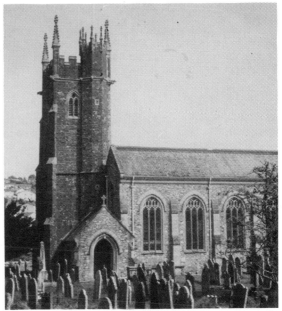

Font at Dean Prior

Dawlish Church

DAWLISH   *St Gregory*   SX 953767

The only features to predate the rebuilding of 1824 by Andrew Patey are the diagonally buttressed 15th century west tower with a polygonal stair turret and white pinnacles, a rebuilt 15th century arcade, the 18th century Royal Arms and a few monuments, notably that to the Reverend John Trosse, d1678. In 1874 J.P. St Aubyn removed the battlements and pinnacles from Patey's nave and built the present chancel and transepts.

DEAN PRIOR   *St George*   SX 731636

The tower has a central polygonal stair turret on the south side with an external doorway. The tower arch is round and unmoulded. The arcades have steep pointed double chamfered arches on low octagonal granite piers, perhaps 14th century work. There is a circular Norman font of sandstone with a band each of crosses saltire and long dragons. There are kneeling effigies of Sir Edward Giles, d1642 and his family. a tablet to Robert Herrick, vicar of Denbury from 1654 to 1674. The surround is later.

DENBURY   *St Mary*   SX 824689

The church reported as "finished" in 1291, but not consecrated until 1318, survives almost complete, although the nave and transepts now have later medieval windows. The chancel has a piscina and Y-tracery in the side windows and intersecting tracery in the three light east window. The tower also has a window with intersecting tracery but is probably 14th century. The north transept once had a squint cutting across the corner of a small vestry which has a cross-shaped loop above the doorway from the chancel. The sandstone Norman font is circular with palmettes. The screen closing off the north transept is said to have come from Dartington old church. The monument by Weston to John Taylor, d1733 has a relief of a naval battle.

DEVONPORT   *St Aubyn*   SS 454546

This church was built in 1771-2 to serve the docks. The west tower is half sunk into the main pediment. The Baroque spire is rather truncated. Thee main windows have segmental tops. The interior has a barrel-vault and a gallery with large Doric columns. A chancel was added in the 19th century.

DIPTFORD   *St Mary*   SX 728568

The tower has diagonal buttresses and a SE stair turret and must be a hundred years later than the fake inscription on the west doorway dating it to 1220. In fact the whole church looks 14th century except for the NE vestry and several buttresses of the 17th and 18th centuries, plus the NE vestry and several windows which are 19th century. A sundial over the south porch entrance is dated 1694. The arcades of four bays have double-chamfered arches on low octagonal piers with foliage carved on the capitals. Parts of the screen are medieval. There is a wall monument to sixteen-year old Anne Taylor, d1763.

Diptford Church

St Aubyn's Church, Devonport

DITTISHAM   *St George*   SX 861551

The chancel has reticulated tracery in the east window and sedilia with a painting of a cleric probably going back to the time of the consecration of 1333. The embattled aisles have 15th century windows with a rood-loft stair-turret on the north side and a two storeyed porch with pinnacles on the south. The porch has two bays of lierne-vaulting with large bosses and blank arcades on the east and west sides, and the doorway has traceried spandrels on both north and south sides. The arcades are of four bays. The west tower has set-back buttresses and a stair-turret and pinnacles. The circular Norman font has a series of arches. Probably there were once columns and figures painted on. The stone pulpit is medieval and there is a screen with early 15th century figures on the wainscoting. The parclose screens with Flamboyant tracery are rather later.

DODBROOKE   *St Thomas a Becket*   SX 739446

A spire on the diagonally buttressed west tower collapsed in 1785. The tall bell-openings have one transom. There is a south aisle with a arcade of six bays and a fine wagon roof. West of the aisle is a porch. In 1878-86 Edmund Sedding restored the church, adding a sanctuary, renewing the tower arch and replacing the destroyed former north aisle with a new one, re-using clustered columns from the abandoned church at South Huish to carry the arcade. The screen was then restored and extended across the new aisle. The square Norman font has five shallow blank arches on each side. There is a tablet to John Beare, d1666, in the south aisle.

Dodbrooke Church

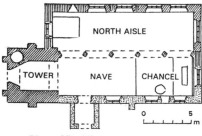

Plan of Doddiscombesleigh Church

Capital at Doddiscombsleigh

DODDISCOMBSLEIGH   *St Michael*   SX 858866

Five 15th century windows in the north aisle contain the best stained glass remaining in a parish church in Devon. The east window shows the Seven Sacraments and the others have saints above coats of arms. The aisle has a five bay arcade with piers of unusually complex section. The western part of the aisle has 13th century masonry with one original lancet and the east jamb of another original opening further east, whilst the west wall has a window with two round arched lights, hidden inside now by the organ. The tower has west buttresses set back from the corners, whilst the north and south sides each have a single centrally placed buttress - a unique arrangement. The south side of the south has been renewed. There are 16th century bench ends with shields in round panels and there is a late 18th century pulpit.

DOLTON   *St Edmund*   SS 570120

Two blocks from a large Anglo-Saxon cross, one square with fine interlace on all sides, the other tapering with more interlace plus symmetrical animals and a human head with moustaches growing into animals, now form the font. The church itself was much repaired and rebuilt in 1848, 1862 and 1874. Widely spaced octagonal piers carry slightly chamfered arches. The west tower has a fine west doorway and diagonal buttresses. It is nalf-engaged by the aisles. Over the south doorway are Royal Arms of 1760. There is a wooden cartouche to Barbara Lister, d1696.

DOWLAND   *St Peter*   SS 568103

The round arched south doorway could be Norman. The exterior was roughcast in 1976 and has little of interest apart from the diagonally buttressed west tower with obelisk pinnacles. Inside are a late medieval timber arcade and ceiled wagon roofs, and bench ends with tracery plus Malchus's ear and St Peter's keys. The small octagonal font with ribbed angles is probably 17th century. One south window has fragments of old glass.

DOWN ST MARY   *St Mary*   SS 743044

This is a small and remote church. Norman are the chancel with one original window and the triangular tympanum over the south doorway showing Daniel in the lions' den. The west tower has set-back buttresses and a stair-turret. There are a few old bench ends with monograms, profiles, a siren with a comb and a cherub with a scourge. The other features and some fine furnishings date from the incumbency of the Reverend W.T.A.Radford 1848-90.

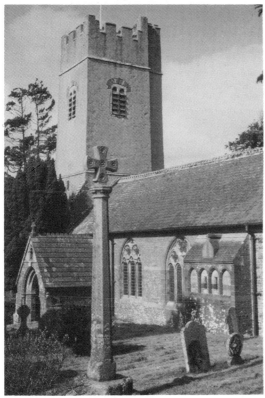

Down St Mary Church   *Doddiscombesleigh Church*

DREWSTEIGNTON   *Holy Trinity*   SX 736909

This is a late medieval granite church of some size with the south aisle and two storey porch embattled, whilst more elaborate windows appear on the north side. The west tower has diagonal buttresses and a 17th century clock. The chancel was rebuilt by Ashworth in 1862-3. There are two traceried 16th century bench ends.

DUNCHIDEOCK   *St Michael*   SX 876877

This is a small, late medieval red sandstone church with a north aisle with an arcade of octagonal piers and a slender west tower with a stair-turret. The octagonal font has tracery on the stem and two quatrefoil panels on each side. The rood screen and parclose screen survive almost complete and there are bench ends with two-tier tracery. There is a monument to Major-General Stringer Lawrence, d1775.

DUNKESWELL   *St Nicholas*   ST 142078

A circular Norman font with figures of a king, bishop, archer, and a beaked animal head under an arcade lies in the church of 1818, enlarged into a cruciform structure by C.F.Edwards in 1868. 3km to the north is a second church, Holy Trinity, on the site of Dunkeswell Abbey, from which have come the coffin and 13th century tiles.

DUNSFORD   *St Mary*   SX 813892

The north arcade has piers of an unusually complex section. The west tower has set-back buttresses and a stair-turret. In the north wall is a 16th century recess. The chancel was rebuilt in 1844-5 by J.Hayward. There are wagon roofs and the stained glass includes some small 15th century figures in the north windows. The other furnishings are mid 19th century. On a tomb chest are recumbent effigies of Sir Thomas Fulford, d1610. Other monuments to members of the Fulford family include that of Francis, d1700, with flaming urns flanking an oval tablet.

DUNTERTON   *All Saints*   SX 376793

The small isolated church is dwarfed by its west tower with set-back buttresses and polygonal pinnacles. The nave has one late 14th century south window. The chancel and the north aisle with a four bay arcade of four-centred arches on piers with decorated capitals and castellated abaci are 15th century. The pulpit is 18th century.

EAST ALLINGTON   *St Andrew*   SX 769484

The west tower has set-back buttresses, a stair turret and battlements upon a corbel-table. The north arcade has five bays and the south arcade four. The capitals are identical throughout but the western two piers on the north are octagonal and perhaps earlier. The screen has oblong Elizabethan panels on the wainscoting. The pulpit stands on a chalice-shaped base and looks like 17th century work in the 15th century style. There are brasses of a mid 16th century kneeling woman and of John Fortescue, d1595, and his wife. There is an incised slab to Edmund Fortescue, High Sheriff, d1624, plus kneeling figures of John Fortescue, d1649, and his wife, d1628, and a plain wall monument to the Reverend Nathaniel Wells, d1762.

Plan of East Budleigh Church

Dunsford Church

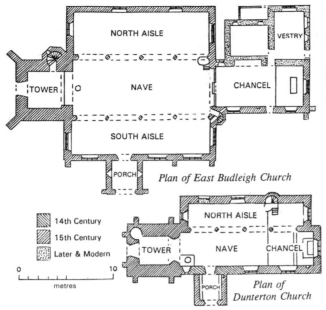

Plan of East Budleigh Church

Green Man at East Budleigh

NORTH AISLE

TOWER   NAVE   CHANCEL

PORCH

Plan of Dunterton Church

14th Century
15th Century
Later & Modern

0   10
metres

EAST ANSTEY   *St Michael*   SS 867265

Everything east of the 15th century porch and doorway, including the vestry and probably the featureless north wall dates from Ashworth's restoration of 1871. The west tower with a NE stair-turret and diagonal buttresses may be 14th century, and there is a 16th century window west of the porch. The pulpit and altar rails are 18th century.

EAST BUCKLAND   *St Michael*   SS 677314

On the south side of the nave and chancel of 1862-3 by R.D.Gould is the diagonally buttressed west tower of the old church with a square NE stair-turret.

Brass at East Allington

EAST BUDLEIGH   *All Saints*   SY 066849

The church is mostly 15th century but the chancel has a 13th century piscina halfway along it, having been lengthened in 1853. Either then or in 1884 two vestries were added. The nave has aisles of four bays, one pier on the south side having a green man on the capital. The south aisle is embattled with a porch in front of a fine doorway with fleurons on the moulding and a squint extends through the rood-loft staircase into the chancel. The west tower has diagonal buttresses reaching halfway up and a polygonal stair turret on the north side. The nave and chancel has ceiled roofs with bosses. The arms of Bishop Lacy appear in stained glass in a north aisle window. There is a panelled font and a screen. There are sixty-three bench ends carved with motifs such as leaves, coats of arms (including those of Raleigh), a ship, shears, angels, faces in profile, and the date 1537. There is a 16th century incised floriated cross-slab in memory of Joan Raleigh with the inscription going backwards.

EAST DOWN   *St John Baptist*   SS 601418

Polwhele claims that the original parish church was at Churchill and this was a manorial chapel until the other church was abandoned. The north transeptal tower has a small plain pointed arch and a 14th century east window. It bears the marks of bullets fired at it during a Civil War skirmish. Within it are very damaged Royal Arms of George II dated 1756. The nave and chancel may be 13th century as the nave has a blocked pointed-headed north doorway of early type and the chancel south windows appear to be of that date. The 15th century south aisle has a five bay arcade with the west respond dramatically leaning back, and with a squint to the chancel beyond the east respond. There are humans and beasts on the second pier capital from the west. The porch goes with it and bears a sundial dated 1709. There are open wagon roofs throughout the church. The font has a tapering hexagonal 16th century shaft and a foot and bowl of c1700. The screen was much restored in 1928. The south chapel altar has Elizabethan panelling. There are slabs to Walter Ley, d1594, and Richard Ley, d1629, and a monument to Edward Pine, d1663.

EAST OGWELL   *St Bartholomew*   SX 838700

The church lies close to the manor house, seat of the Reynells until 1589. The polygonal stair-turret with tiny trefoiled and quatrefoiled windows may be an addition to an earlier tower. One south window in the chancel is 13th century and the south transept may also be that early. The south porch contains a fireplace. The 16th century north aisle has almost semi-circular arcade arches and straight-headed windows. A burial chapel erected by the Reynells east of the transept now serves as a vestry. It contains old heraldic glass, a tablet inscribed "Golgotha R.L. 1633, and three tomb slabs of abbots of Torre brought here after their abbey was dissolved. One is of Thomas Dyare, d1523. The chancel floor level was raised during the restoration of 1884-5 by R.M.Fulford. In the south transept is a tomb chest thought to be that of Richard Reynell, d1585. The tower screen contains 17th century work and the chancel screen is old with Flamboyant details on the wainscoting.

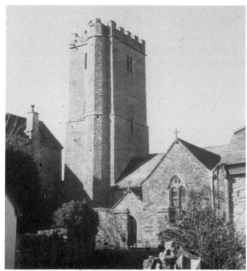

East Ogwell Church

East Portlemouth Church

EAST PORTLEMOUTH   *St Winwalloe*   SX 749384

Essentially late medieval, except perhaps for the slightly earlier low west tower with a modest stair turret, the church lies high above the village and has arcades of five bays and transept project from the fourth bay. The two storey north porch has a straight outer stair to the upper room. The only features of interest inside are the octagonal font and a screen with small figures in the wainscoting.

EAST PUTFORD   *Dedication Unknown*   SS 367164

This former church rebuilt in 1882 now serves as a farm building. It has a damaged circular Norman font and a few old tiles made at Barnstaple in the porch.

EAST WORLINGTON   *St Mary*   SS 775138

The Norman chancel retains one small window and there is a Norman south doorway with three bands of saltire crosses on the inner arch and an outer arch moulding of chevrons with a beast's head stop on the west. The rest is neo-Norman work of 1879 by Clark and Holland for the Earl of Portsmouth.

EGG BUCKLAND   *St Edward*   SX 498583

The west tower has set-back buttresses and big pinnacles. The nave and south aisle with a four bay arcade and a porch are also late medieval but restored and given a new chancel and north aisle in 1864, whilst a NE vestry was added in 1907. An octagonal font with shields and blank arches on the stem is the only old furnishing.

EGGESFORD   *All Saints*   SS 687112

The church was much restored in 1867 for the Earl of Portsmouth but retains a low medieval tower with diagonal buttresses and a north chapel with an arch of c1400 towards the chancel with hollow diagonals on the west respond and shafts on the east respond. The Norman font has rosettes and a scalloped base. Old glass survives in the west window and one south window, with the arms of the Reigny family. There are fine recumbent effigies of Edward, Viscount Chichester, d1648, and his wife, and a monument with a vertical effigy of Arthur, Viscount Chichester, with his wives lying on the two sides of an open pediment. It was made in 1650, although Arthur lived until 1674. There are also memorials to William Fellowes, d1723, and Henry Arthur Fellowes, d1792.

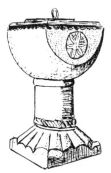

Font at Eggesford Church

Eggesford Church

Ermington Church

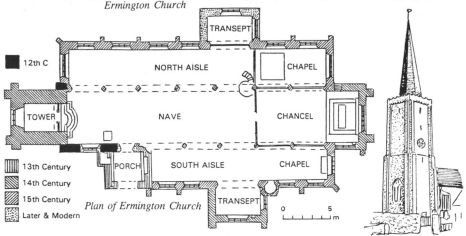

12th C

13th Century
14th Century
15th Century
Later & Modern

Plan of Ermington Church

NORTH AISLE

TRANSEPT

CHAPEL

TOWER

NAVE

CHANCEL

PORCH

SOUTH AISLE

CHAPEL

TRANSEPT

0   5
m

Tower at Ermington

ERMINGTON   *St Peter & St Paul*   SX 638533

Inside above the Victorian south doorway is a Norman rere-arch. The spacious south porch is probably 13th century. Because of it being in the way the south aisle has two bays less than the seven bays of the north aisle. The third arch from the east on each side is higher, an acknowledgement of pre-existing transepts, the ends of which project out beyond the aisles. The south transept has a renewed 14th century window, that on the north is rebuilt except for one 15th century east window. Also 14th century is the east bay of the chancel and the west tower with corner buttresses, small windows and an embattled parapet on a corbel-table, within which rises a twisted spire. A NE vestry no longer survives. The 17th century screen is the only furnishing to have survived a restoration by J.D.Sedding in the 1880s. There is a tomb chest to Christopher Chudleigh, d1570. A brass shows kneeling figures of William Strashleigh, d1583 and his wife. There is a small tablet to Margaret Rich, 1675 and there are several tablets and two helms of the Sweyte family of Traine.

EXBOURNE *St Mary* SS 602019

The early 14th century chancel has a fine east window with niches on the nook-shafts inside. Later medieval are the west tower of granite ashlar with a hood-moulded doorway and niches in the west buttresses and the south aisle with a porch and a four bay arcade with depressed arches. The south aisle windows are straight-headed without tracery. In 1884-6 R.M.Fulford converted the rood-stair turret into a passage connecting the pulpit, vestry and organ chamber. The screen has been much repaired. There is a monument with Ionic columns to Simon Westlake, d1667.

EXETER *St David* SX 914931

An impressive church of 1897-1900 by W.D.Caroe with a NE tower stands on the site of a neo-Grecian church of 1816-17, itself on the site of a Norman chapel.

EXETER *St Edmund* SX 916921

Within a large roundabout between the west end of the walled city and the river lies the ruin of this church which lay beside the eastern two arches of the medieval bridge. All that survives is the undercroft below the nave, chancel and aisle together with part of the tower in the SW corner. There is a record of the tower being rebuilt in 1448-9 but the present structure seems to be mostly of 1834 when the church was rebuilt by the architects Cornish and Julian.

EXETER *St Leonard* SX 924919

A tablet to Thomas Collins, d1761, and a few other memorials survived the rebuilding of the medieval church as a classical style building in 1831 by A.Patey, and a subsequent total rebuilding of 1876-86, creating a large church with a SW tower.

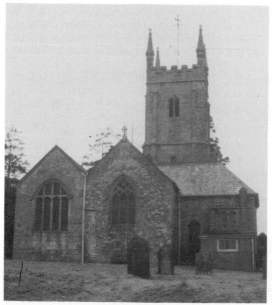

Exbourne Church

St Edmund on the Bridge, Exeter

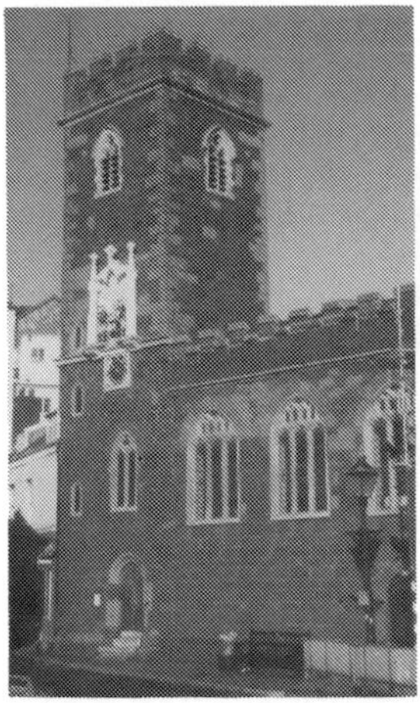

St Mary Steps Church, Exeter

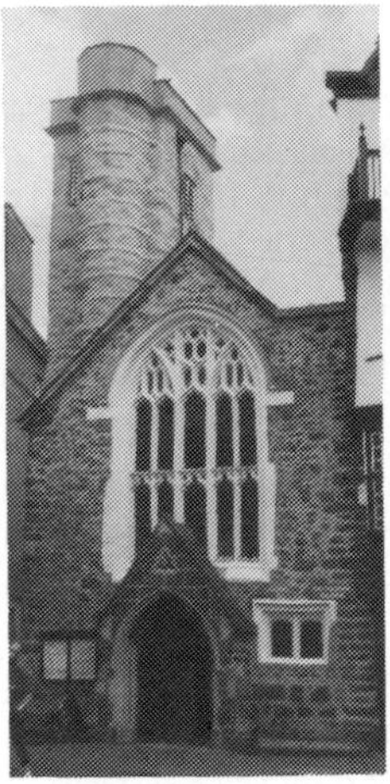

St Martin's Church, Exeter

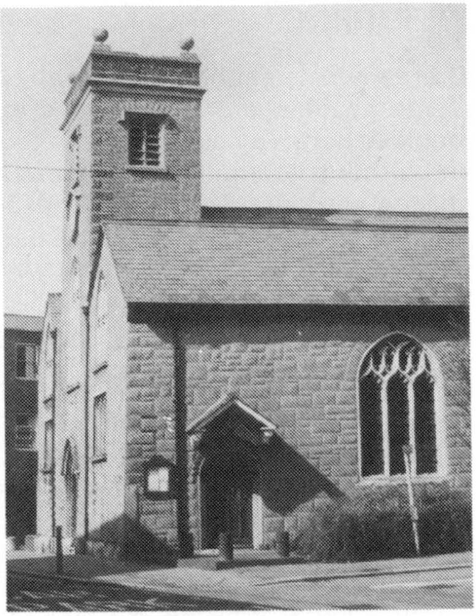

St Mary Arches Church, Exeter

EXETER *St Martin* SX 921926

The church is awkwardly squeezed into a corner of the cathedral close. The nave NE corner has long and short work high up which may be part of the building consecrated in 1065. The chancel arch with fleurons on the abaci is 14th century but the rest of the oddly shaped chancel inclined to the north was rebuilt in the 17th century. The nave is otherwise late medieval with a large transomed west window over a doorway and a small tower projecting from the middle of the north side, with a polygonal staircase turret in the west angle between the two. The reredos of c1710 has arms of Bishop Blackall. The west gallery has the arms of Bishop Trelawney, d1708, and the pulpit and box pews are also of that period. There are late 17th century communion rails with twisted balusters. One south window contains fragments of 15th century heraldic glass. The memorials include monuments to Judith Wakeman, d1643, Winifred Butler, d1673, Edward Seaward, d1703, and Philip Hooper, d1715.

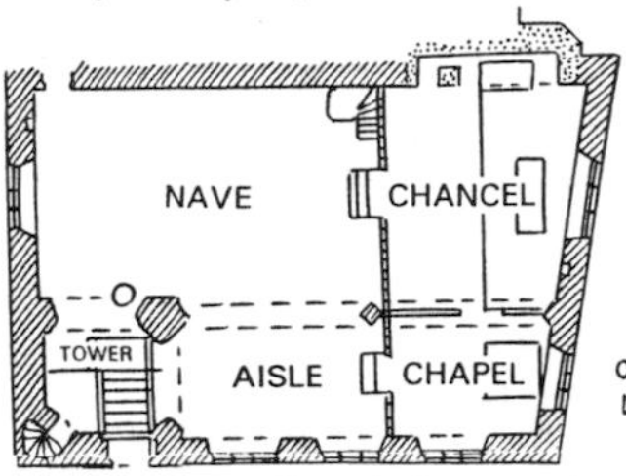
NAVE
CHANCEL
TOWER
AISLE
CHAPEL

St Mary Steps Church, Exeter: plan

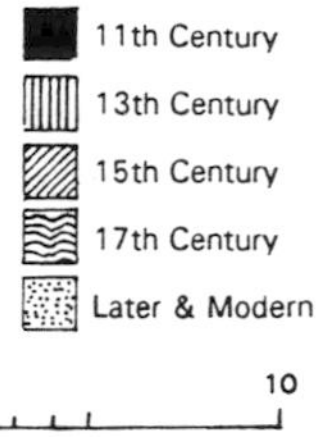
11th Century
13th Century
15th Century
17th Century
Later & Modern
0
10
metres

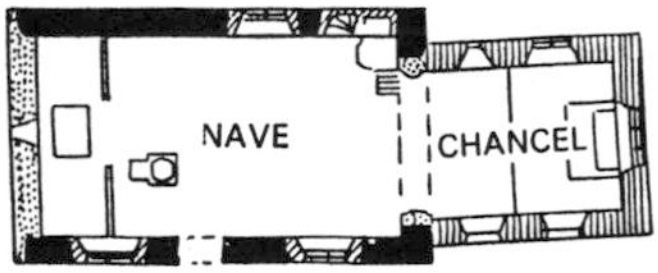
NAVE
CHANCEL

St Pancras' Church, Exeter: plan

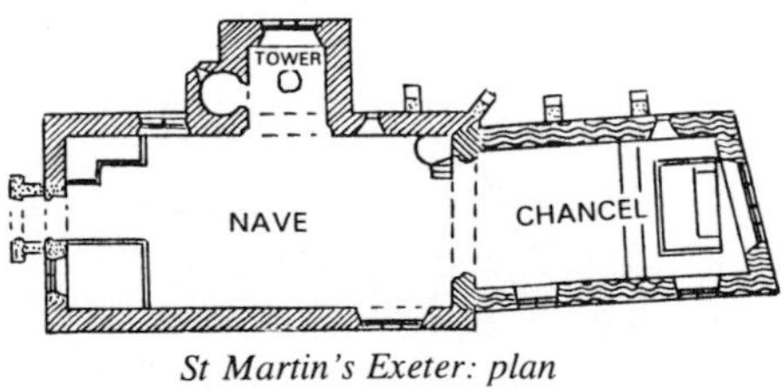
TOWER
NAVE
CHANCEL

St Martin's Exeter: plan

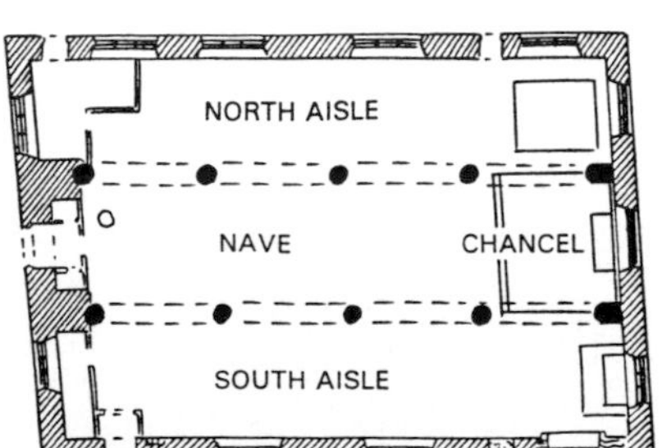
NORTH AISLE
NAVE
CHANCEL
SOUTH AISLE

St Mary Arches Church, Exeter: plan

St Mary Arches Church, Exeter

EXETER   *St Mary Arches*   SX 917924

From the outside this appears as a much altered late medieval rectangular box with a square turret perched on what remains of the tower arch of a former projecting west tower. Inside is a surprise, four bays on each side of double-chamfered arches of the end of the 12th century set on circular piers with scalloped capitals. The church was restored after being gutted by bombing during World War II. More recently it has been converted into a Diocesan Educational Resource Centre with an office divided off by glazing in the NW corner. The reredos of c1700 has Corinthian pilasters and arched panels formerly with the Commandments and Lord's Prayer. Of the same period are the communion rails. Over the south doorway are Royal Arms. The east end of the aisle formed the chantry chapel of Thomas Andrew, twice mayor of Exeter, d1518, of whom there is a recumbent effigy on a tomb chest. There are kneeling effigies of Thomas Walker, d1628 and his wife, monuments to Robert Walker, d1602, John Davy, 1611, and Maria and Christopher Lethbridge, d1659 and 1670 respectively, plus several similar tablets dating from 1666 to 1682.

EXETER   *St Mary Steps*   SX 918922

This church existed by 1199 but the present building is mostly 15th century. It consists of a nave and chancel divided by a 19th century screen and a SW tower and a south aisle and chapel each of one bay with between then a medieval screen brought here from the church of St Mary Major demolished in 1865. The tower contains steps leading up into the church and predates the aisle. Upon it is an early 17th century clock with three armed figures known as Matthew the Miller and his Sons. Below the chapel is a tunnel-vaulted porter's lodge of 1600 used in connection with manning the adjacent west gate of the city wall. There is a Norman font with a cable moulding and a crude palmette scroll and various other motifs.

EXETER   *St Michael & All Angels*   SX 936925

The Norman church at Heavitree served a large parish outside the city walls with several chapels-of-ease. Extended in the 14th and 15th centuries, it was rebuilt in 1541 and in 1844-6. E.H.Harbottle added a tower in 1890 and extended the chancel in 1897. Old parts are the six bay arcade, the screen of the south chapel, and tablets to Sebastian Isaac, 1685, and Thomas Gorges, d1670, and his wife, d1671.

EXETER   *St Olave*   SX 918925

This church has an unusual plan, and is very irregularly laid out. As a result of 15th century widening of the 14th century nave and chancel these parts now embrace a tiny square south transeptal tower built of large blocks. It has a squint into the chancel and could be probably 14th century although an 11th century date has been claimed for it. The late 14th century north aisle has a four bay arcade with double chamfered arches on octagonal piers. The west part of the aisle is flanked by a short but wide outer aisle of the 15th century with a two bay arcade. There is a Norman waterleaf capital with a spirally moulded base and a damaged 14th century relief of the Flagellation. There are Royal Arms of William III.

EXETER   *St Pancras*   SX 921928

This small nave and chancel church now lies in a corner of the paved Guildhall shopping precinct. The south doorway is round-headed and the nave probably contains late Saxon or Norman work, although the windows are later medieval and the west wall has been rebuilt. The Norman font is circular with a thin beaded moulding. The chancel was rebuilt in 1887-9 by J.L.Pearson, a possible Saxon doorway being discovered during the work. There are communion rails brought here from St Stephen in 1977. The pulpit, a fine piece of c1600 with foliage around the panels and caryatids with wreaths, came from All Hallows on its demolition in 1906, along with several monuments, the best being that of I. Loveday Buller, d1711.

St Stephen's Church, Exeter

EXETER   *St Petrock*   SX 920926

This church only became visible from the High Street in 1905, and the north doorway then inserted. The church consisted of just a nave and chancel until the early 15th century when a south aisle and NW tower were added. An outer south aisle was consecrated in 1573 and still further enlarged to the south in 1587 and 1828 when the skylights were provided by Charles Hedgeland, that in the middle of the nave being octagonal. In 1881 John Haywood re-orientated the church by adding a new chancel to the south. The original chancel is now a Chapel of Unity divided off by a glass screen. There are 18th century Royal Arms and tablets to William and Mary Hooper, d1683 and 1658 respectively, Francis and Alexander Worth, d1675 and 1680, John and Faith Mayne, d1680 and 1679, Jonathan and Elizabeth Ivie, d1717 and 1698 (from St Kerian's, demolished in 1873) and Theodore Sheere, d1782.

EXETER   *St Sidwell*   SX 924931

There was a church here by the early 11th century. Being sited by a Roman cemetery and dedicated to a local martyr, an origin as a mausoleum-shrine is likely. The church of 1812 incorporating arcades of 1437 was bombed during World War II and the present building was built in 1957 to a design by Lucas, Roberts and Brown.

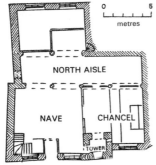

0   5
metres

EXETER   *St Stephen*   SX 921927

A 13th century arch led into an east chapel built over an arch over a street and a crypt which is not now accessible but which is known to have two Norman columns, one with a block capital, the other with a capital with a honeysuckle relief. The main body three bays long may be 17th century and has a west tower with a NE stair-turret. The thin quatrefoil piers of the five bay arcades are of 1826. The oldest of two sets of Royal Arms dates from 1640. There are monuments to George Potter, d1662, "a great benefactor towards the rebuilding of the church", James Rodd, d1678, and Thomas Bulithoe, d1753.

Plan of St Olave's Church, Exeter

14th Century   17th Century
15th Century   Later & Modern

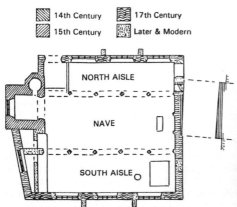

NORTH AISLE

NAVE

SOUTH AISLE

Plan of St Stephen's Church, Exeter

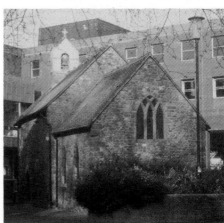

St Pancras' Church, Exeter

Font at St Mary Steps, Exeter

St Thomas's Church, Exeter

EXETER   *St Thomas*   SX 912918

This church, consecrated in 1422, was built to replace a chapel by the west end of the bridge over the Exe. Only the inner north doorway and the arcades of double-chamfered arches on octagonal piers are now medieval. The church was burnt in 1645 and the west tower with thin diagonal buttresses and a polygonal stair-turret and pinnacles, and the south aisle and the east end of the north aisle date from 1657. The western part of the north aisle and porch are of 1821 and the chancel and transepts are of 1828-9 by Patey. The wooden eagle lectern brought here from the cathedral c1840 is an early 14th century piece of some interest. There are Royal Arms of Charles II dated 1682. The largest of the many monuments is that with standing and reclining allegorical figures to Sir Thomas Northmore, d1713.

EXETER   *Other Churches*

Including the cathedral, hospitals and religious houses, Exeter once had over thirty places of worship within the walls. There were 17 parish churches in 1582, when the Corporation petitioned Queen Elizabeth to allow the number to be reduced to five. The plan came to nothing because of the opposition of the diocese, but in 1656 the Commonwealth Parliament agreed to 13 of the churches being sold off, although some of them were returned to ecclesiastical use after the Restoration of 1660. The lost churches included All Hallows over the west gate of the city walls, and St Bartholomew at the east gate. St Peter Minor, St Simon with St Jude, St Edward, St Mary Major and St Michael were set close together in an arc between St Petrock and the cathedral. St Bartholomew. St Paul and St Cuthbert lay in St Paul Street, St Kerrian lay in North Street, and St Lawrence and Holy Trinity lay in near the east end of High Street. All Hallows lay in Goldsmith Street. In South Street lay St George and Holy Trinity. The latter was rebuilt in 1820, and altered in 1884. It is now used as a social club. By the palace gate lay St James. In Fore Street lay St John and St Mary.

EXMINSTER   *St Martin*   SX 946877

The church comprises a nave and south aisle with a four bay arcade of double-chamfered arches on octagonal piers, a chancel and south chapel with a single arch between them and a west tower with diagonal buttresses and a stair-turret. In 1633 the Tothill family had the chapel given a plastered wagon roof with lozenges in panels containing plaster figures of the apostles and evangelists. The south porch was added in 1841. There are old screens dividing off the chancel and chapel, a fine pulpit of c1700 and a white marble late 18th century font. The communion rails are 17th century. The chapel contains a monument with a reclining effigy of Grace Tothill, d1623. In the chancel are kneeling effigies of Otto Petre, and his family of 1608, and a black and gold wall monument to Philippa Cooke, d1690.

FARRINGDON   *St Petrock*   SY 018913

Little apart from the tower with upper and lower stages of two different periods and the recut Norman font predate a rebuilding of 1870-1 by William White.

FARWAY   *St Michael*   SY 173965

The north arcade has 13th century double-chamfered arches set upon short circular Norman piers. There are three full arches plus a fourth cut into by the 15th century tower with a stair-turret on the south side and battlements and gargoyles. The late 13th century chancel has a renewed priest's doorway and window. The three-light 14th century east window has reticulated tracery. In the restoration of 1874-6 by C.F.Edwards the north aisle was rebuilt and the north chapel added at the expense of Louise Prideaux. A bust of Humphrey Hutchins of 1628 commemorates an earlier rebuilding of the aisle, from which the outline of his east window remains. There is an inscription to Richard Prideaux, d1632, and other Prideaux memorials include a recumbent effigy of the lawyer Sir Edmund, d1628, and a tablet to Sir Peter, d1705. In the chancel are tablets to the Reverend Richard Blake, d1788 and his kinswoman Hannah Atkinson, d1796. There is an Elizabethan communion table used as an altar.

Exminster Church   *Farway Church*

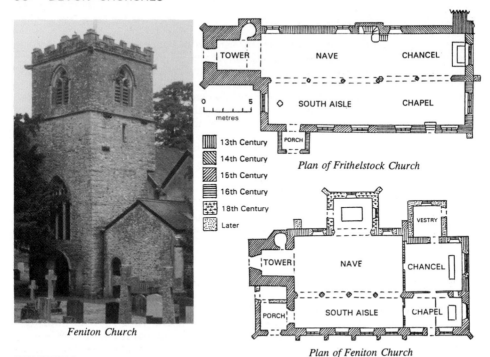

Feniton Church

13th Century
14th Century
15th Century
16th Century
18th Century
Later

TOWER   NAVE   CHANCEL

SOUTH AISLE   CHAPEL

PORCH

0   5
metres

Plan of Frithelstock Church

VESTRY

TOWER   NAVE   CHANCEL

PORCH   SOUTH AISLE   CHAPEL

Plan of Feniton Church

FENITON   *St Andrew*   SY 109994

A south aisle with a four bay arcade and a south chapel with a single wide arch to the chancel were added c1500 to a nave and chancel probably of 13th century date, although their features date from R.M.Fulford's restoration of 1877. A porch with a south entrance lies in the angle between the aisle and the low tower with a polygonal NE stair-turret. The vestry is Victorian but the north projection containing organ is probably 18th century. There are old screens to the chancel and to the south chapel, which contains late 19th century Patteson memorials. A north recess contains an effigy of c1500 showing a corpse in a burial shroud.

FILLEIGH   *St Paul*   SS 664281

The diagonally buttressed west tower and parts of the nave walls alone are medieval. In 1732 the Fortescues of Castle Hill had the church rebuilt on a cruciform plan with a shallow north transept with vestry beyond with an east turret set opposite a wide but shallow south porch. In 1876-7 there was a further remodelling by Clark when a south chapel was added east of the porch and an apsed chancel provided. The many Fortescue monuments include two small late 16th century brasses.

FREMINGTON   *St Paul*   SS 512325

The church was heavily restored by Sir George Gilbert Scott in 1867. Features of interest are the north transeptal tower with lancets on the north side and a blocked pointed arch on the west, the 15th century stone pulpit with traces of original colouring, a fragment of medieval wall painting on the south wall, an Elizabethan communion table and a few wall monuments of no individual merit.

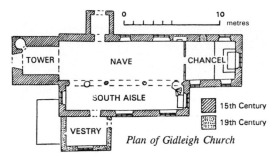

Plan of Gidleigh Church

15th Century
19th Century

Brass at Filleigh

FRITHELSTOCK *St Mary & St Gregory* SS 464195

Here we have a remarkable instance of a parish church and a ruined priory church which were joined together by a late 13th century tower which formed a porch at the west end of the south side of the aisle-less single-chamber priory church probably of the 1230s with a narrower Lady Chapel later added at the east end. The tower formed the NE corner of the 14th century chancel of the parish church with a fine three-light east window with a top circle containing three large cusped and three small uncusped spherical triangles. This chancel was added to an earlier nave to which in the 15th century were added a diagonally buttressed west tower and a south aisle with a three bay arcade with statue niches in the piers of unusually elaborate section. The rood-loft staircase on the north side is also of that period. In the early 16th century a south chapel was added, its two-bay arcade being not quite in line with the aisle arcade, and an embattled porch was added to the aisle. The south chapel east window is of the restoration of 1885-6 by Samuel Hooper. There are ceiled wagon roofs and the furnishings include a Norman font on a round shaft with chevrons, a Jacobean pulpit, some Barnstaple tiles, bench ends with heads in profile and bench fronts with tracery, plus a large set of plaster Royal Arms of 1677.

GALMPTON *Holy Trinity* SX 686405

The church of 1866-7 by Richard Coad was erected to replace the church at South Huish, from which have come the font with a 14th century bowl on a 13th century base and parts of two 15th century alabaster retables with scenes of the Annunciation, Adoration, Betrayal, Scourging, Entombment and Resurrection.

GEORGEHAM *St George* SS 465400

The nave and chancel were rebuilt in 1876-7 to a design by James Fowler for the Hole family. Older parts are the 14th century piscina in the chancel, the west tower with set-back buttresses, a west doorway with continuous mouldings and fleurons and an embattled stair-turret rising above the main parapet, plus the four bay south arcade with a fifth arch to the south chapel, and the aisle masonry and doorway. The south porch has a sundial dated 1773 and could be of that date. The screen between the aisle and chapel with Ionic pilasters and a broken segmental pediment probably dates from 1762. There is a panel of c1300 depicting the Crucifixion with Christ bent in suffering, John and Mary, two angels and two kneeling figures all lacking their heads. In a recess in the south chapel is an effigy of a cross-legged knight assumed to be Mauger of St Aubyn, d1294. Other monuments include one of the late 17th century to John Newcourt, and another erected in 1775 to John Harris.

At Croyde 2km to the WSW is a much altered early medieval chapel, latterly used as a barn. A north doorway, two small windows and the piscina are original.

Gidleigh Church

GEORGE NYMPTON   *St George*   SS 701230

The brick west tower is dated 1673. The nave and north aisle both have straight-headed windows and are divided by a three bay arcade. The aisle east window is 16th century. The roofs of the aisle and chancel retain old bosses. The south and east walls of the chancel date from a rebuilding by E.H.Harbottle in 1882, and the south porch also probably dates from then. The octagonal font is late-medieval. The chancel seats incorporate panels with Flamboyant tracery probably from a former screen. The best of several monuments to the Kerslake family is that of William, d1769, by King of Bath. It has a cherub and a tiny sarcophagus against an obelisk.

GERMANSWEEK   *St German*   SX 438942

The north aisle with a low arcade of four bays is 15th century. The nave, the chancel, south transept and the low west tower with a NE stair-turret are all older but without datable features.

GIDLEIGH   *Holy Trinity*   SX 671884

This granite church on the NE side of Dartmoor comprises a nave with a south aisle with a three bay arcade, a north porch, a west tower now lacking its pinnacles and a chancel, the only part likely to have masonry older than the 15th century. The south doorway now leads into a Victorian vestry. The screen of c1530 has Jacobean replacement uprights and the wainscot figures and colouring are of 1853. The aisle east window contains old stained glass showing the busts of the Virgin and St John.

GITTISHAM   *St Michael*   SY 134984

The chancel arch is 14th century and the nave and chancel are probably of that period. The south aisle was added c1470 by Henry Beaumont, whose initials appear on the middle one of the three bays flanking the nave. An screen divides off a south chapel with one arch leading into a panelled arch for a tomb between it and the chancel. East of this is a recess containing the tomb of Lady Ursula Putt, d1674 and her husband Sir Thomas, d1686. The chapel then extends still further, with its east wall beyond that of the older chancel. Its east window has glass with the Beaumont arms of c1400 and the Putt arms of c1650. Other memorials include alabaster effigies of Henry Beaumont, d1591, and his wife, and a monument to Joane Beaumont, 1627. The upright mullions in the south windows were probably inserted by William Putt, d1662, to repair Civil War damage. His arms appears on a gutter at the east end. There are ceiled wagon roofs with bosses. The west gallery given by Sir Thomas Putt in 1701 is reached by an external stair on the south side of the tower. There are Royal Arms of Charles II and box pews of 1715. The chancel north window contains Flemish stained glass roundels of the 16th or 17th century.

GOODLEIGH   *St Gregory*   SS 599342

Only the late medieval west tower and a small rustic monument to James Acland of Combe, d1655, have survived the rebuilding of the church in 1881 by Ashworth.

Old print of Great Torrington Church

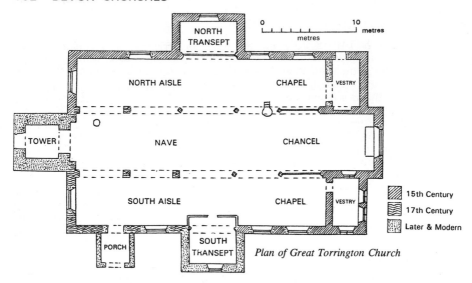

Plan of Great Torrington Church

GREAT TORRINGTON   *St Michael*   SS 495191

An inscription on the outside of south transept records "This church was blown up with powder Feb 16 1645 and rebuilt 1651". This part was originally a tower in which the Royalists had stored munitions, and there is a north transept opposite. The rebuilt parts have square piers with chamfered angles and carry double chamfered arches. The older piers have leaf capitals. The other chief relic of the medieval building is the SE vestry with a quatrefoil pattern on the battlements. The west tower and spire were added in 1828 by W.B.Cock and the windows are mostly of c1861 by William White. There seems to have been some refacing outside and the different periods of work are not easy to distinguish from each other. The late 17th century pulpit has carved cherubs and gilded lions' heads. The tester was returned in 1960 after a period in the Victoria and Albert Museum. The only memorial of note is that to Sarah Gooding, d1698, with angels, columns and caryatids.

HACCOMBE   *St Blaise*   SX 897702

The church lies alone except for the big house, now converted to flats. There are 13th century lancets restored by John Haywood in 1863-4 and an aisle with unmoulded arches on red octagonal piers grafted onto a 12th century nave and chancel. In 1335 a college with six chantry priests was established here by the Archdeacon family whose arms appear on the floor tiles, and from then until the 20th century the church was a peculiar of the Archbishop of Canterbury, excused from the jurisdiction of the bishop of Exeter. There are arms to hold candles or banners in the chancel and aisle. Some early 14th century glass also survives.

Of the late 13th century are two effigies of females in wimples, one holding a book, and an effigy of a cross-legged knight thought to be Sir Stephen de Haccome. On a tomb chest lies a miniature effigy of a youth in civilian dress with angels at the head. The restored effigies of a knight and lady of c1400 are thought to be Sir Hugh Courtenay and his wife Philippa, the Archdeacon heiress. There are brasses of Sir Nicholas Carew, d1469, Thomas Carew, d1586, and his wife Mary, d1589, Elizabeth, d1611, wife of John Carew, and Thomas Carew, d1656 with his family.

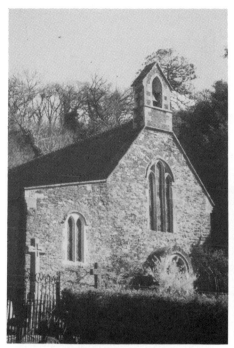

Haccombe Church

Great Torrington Church

Brass at Haccombe Church

Halberton Church   *Halwell Church*

HALBERTON   *St Andrew*   SX 783563

The diagonally buttressed west tower with a stair turret on the south side and the western parts of the arcades with double-chamfered arches on octagonal piers are 14th century. The taller east bays with fleurons on the pier capitals are 15th century, but both parts saw some rebuilding in 1847-9 when the windows were replaced, and there was much refacing done outside in 1887. The plain Norman font has three scallops on each side of the square bowl. The very fine pulpit with fin-like uprights separating the panels, and the rood screen are both early 15th century, whilst the chapel screens look slightly earlier. The monuments include cherub heads and skulls to Richard Clerk, d1728, and a mourning woman by an urn to John Chave, d1796.

HALWELL   *St Leonard*   SX 777532

Only the 15th century north arcade with almost semi-circular arches and the lofty west tower with a polygonal stair-turret in the middle of the south side survived the rebuilding of 1879. A glass and metal screen of the 1970s divides off the west bays.

HALWILL   *St Peter & St James*   SX 427995

Only the nave north wall and the slender west tower with pinnacles survived the rebuilding of 1876-9 by Samuel Hooper.

Porch vault at Harburton

Harburton Church

HARBURTON   *St Andrew*   ST 005129

This large church is embattled on both sides and has arcades six bays long, ceiled wagon roofs and a west tower with set-back buttresses and a central stair-turret. The south porch is vaulted in two bays on coupled arcades, but most, if not all, of this side of the church was refaced during the restorations of 1861 and 1871-2. The circular Norman font has a frieze of rosettes, a band of cable, and a frieze of upright petals. There are old screens closing off the chancel and the chapels, a medieval stone pulpit with nodding ogival canopies with figures added in the 17th century, and carved Royal Arms of Queen Anne. There a monument to Nicholas Browse, d1696.

HARFORD   *St Petroc*   SX 638595

Some 12th or 13th century masonry may survive in the north wall of the nave, where there are traces of a blocked doorway, the slightly narrower chancel, and the north transept, now much altered to serve as a vestry-cum-organ recess. The low unbuttressed west tower with short pinnacles may be 14th century. The semi-circular arches of the four bay south arcade and the form of the windows and priest's doorway indicate a 16th century date for the south aisle. It has a squint into the chancel and a porch in front of the west bay. There are Royal Arms of George II dated 1728 over the south doorway and there are ceiled wagon roofs. A brass of a knight on a tomb chest is supposed to be Thomas Williams of Stowford, Speaker of the House of Commons, d1566, although the armour looks earlier. There are kneeling figures of John Prideaux and his family on a monument made in 1639.

Hartland Church

Harpford Church

HARPFORD   *St Gregory*   SY 091904

The chancel and slightly wider nave are both 13th century but their lancets and later windows have been renewed in a drastic restoration of 1883-4 by Hayward and Son when the south porch and organ chamber-cum-vestry were added and the north aisle rebuilt. The three bay arcade with plain chamfered arches on octagonal piers may be 14th century. The east window and small west tower with a polygonal stair-turret on the north side are 15th century. The altar rail with fluted balusters is of c1670-90.

HARTLAND   *St Nectan*   SS 235247

The 39m high 16th century west tower of four stages with set-back buttresses, gargoyles below the battlements and thin pinnacles has a recess with a statue of St Nectan in the east wall, whilst the west doorway has angel head-stops. The aisles and transepts are all embattled and there are north and south porches but the windows were renewed in a restoration by David Mackintosh in 1848 when the east end was extended. Because of the tall tower arch and the wide spacing of the piers of the late 14th century arcades of six bays of double chamfered arches the interior appears very spacious. The fifth bays correspond to the transepts and the sixth bays are chancel chapels, divided off by a particularly splendid screen with many ribs on the coving, four bands of ornamentation on the cornice and a cresting of iron. There is a reset trefoil-headed piscina in the chancel. The church has an assortment of old wagon roofs, with and without ceilings, and with bosses in the south transept and boards and cross-ribs in the north chapel.

In the upper room of the north porch (called Pope's Chamber) lie a fragmentary pulpit purchased for 33 shillings in 1609, some carved figures probably from the abbey and some 17th century panelling and a helmet from a monument to the Abbott family. The Norman font has a scalloped under edge to the bowl and intersecting arches above, There are vertical chevrons on the shafts and upside down intersecting arches on the base. The north chapel contains an altar with Belgian Flamboyant tracery panels. The canopy above it incorporates further Belgian woodwork of c1300. In the south chapel are bench ends with initials of Hugh Prust, who donated them in 1530. This chapel also has fragments of late 14th century carved scenes probably from a chantry altar. There are plain pews of the 18th century.

A 15th century tomb chest from Hartland Abbey was used as the high altar until the 1920s. It has quatrefoils and roundels with cusping and tracery. There is a brass with a kneeling figure of Anne Abbott, d1610. The stone to Thomas Doctron, d1618 has metal inlaying. The best of the later tablets are those of John Vetty, d1694, Paul Orchard, d1740 and his wife, d1763, and Nicholas Wolferstan, d1763.

HATHERLEIGH   *St John the Baptist*   SS 541046

The church is essentially late medieval with a nave and aisles of five bays without even a screen to divide off a chancel, although a staircase on the south side shows that the two east bays were originally so divided off. The west bays have doorways, with a porch on the south. Several windows look 16th century rather than 15th, including those reset in a 19th century outer chapel on the north side. The west tower has set-back buttresses, a polygonal stair-turret on the north side and shingled spire within a parapet. There are original ceiled wagon roofs with a celure at the east end. The ogival cover on the Norman font is probably 18th century. Parts of the former screen are reused in the pulpit and reader's desk, and the south aisle has a pew with Jacobean panels. The Victorian south aisle west window contains pieces of 17th century Flemish stained glass. An incised slab depicts John Yeo, d1662 and his wife kneeling. There is a tablet to William Wivell, d1695, and several later members of Fortescue family, and another tablet to John Letheridge, d1706.

Font at Hartland Church

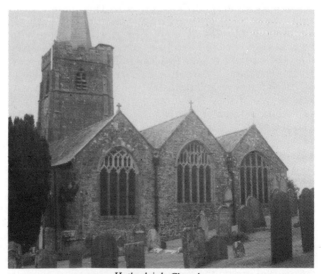

Hatherleigh Church

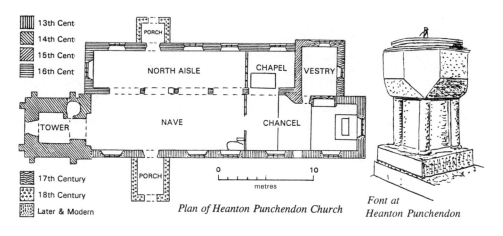

13th Cent
14th Cent
15th Cent
16th Cent

17th Century
18th Century
Later & Modern

Plan of Heanton Punchendon Church

Font at Heanton Punchendon

HAWKCHURCH   *St John*   ST 345005

The north arcade is Norman with heads on the scalloped capital of the pier, and the south arcade is of c1200 with round arches and fine capitals carved with foliage with musical animals, mythical creatures and a bagpiper. The south doorway with a shouldered lintel must be late 13th century and there is a 15th century west tower with a frieze of quatrefoils over the west doorway and pierced stone panels in the belfry windows. The neo-Norman clerestory is part of the rebuilding of 1859-61. There is a Baroque wall-monument to Thomas Moore, 1695 and his two wives.

HEANTON PUNCHENDON   *St Augustine*   SS 502356

This is quite a long church with a late 14th century west tower of ashlar with set-back buttresses. The south doorway looks late 13th or early 14th century, whilst the porch in front may be 18th century. The vestry doorway is 15th century but has evidence of an older doorway above, but the vestry itself is a 17th century rebuild. The aisle is a jumble of 16th, 17th and 18th century features and at some time the original arcade piers have been turned so that their shafts face the diagonals rather than the cardinal points and low four-centred arches with roll mouldings have been built upon them. The south windows date from William White's restoration of 1889-90. Both the nave and aisle have ceiled wagon roofs with bosses. The octagonal font sits on five shafts. The tomb of Richard Coffin, d1523, one-time sheriff of Devon, served as an Easter Sepulchre. There are also monuments to Elizabeth Bassett, d1635, with a kneeling effigy, Arthur Bassett, d1672, with putti on a broken pediment, John Bassett, 1683, Thomas Ballantine, d1693, and Elizabeth Hart, d1695.

HEMYOCK   *St Mary*   ST 135133

Blocked round-headed arches in the north and south walls suggest the Norman tower now lying at the west end was once a central tower flanked by transepts. The layout may have been changed to facilitate the building of the castle closeby to the west. The arcades were rebuilt in 1768 and again in 1846-7 when the south aisle was also renewed, although it retains a cinquefoil-headed piscina. The Norman font is of marble with scalloped sides. Its base with four shafts and scalloped capitals was only discovered during the work of 1847. There is a candelabra of 1773.

HENNOCK *St Mary* SX 830809

The square Norman font has a blank arcade on one side and leaf motifs on the others. The church is otherwise late medieval with a granite west tower aisles of four bays, an unaisled fifth bay sanctuary and an embattled south porch. All the parts except the tower have set-back buttresses and there are ceiled wagon roofs. The screen has early 16th century paintings of apostles and saints. One north window has four original stained glass figures of seraphim.

Hemyock Church

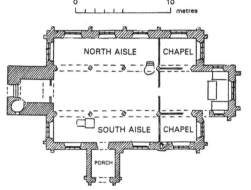

Plan of Hennock Church

South side of Hennock Church

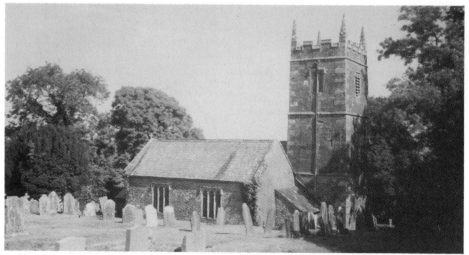

Highampton Church

HIGHAMPTON   *Holy Cross*   SS 490046

The church lies above the village with just one house by it. The font with a band of motifs such as stars and crosses saltire and the south doorway with one order of colonettes are Norman. The west tower has pinnacles. The north aisle may be ancient but its arcade takes the form of two tall granite columns supporting the wall-plate of the nave wagon roof. It dates from 1834, when the chancel was also rebuilt.

HIGH BICKINGTON   *St Mary*   SS 599206

Relics of the Norman church are the square font carved with wheels, rosettes and crosses, the reset plain north doorway (now blocked), and the south doorway with one order of columns, a beast-head corbel, and chevrons on the arches. The lower parts of a south transeptal tower with a pointed arch to the nave and now having a saddle-back roof are probably early 13th century. The north chapel with a two bay arcade with octagonal piers and sedilia with ogival arches is 14th century. Of the 15th century are the north aisle with a four bay arcade and the diagonally buttressed west tower with short pinnacles. There are old wagon roofs. There are many old bench ends with tracery, pairs of saints or prophets, instruments of the Passion, initials in shields, foliage, profiles in medallions and putti blowing trumpets.

HIGH BRAY   *All Saints*   SS 689344

The 15th century tower has set-back buttresses and a polygonal NE stair-turret. The bell-openings could be 17th century. The nave and south aisle both have 16th century straight-headed windows with arched lights and ceiled wagon roofs with crenellated wall-plates. The low arcade has four bays, although both parts are five bays long. The east end was mostly rebuilt in 1873 by Ashworth, when the vestry was added. A bench extends outside along the aisle south wall and the east wall of the porch, and there is here a sundial dated 1717 with initials of church wardens. There is a Norman font with a shallow chevron frieze and palmettes. Three sections of the former rood-screen now lie under the tower.

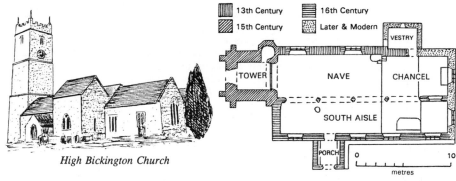

13th Century 16th Century
15th Century Later & Modern

VESTRY

TOWER   NAVE   CHANCEL

SOUTH AISLE

PORCH   0   10
metres

Plan of High Bray Church

High Bickington Church

HIGHWEEK   *All Saints*   SX 852721

This church lies on a hill NW of Newton Abbot and until 1864 ranked only as a chapel-of-ease to Kingsteignton. The diagonally buttressed west tower may have been part of the building consecrated in 1428. The aisles are probably later and have low arcades, and a porch forms the west bay of the south aisle. The north windows are 15th century (one has fragments of old glass), the plain granite south windows are later. The east end is of 1892. The font has tracery panels on the stem and bowl.

HITTISLEIGH   *St Andrew*   SX 734955

The church has an elevated and isolated position. It has a nave and north aisle divided by an arcade of four-centred arches and with ceiled wagon roofs, that in the aisle having bosses and a carved wall-plate. The west tower of granite ashlar has diagonal buttresses. The aisle east window is pointed-headed but the other windows have straight heads. This end of the aisle contains a squire's pew made in 1619 for Thomas Furze of Eastchurch. The square Norman font has incised chevrons.

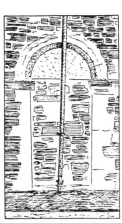

High Bickington Church

High Bray Church

HOLBETON   *All Saints*   SX 613502

The early 14th century west tower has a low NE stair turret and a spire rising to 34m. The wide late medieval nave and aisles have five bay arcades but the windows, roofs and much of the woodwork are of the restoration of 1885-9 by J.D. Sedding for Henry Bingham Mildmay of Flete, when much of the rood screen was renewed. The cornice frieze with recurrent ornamental faces and the tracery suggest a date for the screen of the 1530s and it bears the Tudor badges of the pomegranate, the Tudor rose and the portcullis. There is a monument of 1692 to Andrew Fir.

Holsworthy Church

HOLCOMBE BURNELL   *St John*   SX 858916

A mid 16th century tomb chest serves as an Easter Sepulchre. Other parts which survived a rebuilding by John Hayward in 1843 are the diagonally buttressed west tower, the arcade of double-chamfered arches on low octagonal granite columns, and eight panels from the screen incorporated into the reader's desk. There is a headless medieval alabaster figure of a saint.

HOLCOMBE ROGUS   *All Saints*   SY 056191

The west tower with set-back buttresses, the nave and aisles and the chancel and its chapels are all late medieval, with three light windows, except that the Bluett family chapel north of the chancel has a five light east window. The 17th century Bluett pew still remains and their chapel has a parclose screen brought from St Peter's church at Tiverton in 1854. There is a monument with Richard Bluett, d1614 shown reclining behind and above his recumbent wife. Another monument has recumbent alabaster effigies of Sir John Bluett, d1634 and his wife. Amongst several 18th century monuments are those of the Reverend Robert Bluett, d1749, and Robert Bluett and wife, erected in 1783.

HOLLACOMBE   *St Petrock*   SS 377030

This is an aisless church on a hill-top site. It has a low early tower with a rebuilt saddle-back roof. The nave south side has a lancet and an a Norman doorway with three rosettes on the lintel. The chancel east window of a pair of lancets with a circle above each is also 13th century. The double-chamfered arches into the tower and chancel are of the restoration of 1880-2. There are two fonts, one octagonal and later, the other Norman, and square on five shafts.

HOLNE   *St Mary*   SX 705695

The nave and aisles of five bay with octagonal granite piers carrying depressed double-chamfered arches are late medieval with original roofs, but the battered tower is older. Of greater interest are the screens with paintings on the wainscoting and the pulpit on a goblet shaped foot. It bears arms of Bishop Oldham (1504-19).

HOLSWORTHY   *St Peter & St Paul*   SS 344039

The west tower has pinnacles on the offsets of the buttresses. The piers of the south arcade are too big for their arches. Rebuilding in 1858, 1865, and in the 1880 have left little else of age or interest except the jambs of a Norman south doorway, a few bench ends, 17th century communion rails with twisted balusters, and a much rebuilt 17th century organ and organ case.

HONEYCHURCH   *St Mary*   SS 629029

On the nave south wall are two beast heads from a Norman corbel table. The church still retains its Norman plan of a small nave and tiny chancel, the only additions being a 14th century south porch and a later west tower with set-back buttresses and pinnacles. Part of a Norman window remains over the later priest's doorway and the niche on the nave north wall seems to be the reset outer opening of another. The circular font with chevrons and cable mouldings is also Norman. The chancel arch and one south window are 15th century, a north window is 16th century and the east window is of 1914. The Elizabethan Royal Arms were away under repair in 1999. There are old bench ends, box pews, and a crude hexagonal pulpit and communion rails of the 17th century.   See plan on page 116.

North side of Honiton Church

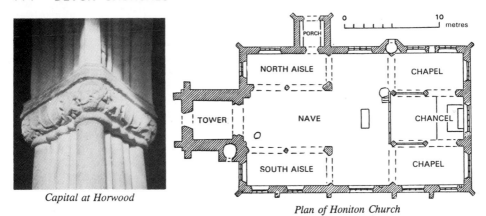

Capital at Horwood

Plan of Honiton Church

HONITON   *St Michael*   SY 109999

The church lies high above the south edge of the town. It was gutted by fire in 1911 but the outer walls survived and the internal layout was unchanged by rebuilding. The west parts were paid for by Bishop Courtenay in the 1480s whilst an inscription on the arcade pier capitals records the east parts as the gift of John and Joan Takell, who died in 1506 and 1529 respectively. The layout suggests gradual additions to a 14th century cruciform plan with shallow transepts although no work of that period remains. Thus the arcades have a wide central bay opening into non-projecting transepts with four-light windows, whereas the nave aisles and chancel aisles forming one rectangular block otherwise have three-light windows. Only the west tower with set-back buttresses and a rectangular SE stair-turret projects from the rectangle. The west doorway has a vine frieze along the jambs and voussoirs.

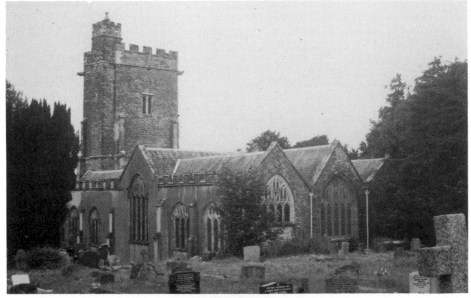

Honiton Church

HONITON   *All Hallows*   SY 163007

This chapel-of-ease was later used as a schoolroom by the adjacent school until it moved to Rousdon in 1938 and it now serves as a museum. Despite rebuilding in the mid 18th century the chapel has a 15th century east window, a circular west window dated 1614 and 16th century four-light side windows.

HORWOOD   *St Michael*   SS 502276

The 14th century chancel has a piscina with a horn-shaped drain and a wooden pier on the north side to help support the roof, which is narrower than that of the nave and does not sit upon the late medieval north arcade of five bays. One arcade pier has flying figures and shields. Only the wall-plates and bosses of the aisle roof are original. The low west tower has a NE stair-turret and a plain round arch towards the nave. The south door is dated 1669. The Norman font with a scalloped under edge has been recut. There are medieval tiles in the chancel and old benches with shields, saints and instruments of the Passion in the nave. The communion rail is Jacobean and the pulpit is of 1635. The north chapel east window contains fragments of old glass. Half a wheel frame for a bell dated 1664 lies in the church. The decayed alabaster female effigy with a horned headdress may be Elizabeth Pollard, d1430.

HUISH   *St James The Less*   SS 533111

A rebuilding of 1873 by G.E.Street left only the small unbuttressed west tower.

HUNTSHAM   *All Saints*   ST 001205

Thanks to a restoration begun in 1854 by Benjamin Ferrey and the addition of a north aisle in 1871 the only old features are the slim west tower with a round-headed tower arch, one 14th century window in the chancel north wall, and a pulpit made up from old bench ends.

Effigy at Horwood Church

HUNTSHAW   *St Mary Magdalene*   SS 506229

The chancel has a south window of c1300. In 1439 an indulgence was offered to those who gave funds for rebuilding the church. The two bay north arcade, the narrower third arch further east, the diagonally buttressed west tower, and the wagon roof may be of about that time. There are image niches on the piers. The chancel arch was inserted either in 1862, when the aisle was rebuilt, or in the restoration of 1876. The south porch and the windows either side of it are also Victorian. There are medieval tiles in the chancel. There is a monument to Thomas Saltren, d1700, and a tablet to Mark Townsend, d1704, and his wife Mary, d1709.

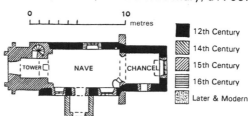

Plan of Honeychurch

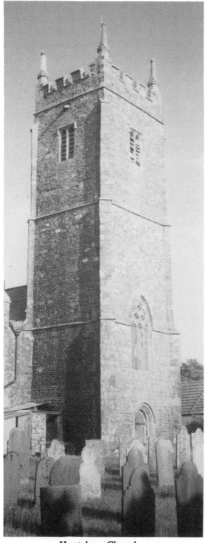

Huntshaw Church

Tablet at Huntshaw Church

Huxham Church

HUXHAM   *St Mary*   SX 946978

The nave of the small church was rebuilt in 1865 by Hayward and the chancel was rebuilt in 1871 by Benjamin Ferrey, but there is a Norman font with a diagonally fluted round bowl with a cable moulding, a frieze of circles, and spots, and the 14th century screen with ogival reticulation is of some interest.

IDDESLEIGH   *St James*   SS 569082

The diagonally buttressed west tower has a west doorway with leaf decoration and gargoyles below the granite battlements. It has been refaced, although the belfry windows look original. The nave, lower chancel and the north aisle with a four bay arcade have suffered much rebuilding in 1720, 1816-18, and 1878-9. The octagonal font is 15th century with a Jacobean cover, there is an old screen now lacking either a coving or cornice, and there is a 17th century panelled pulpit with strapwork. In a recess in the north chapel is an effigy of a cross-legged mid 13th century knight.

IDE   *St Ida*   SX 897904

Only the red sandstone tower with a polygonal SE stair-turret is medieval, the rest being a wide box of 1834 by Henry Hooper lying on the foundations of a medieval nave and north aisle. Screens divide a chancel from side-chapels at the east end.

IDEFORD   *St Mary*   SX 894774

The church was mostly rebuilt in 1850-2 by Wightwick and Damont. Old parts are the west tower, the wagon roof with a celure where the screen used to be, the arcade with double-chamfered arches on octagonal piers, the octagonal font, and a Norman gabled lintel carved with a serpent, a tree of life and what looks like a cock. Several windows have medieval heraldic glass and the pulpit and chairs incorporate panels from the former screen.

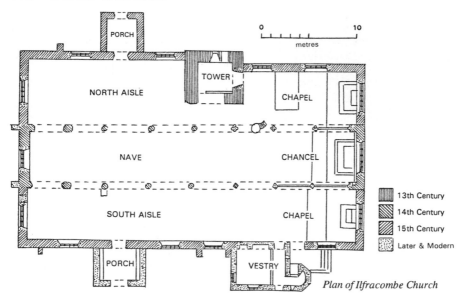

PORCH

TOWER

NORTH AISLE

CHAPEL

NAVE

CHANCEL

SOUTH AISLE

CHAPEL

PORCH

VESTRY

0   10
metres

|||| 13th Century
\\\\ 14th Century
//// 15th Century
..... Later & Modern

Plan of Ilfracombe Church

ILFRACOMBE   *Holy Trinity*   SS 514474

The rectangular north transeptal tower with a lancet and doorway facing north is 13th century. The west bay of the nave with elongated arcade piers may represent the enlargement ordered in 1321 by Bishop Stapledon. The east end of the chancel is also of about that time. During the 15th and 16th centuries the aisles were rebuilt larger and extended as chapels up to the chancel east wall, thus enclosing the west and east sides of the tower. The outer walls and windows were mostly rebuilt during a restoration of 1861 by Hayward when the south chapel arcade was rebuilt and the south porch added, whilst the vestry was added in 1894, but the fine wagon roofs with a celure at the nave east end are original. They have angels and corbels with mythical beasts. The 15th century north porch has an open wagon roof.

Ilsington Church

St Nicholas Chapel, Ilfracombe

The Norman font has three rosettes on each side and scallops under the bowl. The south door is late medieval and retains an original knocker. The Elizabethan pulpit has two tiers of arched panels on short columns. The stained glass is all Victorian. There is a tapered 12th century tomb slab with an incised cross. Marie Selwood, d1635, has a medieval style tomb slab with interlace. The best of many wall-monuments is that of Richard Bowen, d1797. It has a trophy over a sarcophagus.

ILFRACOMBE   *St Nicholas*   SS 526478

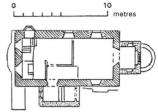

Attractively located on a rock by the harbour is a small 14th century chapel now subdivided with sash-windows and east and south porches. The fish weathervane is dated 1819. The bay window near the west end of the north side contained a perpetual light to help guide ships safely into the harbour.

Plan of St Nicholas Chapel, Ilfracombe

ILSINGTON   *St Michael*   SX 785761

The chancel and the north and south transepts are 13th or 14th century, the south transept having a tiny west lancet and the north transept a niche containing a decayed female effigy of c1300. The transepts are irregularly laid out and lean towards the east. The aisles with five bay arcades and the unbuttressed west tower are 15th century. The south side has a two storey porch and is all embattled. The upper walling over the arcades is left out in the fourth bay to allow the meeting of the wagon roofs of the nave and transepts. There is a stair turret on the north aisle NW corner. The only old furnishings are the screen with leaf friezes and Devon's only medieval examples of stall ends with poppy heads.

Ilfracombe Church

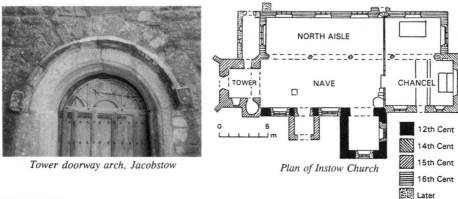

Tower doorway arch, Jacobstow

NORTH AISLE

TOWER   NAVE   CHANCEL

0   5
└──┴──┴──┴──┴──┘ m

Plan of Instow Church

■ 12th Cent
▨ 14th Cent
▧ 15th Cent
▤ 16th Cent
▧ Later

INSTOW   *St John Baptist*   SS 480310

The block-capital shaped font is Norman and the nave south wall and south transept may also be of that period. All the windows of the early 14th century chancel are renewed. Of the 15th century are the south porch with a renewed outer entrance and the diagonally buttressed west tower with a lofty SE stair-turret. An inscription on two of the three piers of the north arcade tells up that the aisle was built in 1547 by Richard and Emma Waterman. It has a ceiled wagon roof. There are medieval tiles in the chancel. The monuments include an effigy of John Downe, d1640, in a gown leaning on a skull, and Humphrey Sibthorp, d1797, who was buried at Bath Abbey.

INWARDLEIGH   *St Petrock*   SX 560995

The church has a low west tower with diagonal buttresses and a nave and north aisle with straight-headed windows. The nave south wall was rebuilt during a restoration by Tait and Harvey in 1898. There are a few Barnstaple tiles, one window has fragments of 14th century stained glass, and there a Norman font of block-capital shape with rosettes and other motifs on the shaft and base.

IPPLEPEN   *St Andrew*   SX 834665

Except for a Norman tympanum with traces of a bird and cross over a small north doorway, this is an all-15th century church with a contemporary fittings including a screen with painted figures on the wainscoting, a pulpit with a Georgian stair, fragments of glass in the east window, and an octagonal font with quatrefoils, shields and three statuettes on the pillar and bowl. The west tower rises to 27m and has eight low pinnacles. Both aisles are embattled with staircase turrets on the western corners and the south side has a two storey porch. The restored east window of the south aisle has a star-shaped motif in the top of the tracery. The arcades of six bays have double-chamfered arches on red sandstone octagonal piers with white capital with fleurons, some left unfinished. There is a chandelier of c1765 from Stone in Staffordshire and a cartouche of 1727 to the Neyle family.

JACOBSTOW   *St James*   SS 586016

This aisleless church with a round-headed south doorway was much restored in 1902. The west tower has diagonal buttresses and pinnacles. The square font of uncertain date has chamfered angles.

KELLY *St Mary* SX 396814

Of a 14th century chancel all that remains is the south respond of the chancel arch with a head on the capital. A new chancel arch was provided in the 15th century when a north aisle and north chapel were added with a five bay arcade and also a west tower with set-back buttresses and polygonal pinnacles which were rebuilt in 1835 after a lightning strike. A plaque records the rebuilding of the chancel in 1710 by John Bollon, and the round headed south windows have round ends to the hoodmoulds with that date and the initials of rector Richard Edgcumbe, whose monument lies between these windows inside. The nave has one 16th century south window set in a wall that may go back to the consecration recorded in 1259. The south porch and the vestry west of it are Victorian. The stained glass includes some late 15th century figures in the chapel east window. There are incised slate slabs to members of the Kelly family who died in 1594, 1605 and 1627.

Ipplepen Church

13th Century
14th Century
15th Century
18th Century
Later & Modern

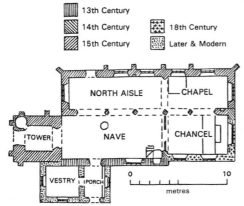

NORTH AISLE — CHAPEL

TOWER — NAVE — CHANCEL

VESTRY | PORCH

0   10

metres

Plan of Kelly Church

Kelly Church

Kenn Church

Kentisbury Church

KENN   *St Andrew*   SX 922857

The sandstone church is all embattled. The overall impression outside is late medieval, whilst the interior was refurnished during restorations of 1863, 1866-9, 1882 and 1887-90 and there is much stained glass of that period. In fact the chancel with a five-light window with intersecting tracery, the diagonally-buttressed west tower, the five bay arcades of double- chamfered arches on octagonal piers, and the stained glass figures in the vestry east window are all 14th century and the font is Norman. The screen encases the piers and has been much renewed but retains poor quality 16th century paintings of saints. The bench ends have two-tier tracery.

KENNERLEIGH   *St John Baptist*   SS 819074

The small church was heavily restored in 1847-8. The oblong west tower has a 19th century pyramidal roof and pyramid-covered corner pinnacles. The piers of the four bay arcade have capitals only on the shafts. The chancel retains its original ceiled wagon roof. Fragments of the old screen cornice have been re-used in the vestry.

KENTISBEARE   *St Mary*   ST 068081

The nave may be 13th century but has 15th century north windows, one at the east end having fleurons round the arch and busts as head-stops. The north doorway also has fleurons and a canopied niche above. Of the 14th century are the chancel and the north tower with a stair turret. Both have buttresses with a chequer pattern of blocks of pink and grey stone. The 16th century south aisle is as wide as the nave and has a ship and a woolpack carved on one of the pier capitals. These refer to the donor John Whyting, whose tomb chest lies in the south chapel and whose arms appear on the rood screen. The parclose screen is of the same period. There are old wagon roofs, that in the chancel plastered in 1757. The vestry was added in 1865-6. The pulpit was once dated 1736 and goes with the reader's desk. The parapet of the west gallery of 1632 has painted figures and texts with carved strapwork below. The Elizabethan panelling in the south chapel is from Bradfield. There are indents of two missing brasses. There is also a monument to William Eveleigh, d1697.

Porch at Kenton

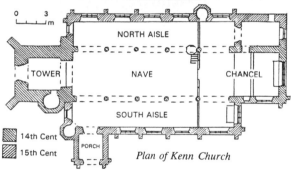

Plan of Kenn Church

0   3
└──┘m

NORTH AISLE

TOWER   NAVE   CHANCEL

SOUTH AISLE

▨ 14th Cent
▧ 15th Cent

PORCH

Screen at Kenton

KENTISBURY *St Thomas* SS 623439

In 1873-4 the church was rebuilt by E. Dolby for the absentee rector and patron the Reverend Thomas Openshaw, leaving from the medieval period only the south doorway and porch and the west tower with set-back buttresses and a NE stair-turret. There are two 18th century slate tablets with long inscriptions refering to the Richards family, who were patrons and rectors from 1598 until 1773.

KENTON *All Saints* SX 958833

Of the early 16th century are the 36m high west tower with a panelled tower arch, set-back buttresses and large three-light bell-openings with a transom and a four-light west window with niched pinnacles below, and the embattled two storey porch with an ornate niche over the square-headed outer portal and small niches above the gargoyles. The nave and aisles with seven bay arcades are of c1500 so the newly-built aisle in which William Slighe wished to be buried in 1379 no longer exists. The pulpit is original but was much restored in 1882. The screen has rustic painting on the wainscoting and a modern loft above. It bears the arms of Bishop Peter Courtenay (1478-86). Old bench end panels with angels holding shields are reused in a doorway into the north chapel. This chapel also has and old parclose screen. The monuments include a seated figure of Dulcebella Hodges, d1628.

Kingsbridge Church

KILMINGTON   *St Giles*   SY 274980

The embattled west tower with a stair turret and a doorway with a four-centred head, plus monuments to Thomas Southcott, d1715 and Agnes Tucker of Coryton, d1788, alone has survived the rebuilding of 1862 by C.F.Edwards.

KINGSBRIDGE   *St Edmund*   SX 739446

The 13th century central tower has slightly chamfered pointed arches. The bell-openings and embattled parapet on a corbel table surrounding the base of the spire are early 14th century. The consecration recorded in 1414 probably refers to the building of either the south chapel with a two bay arcade and a priest's doorway that cuts into a buttress, or the north chapel with just a single arch. Both chapels have old parclose screens in the Flamboyant style. The three bay nave and aisles with octagonal piers were rebuilt in the 19th century when most of the exterior was restored and in 1849 a big chapel was added west of the south transept. The octagonal font with two shallow pointed arches on each side may be 13th century. The pulpit and reader's desk incorporate Flamboyant arcading from the former rood screen. There is a monument to the Reverend George Hughes, d1667.

KINGSKERSWELL   *St Mary*   SX 876678

Of c1400 are the south aisle and chapel with an arcade of double-chamfered arches on octagonal piers, all sandstone except for the limestone moulded capitals, plus the mutilated effigies of what may be Sir John Dinham and his two wives, now in the north aisle. The shallow and low embattled transept is probably contemporary and has a recess with blank arcading with cusping cut into by the later south window. The north aisle is two or three generations later. The west tower is unbuttressed and has a stair-turret. The east window contains fragments of old glass and the chancel stalls incorporate parts of the wainscoting of the former screen.

KINGS NYMPTON   *St James*

SS 682195

The featureless north wall of the nave, the north transept with a plain pointed arch towards the nave, the chancel of the same width as the nave and the roughcast tower with small bell openings and a recently renewed spire may all be 13th century. On the south side is an embattled aisle of five bays with a porch and a tall arcade with capitals only on the pier shafts. The doorstep of the inner south doorway is a granite cross-slab re-used. A coffin-shaped doorway leads into the 16th century NE vestry. The nave and aisle have medieval wagon roofs, and there is a celure over the screen, which has a ribbed coving and three bands of ornamentation on the cornice. In 1755 the chancel roof was plastered to allow the then incumbent, Lewis Southcombe, to paint it with sky, clouds, and a large cross. All probably of the early 18th century are the baluster font with a fluted bowl, the large reredos with Ionic balusters and the communion rail with alternating twisted balusters and columns. There is Jacobean panelling inn the south chapel. In the chancel is a tablet to Jacob Smith, d1667.

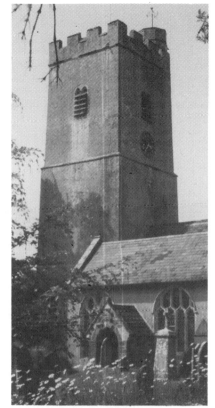

Kingskerswell Church

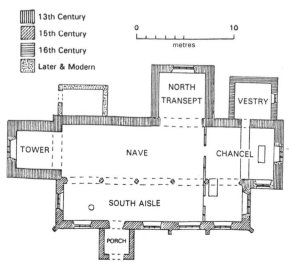

13th Century
15th Century
16th Century
Later & Modern

0   10
metres

TOWER

NAVE

NORTH TRANSEPT

VESTRY

CHANCEL

SOUTH AISLE

PORCH

Plan of King's Nympton Church

Kingsbridge Church

Kingsteignton Church

KINGSTEIGNTON   *St Michael*   SX 872728

The crude plate tracery of the west window of the tower with set-back buttresses is probably 17th century. The nave and aisles with arcades of five bays are 15th century and the very fine south doorway and font with tracery and leaves are of that date, but the windows were all renewed in restorations of 1824 and 1865, whilst one of the two SW corner buttresses is dated 1776. Only the wainscoting survives of the screen. The earliest of the ledger stones is of 1670.

KINGSTON   *St James*   SX 634478

The south transept may be late 13th century but has suffered from a drastic restoration of 1892-1905 which has left only an octagonal font with quatrefoils, and one bench end from the old furnishings. The rounded-headed south doorway is probably still older, whilst there is a 14th century west tower with diagonal buttresses. The battlements and those of the higher stair turret set on corbel-tables. The north aisle with three light windows without tracery must be later than the consecration recorded in 1422. The chancel has a piece of carved wall-plate.

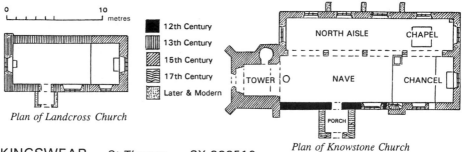

Plan of Landcross Church

Plan of Knowstone Church

12th Century
13th Century
15th Century
17th Century
Later & Modern

KINGSWEAR   *St Thomas*   SX 883510

Only the diagonally-buttressed tower survived the rebuilding of 1847 to a design by Hayward.

KNOWSTONE   *St Peter*   SS 828231

The nave south wall with a plain round-headed doorway is Norman. The rood-loft staircase on the south side, the chancel east of it and the diagonally-buttressed west tower with a polygonal stair-turret are 15th century. The north arcade of four round arches on square piers is 17th or 18th century but the aisle must be older since it has a medieval wagon roof. The coved ceiled roofs of the nave and chancel are whitewashed. The pulpit includes one panel from the former screen. There is a monument to John Culme, d1691.

LAMERTON   *St Peter*   SX 451771

The only features older than the fire of 1877 are the diagonally buttressed west tower with a polygonal stair turret and crocketed pinnacles, the Jacobean font cover and the monuments to Hugh Fortescue, d1650 and his wife, and the Tremayne brothers of Collacombe, erected in 1588 but repaired and altered in 1707.

LANDCROSS   *Holy Trinity*   SS 462238

This is a small single chamber probably of early date with a 15th century east end. A slate-hung turret projecting from the west wall replaces a tower destroyed by lightning c1820. The pulpit has early Renaissance panels and there are 16th century bench ends with shields, profile heads, leaves and tumblers.

LANDKEY   *St Paul*   SS 591311

The chancel was restored in 1868-9 by William White but retains one small lancet on the north side and a squint from the south transept. The rest is 15th century with embattled transepts with gargoyles, a porch beside the south transept with fleurons on both doorways, a north aisle with a three bay arcade, an octagonal font with quatrefoils and tracery panels on the stem. There is also a west tower with set-back buttresses and a polygonal stair-turret rising above the main battlements, below which are gargoyles. The nave, north aisle and porch have ceiled wagon roofs. In the nave the beams rest on head-stops and there are more of these on the window hoodmoulds. There are effigies of three members of the Beaupel family, a knight and wife of c1300 and a slightly later lady. There is a monument with a semi-reclining effigy of Sir Arthur Acland, d1610, set above and behind his recumbent wife.

Langtree Church

Screen at Lapford

LANGTREE   *All Saints*   SS 451156

The chancel south wall was rebuilt in 1865-6, and there are plaster Royal Arms and a pulpit of the late 17th century with garlands and cherub's heads, whilst two chancel chairs have Flemish reliefs showing Christ carrying the Cross and Christ crucified. Otherwise the features are mostly 15th century. The west tower has boldly projecting clasping buttresses and a stair turret on the south side rising above the main battlements. The wide nave has a north aisle of four bays and there is a north chapel of two bays. The north windows are straight headed. The chancel east window is particularly interesting. The octagonal font has patterns in the panels.

LAPFORD   *St Thomas of Canterbury*   SS 732084

The best features are the nave roof with angel corbels and a foliated wall plate plus a celure with cross-ribs and roses-en-soleil, plus the screen of the 1530s or 40s with Renaissance details and a cornice with four decorative strips and cresting. The empty panel is assumed to have been a reredos for an altar. There is also a parclose screen. The south door was very ancient and has an original knocker, and there are many 16th century bench ends with initials, monograms of the St John family, profile heads, and the symbols of Christ's Passion. The west tower with diagonal buttresses, an image niche on the south side and a polygonal SE stair turret is probably 15th century, whilst the north aisle with its lofty arcade of granite piers and straight-headed windows without cusping is 16th century. During a restoration by Ashworth in 1888 the east end was rebuilt, several windows replaced, and a vestry added.

LEW TRENCHARD *St Peter* SX 456861

The Baring Gould monuments in the north chapel were assembled here by the folklore expert and antiquarian Sabine Baring Gould, rector and squire here for over 40 years until he died in 1924. He has a plain headstone in the graveyard and was responsible for refurnishing the church, re-roofing it, and adding the vestry. The building has a small nave with a narrower chancel and a two bay arcade with concave sided piers to a north aisle, the third bay beyond the screen opening to the north chapel. Only the top stage of the unbuttressed west tower is of granite ashlar. It has obelisk pinnacles. There are a few 16th century bench ends with motifs such as instruments of the Passion, a fool and a bust of a woman, and some old panels are re-used in the chancel stalls. The 16th century wooden eagle lectern was carved in Brittany.

LIDWELL SX 923762

This well chapel lies on the edge of some woodland with the ground rising steeply outside the west doorway, which is fitted with a draw-bar slot. This wall stands complete but only foundations remain of the side-walls and nothing of the east wall.

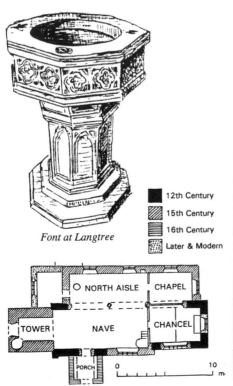

Font at Langtree

■ 12th Century
▨ 15th Century
▤ 16th Century
▨ Later & Modern

Plan of Lew Trenchard Church

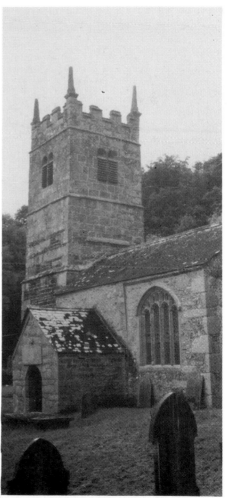

Lew Trenchard Church

Little Torrington Church

Lifton Church

LIFTON   *St Mary*   SX 386850

The whole church is of c1500-50, the only older feature being a Norman font of the Cornish type with corner heads with intersecting arches between them. The only other furnishings of note are four bench end panels with arabesques in shields. The west tower has set-back buttresses with large polygonal pinnacles and three-light bell-openings. There are arcades of six bays with castellated abaci on the piers, the two bays which served the chancel chapels, having lower arches. The north porch is embattled and of two storeys. There is a cartouche to John Dynham, d1641, and a large monument has alabaster kneeling effigies of Sir William Harris, d1590, Sir Arthur Harris, d1618, and Lady Harris, d1630.

LITTLEHAM   *St Swithin*   SS 443235

A 13th century lancet survives in the chancel north wall. The north transept leans towards the west and has a 15th century lancet in the north wall but the masonry is older as there is a wall painting of Christ of the Trades of c1300. Also 15th century are the south aisle, the west tower with clasping angle buttresses, and the font. The bench ends with early Renaissance scrolls must be 16th century. The screen dates from the second of two restorations in 1874 by White and 1891-2 by Temple Moore.

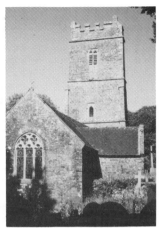

Littleham in South Devon   *Littleham in North Devon*

LITTLEHAM   *St Margaret & St Andrew*   SY 029813

The trefoil-headed piscina is evidence of the 13th century date of the chancel and there is a blocked lancet in the south wall (not now visible). The low two bay arcade of the south chapel looks 14th century. The north aisle was begun in 1528 but was partly rebuilt in 1883-4 by R.M.Fulford, whilst one window contains late 15th century stained glass with figures of Christ showing his wounds, St Roche and St Michael. The nave and west tower with diagonal buttresses may be slightly older·than that but the nave south windows are now of 1911. The chancel roof has old bosses re-used. There is a much restored rood screen, and the parclose screens have early 16th century linenfold wainscoting. There are many 19th century monuments to Exmouth residents, including one to Lord Nelson's widow, d1830.

LITTLEHEMPSTON   *St John*   SX 813627

The 15th century west tower has set-back buttresses plus another in the middle of the north wall, balancing the polygonal stair turret on the south side. The rest of the church also appears to be of that date although there is renewed 14th century type tracery in the chancel, where the north window has 15th century stained glass moved here from Mardon, and there are three 14th century effigies, a knight on the north side, and a knight and lady on the south side, thought to be members of the Stretch family. Both aisles are of ashlar and embattled and there is an embattled two storey porch on the south side. The south doorway with traceried panels is particularly good. A screen with leaves, grapes and birds carved on the cornice cuts off the east bay of the five bay arcades. The seven sided font with ribs is Norman.

LITTLE TORRINGTON   *St Giles*   SS 491169

The narrow roughcasted west tower has thin diagonal buttresses. The pinnacles are probably after 1438 when an indulgence was granted for rebuilding the belfry after it was struck by lightning. The south arcade is of four bays with granite piers. The porch is old and has a niche over the doorway, but the aisle has been rebuilt and so has the chancel. The font has what looks like a Norman bowl set on a 16th century base, whilst the cover is Jacobean. The earliest monument is Henry Stevens, d1802.

LODDISWELL   *St Michael*   SX 721487

The diagonally buttressed west tower with a broad stair turret not reaching as high as the battlements on a corbel table may be as early as the 1290s. Of about the same period are the nave, north transept and chancel. The addition of a 16th century south aisle has swept away a south transept except for the east respond of the arch into it. There is a porch at the west end of the aisle, one window of which contains heraldic glass. The small circular Norman font has a frieze of voluted palmettes and a narrow band of saltire crosses. There is a slate slab of 1616 with a black-letter inscription, an unusually late use of this type of lettering.

LOXBEARE   *St Michael*   SS 911161

In c1850 the chancel was given a new east window and largely rebuilt. It is slightly lower and narrower than the nave but internally only a step divides the two. The nave has a Norman south doorway with chevrons, now covered by a shallow porch. The low west tower with a NE stair-turret contains three 15th century bells. There are tablets in the chancel to Daniel Cudmore, d1645, and Zachri Cudmore, d1657,. and over the doorway are Royal Arms of George II dated 1725. The communion rail and west gallery contain Jacobean work, whilst the pulpit and tester are of c1660.

LOXHORE   *St Michael*   SS 617387

The short north aisle has an arcade with two wooden piers supporting an entablature. This part contains a tablet to Philip Hammond, d1704 and Royal Arms of 1714 and may be of that period, although there is also a tablet to Edward Hammond, d1653, and the ribs and bosses of the wagon roof look still older than that. The chancel is entirely of 1882 by E.Dolby and the nave also has Victorian windows, but the porch is 15th century, whilst the diagonally buttressed west tower may be 16th century. The square Norman font has a 16th century cover with a crocketed top. There are brass inscriptions to Richard Carpenter, d1627, and Mary Weber, d1671.

Loxbeare Church

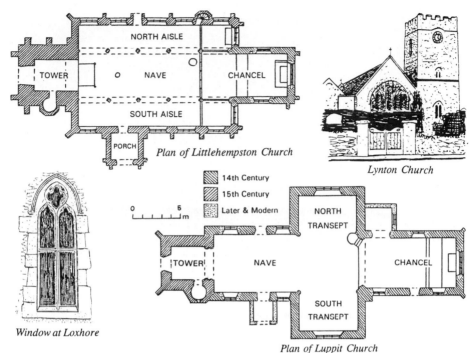

Plan of Littlehempston Church

Lynton Church

14th Century
15th Century
Later & Modern

Window at Loxhore

Plan of Luppit Church

LUFFINCOTT   *St James*   SX 333947

According to an inscription the west tower with obelisk pinnacles was rebuilt in 1791 by the mason Richard Sillifant, but he must have reused materials from a medieval structure. The north side of the single chamber nave and chancel has sash windows of 1761, although a medieval carved wall-plate remains above them and there is a boarded wagon roof with carved bosses. The panelled south door is also 18th century. The octagonal granite font is in a poor condition.

LUNDY   *St Helena*   SS 138439

The existing church was built in 1896 by J.Norton for the Rev H.G.Heaven. Foundations of the 13th century chapel of St Elen lie in the old burial ground.

LUPPITT   *St Mary*   ST 169068

The church preserves its 14th century plan of a nave with a chancel arch leading into a narrower chancel and a pair of wide but shallow transepts. The chancel was mostly rebuilt in 1880-1, the nave was given new windows in 1870-1, and the south transept was repaired in 1884, so the outside has little of interest apart from the diagonally buttressed west tower with polygonal SE stair-turret. Of greater interest are the way the late medieval wagon roofs meet in a spectacular manner in the middle with a central boss, the Norman pillar piscina in the chancel and the Norman font with heads at the corners with a centaur fighting two dragons, a martyrdom in which two men drive a nail into a detached human head, a group of dogs and a tree with dishevelled foliage. There is also a late brass inscription with part of a female figure of the 1430s on the reverse.

Screen at Lustleigh Church

LUSTLEIGH   *St John*   SX 785813

The church lies in a circular churchyard in the middle of the village. The 13th century chancel has an original lancet and a tomb recess on the north side and three sedilia and a piscina on the south. Flanking much of the south side of the nave, leaving only space for a narrow porch added to the west of it, is an early 14th century transept containing the effigy of a cross-legged knight of that period in the south wall. There is an unbuttressed west tower with obelisk pinnacles of late 14th or 15th century date, whilst the four bay north aisle with fragments of stained glass in the north windows and the screen with statuettes in the wainscoting are 16th century. The aisle contains recesses with effigies of a knight and lady of c1300. A Norman font is incorporated into a later font with six shafts, and there is a late 6th century stone inscribed Datidoci Conhinoci Filius (Datwidoc, son of Conhinoc).

LYDFORD   *St Petrock*   SX 509848

This is not a large church when one considers Lydford's former importance, and the north aisle and vestry were only added in 1889-90 by S.Hooper. Excavations have revealed traces of an oratory on the site. The 13th century chancel retains an original piscina and one north lancet. The south doorway and porch and one trefoiled window to the west also look 13th century. Otherwise the aisle is 15th century and modest but with three widely spaced arcade arches, and there is a squint towards the chancel. The tower with set-back buttresses is also 15th century. There is a tub-shaped Norman font. Two windows contain fragments of medieval stained glass.

LYMPSTONE *St Mary* SX 993843

Features to have survived a rebuilding by John Ashworth, and the lengthening of the chancel and addition of a south chapel in 1928 by Harold C.King, are the red sandstone west tower with set-back buttresses and a stair-turret, the chancel arch, the five bay north arcade, and a monument with busts of Nicholas Lee, d1759, and his wife.

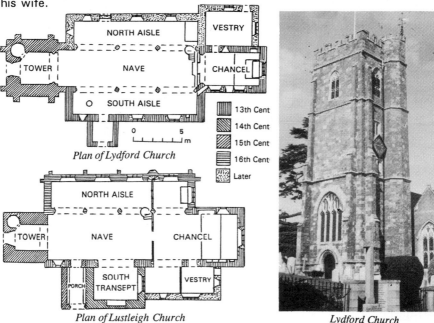

Plan of Lydford Church

▥	13th Cent
▧	14th Cent
▨	15th Cent
▤	16th Cent
▦	Later

Plan of Lustleigh Church

Lydford Church

Lympstone Church

Mamhead Church

Manaton Church

LYNTON   *St Mary*   SS 721495

The tower at the west end of the south aisle and the Norman font on a 15th century octagonal stem with eight piers are the only relics of the medieval building. The Elizabethan font cover, the south aisle outer wall of 1741, the Royal Arms of William III dated 1833, and the wooden tablet to Thomas Grose, d1734 painted with a choir of angels also predate the additions and rebuilding of 1868-9, 1893-5 and 1905 resulting in a wide nave with north and south aisles. See view on page 133.

MALBOROUGH   *All Saints*   SX 707399

The low rendered west tower of the end of the 13th century with a broach-spire seems rather modest for the rest of the otherwise spacious 15th century church with windows of three or four lights with four-centred heads without tracery. There are arcades of six bays with the arches almost semi-circular, plus two bays of differing widths for the chancel chapels. The south side has a rood-loft stair-turret and a two storey porch vaulted in two bays with four heads meeting at the chins on the central boss. The only old furnishings are the chapel parclose screens and the Norman table-top type font on five shafts and with five blank arches on each side.

MAMHEAD   *St Thomas*   SX 931808

The church lies alone within the landscaped estate. The chancel has one south lancet and the nave and south transept may also be of 13th century origin, whilst the diagonally buttressed tower may be no later than c1300. The north aisle is 15th century and has an arcade of semi-circular arches on octagonal sandstone piers which were encased in cement during a drastic restoration of 1830-1, when the vestry was added. There are no pre-19th century furnishings or monuments.

MANATON   *St Winifred*   SX 749813

The whole church is of c1480-1500 with arcades of four bays with granite piers, ceiled wagon roofs, and the south side embattled, of granite ashlar, with a vaulted two storey porch. The restored screen has early 16th century painted panels of saints with their faces gouged out at the Reformation. One north aisle window has original stained glass figures. There are many ledger stones.

MARIANSLEIGH   *St Mary*   SS 744221

As a result of the church being gutted by fire in 1932 two arches with circular piers of a blocked 13th century south arcade were discovered. The west tower with low diagonal buttresses and a low, unmoulded tower arch is not much later. From a north transept of that period there remains part of the east wall with a piscina, now part of a late medieval aisle with straight-headed windows.

MARLDON   *St John*   SX 866630

The 13th or 14th century west tower has a pronounced batter. The aisles are embattled, with a rood-loft stair turret on the north and a vaulted two storey porch on the south. The windows were mostly restored in 1884 by Fulford. The aisles are of five bays, plus two extra on the south side for a chapel built by the Gilbert family of Compton Castle c1520. To the chapel was transferred a shelf-piscina from the breached chancel south wall. Only some loose fragments remain of a former stone screen. There is a small effigy of the knight, probably Otho Gilbert, d1492, to whom there is a cenotaph originally part of the screen. There is an octagonal font.

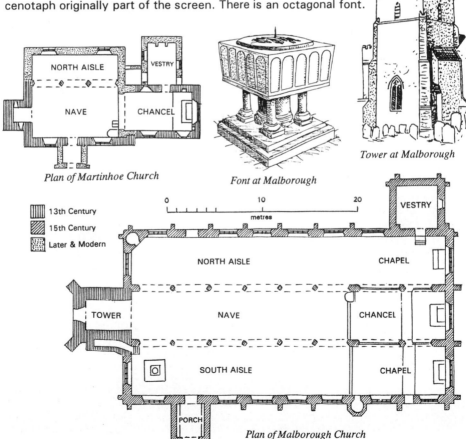

Tower at Malborough

Plan of Martinhoe Church

Font at Malborough

13th Century	
15th Century	
Later & Modern	

0   10   20
metres

NORTH AISLE

VESTRY

TOWER

NAVE

CHANCEL

CHAPEL

SOUTH AISLE

CHAPEL

PORCH

Plan of Malborough Church

MARTINHOE   *St Martin*   SS 668487

The nave and chancel each have an original 13th century south window of two lancets, with trefoiled heads in the chancel, and other windows are renewals of lancets of that period, to which also probably belongs the tiny west tower. The chancel arch, the north vestry, the south porch and the north aisle of three bays are of the 1850s and 60s. Originally the chancel arch was further east. Some tracery of the wainscoting is all that remains of the rood screen.

MARWOOD   *St Michael*   SS 544376

The church is long and the position of the 14th century south doorway suggests a later lengthening of the nave to meet up with the fine 15th century tower with set-back buttresses and a NW stair-turret. The chancel has 13th century lancets on the north side and traces of the jambs of two more on the south, but it was mostly rebuilt by Hayward in 1858-9. The south transept is also 13th century, with a lancet on the east and a plain pointed arch to the nave. The outer wall of the 16th century aisle overlies the battered base of a former north transept then swept away. The aisle has window of three lights with four-centred heads under a square head and a five bay arcade. East of it is a late 16th century vestry. There are wagon roofs in the nave and aisle, the latter with moulded ribs and bosses. The east bay of the aisle is closed off by a very fine contemporary screen with early Renaissance motifs. The back of the loft still survives. On the wainscoting panels of the door is an inscription recorded it as the gift of Sir John Beaupel, rector in 1520. There are old bench ends with initials, shields and saints. The mid 17th century pulpit has baluster legs. Old panelling has been used in the reredos. There are large plaster Royal Arms of George III in the aisle. The porch sundial is of 1762 and there are monuments to William and Anthony Peard, d1652, and William Parminter, d1737.

Martinhoe Church

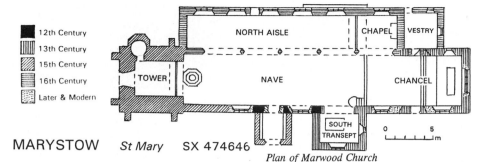

■	12th Century
▦	13th Century
▨	15th Century
▤	16th Century
▦	Later & Modern

Plan of Marwood Church

MARYSTOW   *St Mary*   SX 474646

Norman are the square font with intersecting arches and corner heads and the south doorway ornamented with billet and saltire crosses. The early 14th century chancel has one original south window and trefoil-headed double sedilia. The granite ashlar west tower with four diagonal buttresses is 15th century but was partly rebuilt in 1824. The north aisle has a six bay arcade and one four-light 16th century window. The east end is largely filled by a monument with recumbent effigies of Sir Thomas Wyse, d1629, and his wife. Beyond this end is a narrow Victorian aisle of two bays. The south side has one 15th century window and another of the 16th century and there is a porch with a fireplace, now lacking a chimney since a roof renewal.

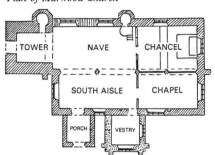

Plan of Mary Tavy Church

MARY TAVY   *St Mary*   SX 519788

The nave may have early masonry. The rest is late medieval, comprising a chancel as wide as the nave, a south aisle as long as the building, with a four bay arcade, an ashlar south porch with a wagon roof, and a granite ashlar west tower with a high polygonal NE stair-turret and obelisk pinnacles. One window on the south side has an image niche. The transept projecting from the aisle was added in 1893.

MEAVY   *St Peter*   SX 540673

Meavy Church

The north respond of the chancel arch with red and white stone and two rams' heads at the corners is Norman. The battered oak tree outside is said to be just as old. The chancel east window with three sharply pointed lights under one head and the reset windows with Y-tracery in the chapel are of c1300. The 15th century west tower has a rectangular NE stair-turret, a granite plinth, and low pinnacles. The south aisle and its arcade are 15th century but the transept is older. The nave wagon roof is open but the others are ceiled.

Meavy Church

MEETH   *St Michael*   SS 548084

The Norman nave has one original north window and a south doorway with slight decoration on the arch outer moulding. The square font on five shafts is also Norman. The porch has a wagon roof with leaf bosses. The west tower with a NE stair turret may be late 16th century. The chancel and the organ-chamber-cum-vestry on the north side are Victorian. The plaster Royal Arms of Queen Anne are dated 1704.

MEMBURY   *St John*   ST 276030

The 13th century chancel has an original north lancet and an internally nook-shafted east window with triple lancets. The priest's doorway and the blocked nave north doorway may also be of that period. The north transept appears to be a late medieval rebuild of an older structure since it contains a female effigy of c1300. The reset animal heads biting a roll moulding used as label stops on the windows on the 15th century embattled south aisle have come from a Norman doorway assumed to have been destroyed when the aisle and porch were added. The arcade is of four bays to the nave with an extra arch to the chancel. The old SE corner of the nave is pierced by a squint looking from the south chapel into the nave. The west tower has set-back buttresses and a SE stair-turret and there are goat-gargoyles at the top. A screen with early 16th century linenfold panelling divides the aisle from the south chapel. The south aisle has a monument to Shilston Calmady, d1645, The south chapel has monuments to the Frys of Yarty, notably Nicholas, d1632, and his wife, Robert, d1725, and the seventeen year old Frances, d1723.

MERTON   *All Saints*   SS 526120

The north aisle was rebuilt in 1872-5 by R.M.Fulford but it retains a late medieval five bay arcade and its east window contains fragments of old glass. The south transept must be earlier but the only ancient feature there is a recess for an effigy. The tower has set-back buttresses and obelisk pinnacles. The square Norman font has three scallops under each side.

MESHAW   *St John Baptist*   SS 759197

The church is of 1838 by R.D.Gould with a sanctuary added in 1878, but it contains a monument to James Courtenay, d1685, and has a west tower of 1691.

MILTON ABBOT   *St Constantine & St Aegidius*   SX 407793

This is late 15th century a church unless the diagonally buttressed west tower with a stair turret is slightly earlier. The rest forms a plain rectangle with arcades of four bays with the arches almost round-headed. The north side has original windows and rood-loft stair projection. The south side has restored windows and a porch at the west end and a smaller Victorian porch at the east end covering the priest's doorway. Corbels on the eastern set of piers mark the position of the former screen and loft. There are three 19th tablets to the Edgcume family in the south aisle and also a tablet to Gulielmus Salmon, d1750.

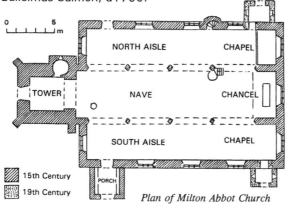

Plan of Milton Abbot Church

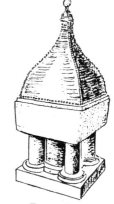

Font at Meeth

Milton Damerell Church

MILTON DAMERELL   *Holy Trinity*   SS 385107

The oldest part appears to be the late 13th century north chapel with a window with three trefoil-headed lights in the east wall. The early 14th century chancel has an original piscina, windows with cinquefoils on the south wall and a three light east window with reticulation. The tower may be of the about the same period but it was rebuilt in 1892. The nave is wide and has a large 16th century south window. The north aisle has a three bay arcade with crudely ornamented capitals on the piers. There are old tiles, Royal Arms of 1664, and a pulpit of about that period.

MODBURY   *St George*   SX 655516

The 14th century west tower has corner buttresses and a spire which was rebuilt in 1621, probably in the same way as it was before, after being struck by lightning. The arcades with their thick, short piers are also 14th century, whilst the recesses in the south transept or Champernowne chapel are probably of c1300. They contain battered effigies, one now unrecognisable, the other a knight of c1460. Two more very damaged effigies lie in a 14th century recess in the north transept or Prideaux chapel. Of the late medieval period are the aisle outer walls with windows without tracery, the arches into the transepts and chancel chancels, and the chancel set over a vestry. The east end was restored by William White c1860. The pulpit has been made up from Flamboyant panels from the former 16th century screen. In the north chapel is a large inscribed slab to Oliver Hylle, d1573. High above the south arcade is a 17th century monument with kneeling figures with an illegible inscription. In the north aisle is a monument to John Swete of Traine, d1690.

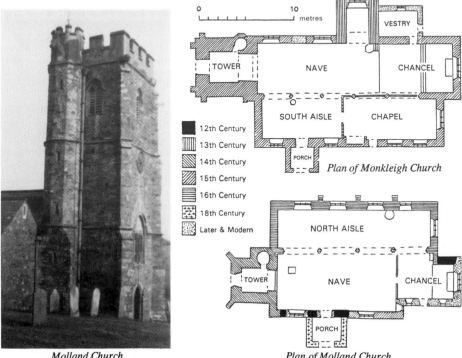

0   10
metres

VESTRY

TOWER   NAVE   CHANCEL

SOUTH AISLE   CHAPEL

■ 12th Century
▥ 13th Century
▨ 14th Century
▨ 15th Century
▤ 16th Century
▦ 18th Century
▒ Later & Modern

PORCH   *Plan of Monkleigh Church*

NORTH AISLE

TOWER   NAVE   CHANCEL

PORCH

Molland Church   *Plan of Molland Church*

MOLLAND   *St Mary*   SS 808284

The square Norman font has a scalloped under edge. The small chancel has been mostly rebuilt in the 19th century but the north wall could have Norman work, whilst the east window is 15th century work reset. The diagonally buttressed west tower with a rectangular NE stair-turret (it is polygonal above) and figures high up may be of c1400. The nave south windows are perhaps 15th century and the porch could be 18th century, whilst the north aisle is early 16th century. It has windows of three lights with four-centred arches under a square headed with a hood-mould and an arcade of three bays to the nave plus one to the chancel. The east pier has a niche and there are wreathed capitals. The aisle roof has tie-beams but is coved. The screen has a solid tympanum with Royal Arms and Ten Commandments painted in 1808. Part of the old screen remains in the reredos and there are communion rails of c1700. The three-decker pulpit has a sounding board with a marquetry stair and a trumpeting angel on top. There are fragments of a late medieval tomb chest with quatrefoils and the Courtenay arms. Other Courtenay monuments include John, d1660, John, d1724, and John, d1732. There is a tablet to David Berry, d1664.

MONKLEIGH   *St George*   SS 457208

The small north transept is probably early and intended to be carried up as a tower. Sir William Hankford, Chief Justice of the King's Bench, d1423, left money for completing the five bay arcade and the rest of the church is probably of about that time. His tomb chest lies in a fine recess in the south wall within the two and a half bays closed off as a chapel by a fine screen, original on the west and an imitation of 1879 towards the chancel. Some of the aisle windows have tracery with intersecting round-headed arches cut by mullions. The west tower has set-back buttresses and a polygonal NE stair turret and pinnacles. Made up from an old bench end is a lock box carved with a monster and tracery and there are benches in the chapel assembled from 15th and 16th century panels. The Norman font has fluting on both the bowl and the top of the shaft. The communion rails are 17th century and the chapel east window has fragments of 16th century glass. Both the chancel and chapel have old tiles. In the chancel is a brass of a 16th century kneeling knight together with fragments of a lost 16th century monument. There are half-figures of William Gaye, d1631, and his wife and slate plates depicting Henry Hurding, d1627 and his family and Jane Coffin, d1646, with a baby (she probably died in child-birth).

MONK OKEHAMPTON   *All Saints*   SS 581055

The church was entirely rebuilt in 1855 by F.Harper except for the low west tower with large pinnacles, and a cusped arch in the chancel from a tomb recess.

MONKTON   *St Mary Magdalene*   ST 188031

A rebuilding in 1863 by Hayward has left only the restored medieval west tower.

Brass inscription at Monkleigh Church

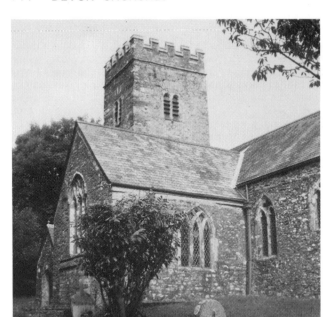

Moreleigh Church

MORCHARD BISHOP   *St Mary*   SS 773075

The church may be of the mid 15th century when an indulgence was granted to those contributing towards rebuilding. It has a west tower with set-back buttresses, a large four-light west window, short pinnacles rising to 28m and a polygonal NE stair-turret. There are sandstone arcades of three bays, plus a fourth bay of limestone for the chancel chapels. The outer walls were rebuilt above the footings except for the SE corner in 1887-91, whilst the chancel was rebuilt in the 18th century, having round arched windows and panelling. In a tomb recess in the south chapel are effigies said to be William Eyston, d1505, and his wife, who gave money for completing the aisle. The screen has been reconstructed on the basis of a few original surviving parts. The communion rail is of 1768, and the reredos is of about the same period.

MOREBATH   *St George*   SS 955251

The saddleback roof and upper part of the early west tower date from William Butterfield's restoration of 1875-82. His also are the south windows and all the furnishings. The north aisle may be late 14th century as the north windows have ogee-hexagon tracery. There are several late 18th century tablets to the Bere family, and there is a monument to Nicholas Sayer, d1713 and his family.

MORELEIGH   *All Saints*   SX 761526

This is a small church with a low early tower. The late medieval south aisle has an arcade of three bays. The circular Norman font has one frieze of two intertwined wavy lines. Part of the old screen now serves as a reader's desk. The pulpit and tester are 18th century.

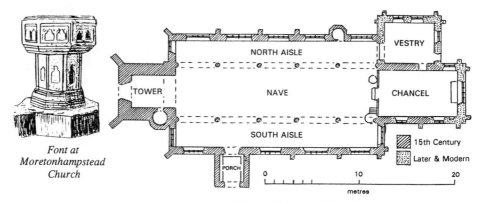

Font at Moretonhampstead Church

Plan of Moretonhampstead Church

MORETONHAMPSTEAD   *St Andrew*   SX 755861

The tower with a polygonal SE stair-turret was under construction by 1418. Both it and the western corners of the roughly contemporary aisles have diagonal buttresses. The aisles extend for five bays, and then the chancel has two more, but its east end and the large vestry north of it are Victorian. A rood-loft stair-turret in the north side shows that the former screen divided off the fifth aisled bay. The embattled south porch is of two storeys. The side windows have been renewed.

Moretonhampstead Church

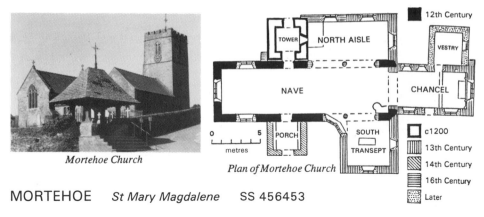

Mortehoe Church

Plan of Mortehoe Church

■	12th Century
□	c1200
▥	13th Century
▧	14th Century
▤	16th Century
▦	Later

MORTEHOE *St Mary Magdalene* SS 456453

The north and south doorways could go back to 1170, when William de Tracey is supposed to have founded the church to atone for his part in the murder of Thomas Becket, Archbishop of Canterbury. That on the north now leads to a tower built against this side a generation or two later. The chancel is 13th century although its north lancets are renewed. The south transept is also probably 13th century although its features are later. It contains a tomb chest thought to be of William de Tracey, d1322, a rector who founded a chantry here in 1308. On the lid is an incised effigy of a priest with a chalice. A vaulted passage to the nave has been created by building a pier in line with the west wall. The pier is dated 1618 but may be older. The north transept was later extended west to meet the tower and given a two bay arcade, probably in the 16th century. There are 48 bench ends carved with heraldry, saints, initials, profile heads in roundels and the Instruments of the Passion. There is a rustic-looking cartouche to Mary Newell, d1700.

Interior of Mortehoe Church

Musbury Church

MUSBURY   *St Michael*   SY 276946

The chief item of interest is the monument erected in 1611 by John Drake, d1628. In front of the kneeling effigies of John and his wife, are similar effigies of his father Sir Barnard, d1611, and his grandfather John, d1558, with their wives. There is also a monument to John Anning, d1793. The church has a 15th century west tower with diagonal buttresses and a SE stair-turret, and part of the south aisle is 16th century but the south porch, chancel and north aisle were all rebuilt in 1874-6 by Hayward.

Interior of Musbury Church

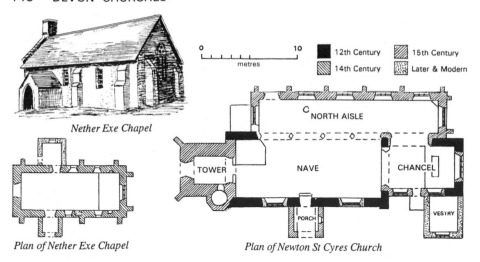

Nether Exe Chapel

0   10
metres

■ 12th Century   ▨ 15th Century
▧ 14th Century   ▒ Later & Modern

NORTH AISLE

C

TOWER   NAVE   CHANCEL

PORCH

VESTRY

Plan of Nether Exe Chapel   *Plan of Newton St Cyres Church*

NETHER EXE   *St John the Baptist*   SX 932998

This is a small 14th century chapel lying alone in a field near the river Exe. It has a piscina with a trefoiled arch and doorways to the west and south, the latter with a porch. There are just two small windows on each side and a three light east window. There is a Norman font with a scalloped underside set on round shafts rising from a square base with a scalloped top. There is a cartouche to Mary Young, d1771.

NEWTON ABBOT   *St Leonard*   SX 858713

In the town centre is a grey limestone tower of two stages which is all that remains of the medieval chapel-of-ease to Wolborough. It was replaced in 1835 by a new church of St Leonard in Wolborough Street, to which a chancel was added in 1876.

NEWTON ABBOT   *St Mary*   SX 857713

A church of 1904-5 by E.H.Sedding in Waverley Road, Abbotsbury, has a central east window and a piscina and pulpit from the former St Mary's chapel-of-ease to Highweek church in Highweek Street. The chapel still exists and has a 15th century tower, but has long been used for secular purposes, mainly as a school. The window is of interest since it has in the tracery a curvilinear star-shape and their are crocketed niches and badges of the families of Yarde and Ferrers.

NEWTON FERRERS   *Holy Cross*   SX 551481

Only the late medieval west tower and arcades, plus an early 14th century piscina in the chancel survived the rebuilding of 1885-6 by G.Fellowes Prynne.

NEWTON POPPLEFORD   *St Luke*   SY 086897

Only the small west tower remains of this 14th century chantry chapel, later a chapel-of-ease to Aylesbeare. The rest was rebuilt in 1826, when a south aisle was added. The octagonal wooden posts close to the north wall to give the illusion of an aisle there were inserted in 1875 by R.M.Fulford, who also remodelled the chancel.

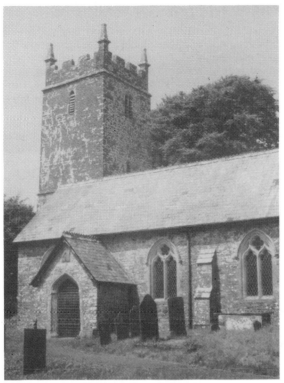

Newton St Petrock Church   *St Leonard's Tower, Newton Abbot*

NEWTON ST CYRES   *St Cyriac & St Julitta*   SX 879980

The south doorway has a chamfered round-headed Norman rere-arch and the SE corner of the nave looks Norman also. The windows of the nave and chancel are 19th century. Of the 15th century are the ashlar south porch with a wave-moulded doorway, the diagonally buttressed west tower with a polygonal SE stair-turret, and the north aisle with a four bay arcade to the nave and a wider panelled arch to the chancel. There is an 18th century marble font and also the base of a four-columned Norman font. The pulpit with a large tester is late 18th century. There are rare Royal Arms of James II, dated 1685. The clock dates from 1711. The lectern and aumbry have two carved panels probably of Flemish workmanship. There is a monument with an effigy of John Northcote, d1632, flanked by busts of his wives, and there is a small effigy of the seventeen-year-old Sherland Shore, d1632. Monuments to the Quicke family include those of Thomas, d1701, John, d1704, and his wife, d1706, John, d1776, and Andrew, d1793.

NEWTON ST PETROCK   *St Petrock*   SS 411123

The nave north windows and the south aisle with its arcade of four bays are late medieval. Older are the west tower with a plain pointed arch towards the nave, and the circular Norman font. There are 16th century bench ends with initials, heraldry, Renaissance scrolls and other motifs. The communion table is Elizabethan.

NEWTON TRACEY   *St Thomas of Canterbury*   SS 529269

The tiny nave and chancel are both 13th century, with restored lancets in the chancel, and also the cushion-capital shaped font with cable mouldings round the waist and stiff-leaf foliage in low relief at the angles. A two bay arcade probably also of 13th century date with a round piers was discovered and opened out again when the north aisle was added during the restoration of 1867 by R.D.Gould. The west tower has a 15th century west doorway carved with arms of the families of Pollard, Bourchier and St Leger. Both the west and south doors have old ironwork.

NORTHAM   *St Margaret*   SS 448291

This is a large church on a commanding site high above Bideford, the tall tower serving as a landmark for shipping in Barnstaple Bay. The tower has diagonal buttresses, a polygonal stair-turret on the south side, and a west doorway with fleurons. The wide nave has a wagon roof on angels with bosses on which appear the symbols of the Passion. The south transept has an old wagon roof. According to an inscription on one of the octagonal piers of the five bay arcade with double chamfered arches the north aisle was added in 1593. The chancel was entirely rebuilt in 1865. The 13th century font has pointed blank arches on each side. There are several minor late 18th and early 19th century monuments, but none of importance.

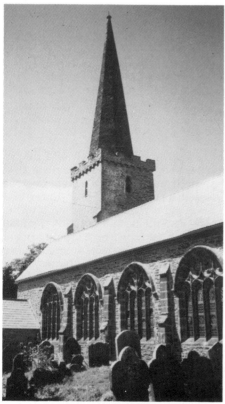

North Huish Church

Northleigh Church

Interior of North Bovey Church

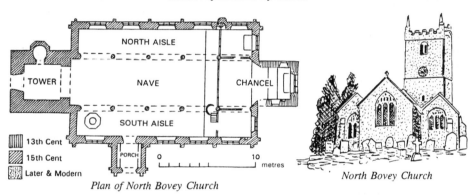

NORTH AISLE

TOWER

NAVE

CHANCEL

SOUTH AISLE

||||| 13th Cent

///// 15th Cent

▒▒▒ Later & Modern

PORCH

0   10

metres

Plan of North Bovey Church

North Bovey Church

NORTH BOVEY   *St John*   SX 739838

The narrow chancel must be 13th century but the rest is late medieval with aisles of five bays with the fifth bay cut off by an original screen, the arches being double-chamfered with octagonal piers. There is a south porch and a tower of huge granite ashlar blocks with a polygonal stair-turret in the middle of the north side. There are ceiled wagon roofs in the aisles and chancel. The screen has statuettes around the central doorway and there are also old parclose screens and bench ends with two-tier tracery and leaf motifs. One north window retains some original stained glass.

NORTH HUISH   *St Mary*   SX 711566

The west tower with battlements on a corbel table and low diagonal buttresses is early 14th century. The top is now slate-hung and a spire has been added. There is a 13th century piscina in the chancel and the north transept may be of that date also. The 15th century south aisle was divided off by a concrete wall in 1984 and the medieval rood screen then re-erected as an entrance screen. There are old roofs in the nave, aisle and south porch.

NORTHLEIGH   *St Giles*   SY 196959

There is a plain Norman south doorway. The rest is late medieval with a vestry added beyond the north chapel either in 1858 when the chancel was rebuilt, or in 1868-9 when the nave and aisle were given new roofs and windows and a porch added. The low arcade is of three bays plus one more for the chapel The west tower has diagonal buttresses and a NE stair-turret. Original screens divide off the chancel and north chapel from the other parts. There are old bench ends in the nave. The north chapel east window has escaped restoration and contains some 15th century stained glass.

NORTHLEW   *St Thomas of Canterbury*   SX 505992

This is a small church with arcades of four bays, the easternmost opening into chancel chapels. The south windows have four lights with late medieval tracery, whilst the north windows are straight-headed and without tracery. There are old unceiled wagon roofs, that in the north chapel having bosses with leaves sticking out in four directions, while that in the south aisle and chapel has angels against the wall-plate. The square font with saltire crosses and rosettes on five columns and the lower part of the west tower with small original north and south windows are Norman. The bench ends have tracery and initials on shields, and one is dated 1537. Only the wainscoting is original of the screen.

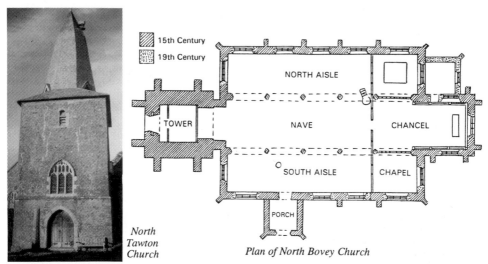

North Tawton Church

Plan of North Bovey Church

15th Century
19th Century

NORTH AISLE

TOWER   NAVE   CHANCEL

SOUTH AISLE   CHAPEL

PORCH

Doorway impost at Nymet Rowland

NORTH MOLTON   *All Saints*   SS 737300

The lofty west tower has set-back buttresses and a niche on the south side with a figure of the Virgin. The tall pinnacles have been removed. The east buttresses connecting tower with the nave look as if they could have been part of an earlier and more modest tower. Everything else seems late medieval apart from the Victorian NE vestry. There are five bay arcades with a clerestory above and with the last bay divided off by a screen now lacking its coving and spandrels. The parclose screens are also medieval and of different designs. There are diagonal corner buttresses on the aisle and the south porch. The windows were renewed in the 1880s by John Ashworth. The octagonal font with figures on the shaft and pointed quatrefoils and panelling on the bowl, and the pulpit, a timber version of the stone one at South Molton, are both 15th century. The chancel panelling is probably mid 17th century. It has arms of the Parker family and came from their seat of Court House in the 1840s. There is a clock of c1720. The north chapel east window has 18th century glass. In the south chapel is a large monument with a recumbent effigy of Sir Amyas Bamfylde, d1624, with his wife seated at his feet and seventeen children shown kneeling against the tomb chest and against the back. There is also a monument to John Burgess, d1752, and his wife, d1772.

NORTH TAWTON   *St Peter*   SS 664018

The arcades of six bays have granite piers and almost semi-circular arches. The nave and aisles have old unceiled wagon roofs. The shingle spire on the 13th century west tower was restored in 1900. The sanctuary is an addition of 1832. There are old bench ends, and others with tracery panels with roses in leaves in the spandrels have been reused at the east end. One north window contains 15th century stained glass showing angles with shields, one having the Champernowne arms.

NYMET ROWLAND   *St Bartholomew*

SS 711082

The Norman south doorway has modest decoration on the imposts of the arch. Also Norman is the cup-shaped font with cables and semi-circles on the shaft. The decoration on the north side of the bowl is probably later. The three bay north arcade is of timber. The west arch has started to come apart and is held by a later post in the middle. A large round-headed south window is dated 1636. The north aisle has an original wagon roof and contains Royal Arms of George III dated 1792. The chancel east wall was rebuilt during Samuel Hooper's restoration of 1874.

Font at Nymet Rowland Church

OAKFORD   *St Peter*   SS 911213

Only the monuments to the Spurway family, the earliest being of Margaret, d1691, and the diagonally buttressed west tower with a stair-turret and later obelisk pinnacles, survived the rebuilding of the church in 1838 by R.S.Pope.

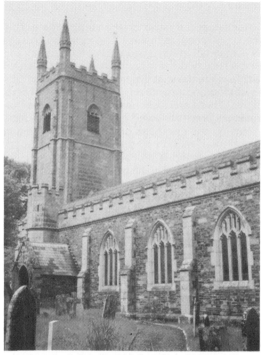

All Saints' Church, Okehampton   *St James' Chapel, Okehampton*

OFFWELL   *St Mary*   SY 194996

The nave and chancel date from c1200, with one original south window and a plain chamfered round arch between them. A 14th century south doorway has been renewed. The 16th century north aisle has three arches to the nave and one panelled arch to the chancel. One capital has naked figures. The west tower has diagonal buttresses and a NE stair-turret. The pulpit of 1724 has figures of evangelists added in 1784. The reader's desk includes a richly carved Flemish panel. The box pews of 1798 were altered in 1853. Re-used under the tower are is part of a medieval screen from St Mary Major at Exeter. There is a tablet to Joanna Southcott, d1696.

OKEHAMPTON   *All Saints*   SX 582951

The tower with set-back buttresses and crocketed pinnacles, and the arcades survive from the building under construction in 1448. The rest was rebuilt in 1842-4 by Hayward after a fire but is said to reproduce what was there before.

OKEHAMPTON   *St James*   SX588952

This is a modest chapel-of-ease without a graveyard, standing isolated in the middle of east end of Fore Street. Only the small west tower with set-back buttresses and obelisk pinnacles survived the restoration of 1862 by Ashworth, the blocked arcade of three bays with octagonal piers being a facsimile. The pulpit dated 1662 and the reader's desk incorporate woodwork of the 15th, 16th and 18th centuries.

OTTERTON   *St Michael*   SY 080852

This is a very large church with a wide nave and aisles, entirely the work of Benjamin Ferrey in 1869-71 for Lady Rolle except for a 13th century tower on the south side of the chancel. The tower is said to have stood between a parochial nave and a choir used by a Benedictine priory until it was suppressed as alien in 1414, yet the tower's only original arch faces north to the chancel and the east wall is solid.

Pier capital, Ottery St Mary

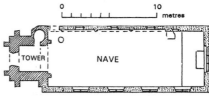

Plan of St James' Chapel, Okehampton

Otterton Church

Dorset Aisle at Ottery St Mary

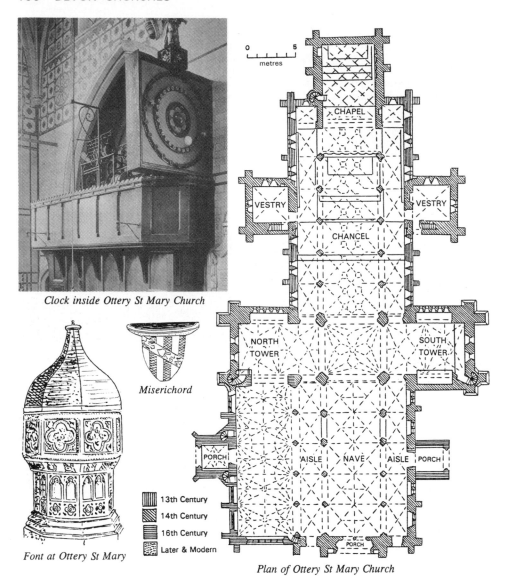

Clock inside Ottery St Mary Church

Miserichord

Font at Ottery St Mary

13th Century
14th Century
16th Century
Later & Modern

Plan of Ottery St Mary Church

OTTERY ST MARY   *St Mary*   SY 098956

Bishop Grandison acquired Ottery St Mary from the cathedral of Rouen and in 1337 established a college which eventually had as many as forty members. The outer walls of the aisles of the collegiate choir with their modest two lancets are probably a left-over from the previous church on the site and there is the same arrangement of twinned lancets in the nave aisles, despite this being very out of date for the 1340s and 50s. The wide Dorset aisle beyond the nave north aisle is of c1510-25, otherwise the whole church dates between 1337 and when the bishop died in 1369.

Ottery St Mary Church

In plan Ottery church is like a scaled-down version of Exeter cathedral. The building is comparatively low, has two transeptal towers, and is 50m long. The nave is five bays long and has a vaulted recessed west entrance with splayed sides. This may have been the principal entrance as the existing south doorway and porch are 16th century and the door itself there is dated 1575 on the ironwork. Originally there was a cloister on this side with a chapter-house on the east side of it. There is another entrance, used by the townsfolk, through a two storey porch beyond the Dorset aisle. There are three-light windows of the usual late medieval type in the Dorset aisle and it is covered by a fan-vault with pendants of spiral openwork bars. The arms of Bishops Oldham and Veysey appear in the north porch, whilst the moulding below the parapet has the Stafford family knot emblem, one of the major benefactors being Cicely, Countess of Wiltshire, who married Henry, Lord Stafford in 1503. The six-light west window in this aisle was renewed in 1843.

The east end forming the collegiate choir is longer than the nave, for although the main altar is in the fifth bay with a wall behind it, there is a sixth bay forming an ambulatory which gives access to a Lady Chapel three bays long with a very unusual east grouping of eight lancets. The choir aisles extend as a seventh bay to flank the first bay of the Lady Chapel. The aisles are comparatively narrow and a covered with quadripartite vaults. Projecting from the fourth bays of the choir aisles are two storey vestries, the lower rooms vaulted and the upper ones reached by straight stairs in the thick west walls. The transeptal towers have recesses for altars lighted by groups of five lancets. The south tower has a west recess as well but its northern counterpart has been broken out at the back to allow access from the Dorset aisle. The towers have pierced parapets which are a replacement of 1872, within which the north tower has a short lead spire with an old weathercock with trumpets.

The glory of the church at Ottery are the vaults, especially the choir vault, which is thought to be the work of William Joy, known to have been at work at Wells an Exeter in the 1340s. It is characterised by predominant curves and a four-petalled pointed rosettes with liernes connecting them to the wall-shafts supporting transverse arches. The ribs are not load bearing and form decoration on the surface of what is in effect a glorified tunnel-vault, above which are scissor-braced roofs. The bosses are carved with figures of Bishop Grandison, St John the Baptist, St Anne and the Virgin, the Coronation of the Virgin, Assumption of the Virgin, Coronation of the Virgin, and the Last Judgement.

In the Lady Chapel lie stalls with miserichords on which are carved Bishop Grandison's arms. He also provided the gilded wooden eagle lectern. The features on the wall behind the main high altar were hacked off at the Reformation and had to be restored in the 19th century and the 1930s. The choir has original parclose screens with straight tops and cusped ogival arches. The clock in the south transept may be a 15th century remodelling of an older timepiece. The face shows the phases of the moon as well as the hours. The pulpit of 1722 has figures of the evangelists.
Opposite each other under the fourth arches of the nave arcades are tomb chests with effigies of Otho de Grandison (the bishop's brother), d1358, and his wife Beatrice, d1374. Three brasses at the east end of the south aisle to the Sherman family bear the dates 1542 and 1583. On the north side of the choir is the tomb of John Haydon of Cadhay, d1587, possibly a conversion of an older Easter Sepulchre. In the south chapel are three monuments of c1620 to members of the Sherman family. At the east end of the Dorset aisle is a standing figure of John Coke, d1632. In the north transept is a monument of 1794 to William Peere-Williams of Cadhay.

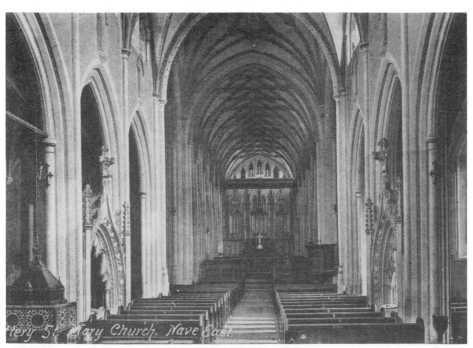

Interior of Ottery St Mary Church

Interior of Paignton Church

PAIGNTON   *St John*

SX 886609

Paignton belonged to the bishops of Exeter, ruins of whose palace lie close to the south of the church, and in consequence is a building of some size 58m long. The chancel may contain Norman masonry, and there is a circular Norman font with palmettes, but otherwise the only relic of a large and fine church of that period here is the doorway reset in west wall of a 15th century tower with set-back buttresses. The doorway features polychrome masonry with alternating strips of red and white on the door surround, the outer order being red with saltire crosses on scalloped capitals, whilst the white inner order has chevrons and foliage capitals.

Norman doorway at Paignton

The arcades are late 13th century with double-chamfered arches on sandstone piers with white capitals. The east bays are 15th century and the renewed four-light windows, the battlements and the transepts are of that period. The 14th century porch is vaulted. The sedilia were reconstructed from old fragments in 1870. Between the south aisle and transept lie the 15th century two bay screen and monuments known as the Kirkham chantry. The openings are fan-vaulted with pendants and there are pinnacles with angels. The tomb chests each have effigies with a knight and wife said by Prince in 1701 to be Kirkhams although this remains unverified. The late medieval stone pulpit has figures under ogival canopies. In a recess in the south aisle is a 15th century cadaver. A similar recess in the north aisle now lies empty. In the Kirkham chapel are two kneeling figures facing each other.

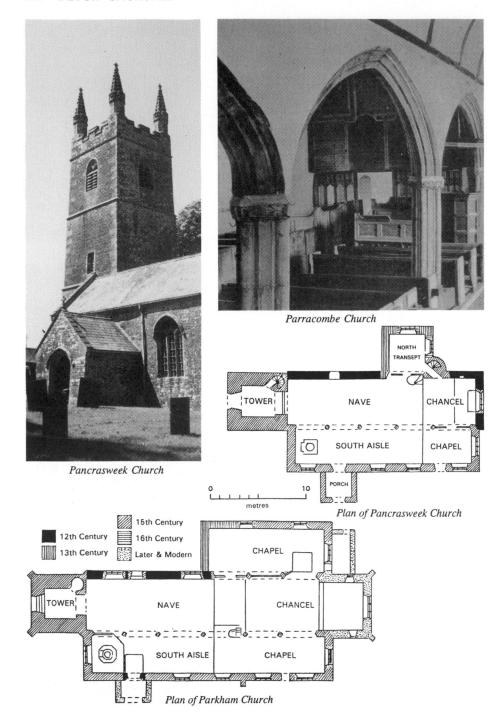

Parracombe Church

Pancrasweek Church

NORTH
TRANSEPT

TOWER   NAVE   CHANCEL

SOUTH AISLE   CHAPEL

PORCH

0   10

metres

Plan of Pancrasweek Church

12th Century   15th Century
13th Century   16th Century
                Later & Modern

CHAPEL

TOWER   NAVE   CHANCEL

SOUTH AISLE   CHAPEL

Plan of Parkham Church

PANCRASWEEK *St Pancras* SS 297058

The north side of the church is early, with no openings in the nave, a transept with a squint, and a chancel with a small blocked window. The south aisle has a granite arcade of five bays and has original windows of three and four lights still with their original iron stanchions to protect the glass. The aisle east window has old glass from Muchelney in Somerset. The west tower has large cusped pinnacles. There are 17th century railings around the octagonal font. The pulpit is Jacobean.

PARKHAM *St James* SS 388215

It is likely that the church was originally cruciform and that the north chapel was expanded out of a former north transept. The three arches of its arcade are more steeply pointed than the six arches of the south arcade and are probably earlier. The south aisle has a chequerwork parapet and reset in the walling is a Norman doorway with one order of colonettes and with one beakhead surviving at the top. The diagonally buttressed west tower has big polygonal pinnacles. The east end seems to have been rebuilt during the restoration of 1875 by R.W.Drew. There is a plain Norman font. The communion rail is late 17th or 18th century. There is a monument to Thomas Saltren, d1753.

PARRACOMBE *St Petrock* SS 675450

The old church lies alone and is now cared for by the Redundant Churches Fund, services being held in Christ Church of 1878 by W.C.Oliver in the village. Since the old church was neither restored nor demolished it is a rare survival showing what a church was like two centuries ago. The nave and chancel are 13th century with a twin lancet in the east wall, and the diagonally buttressed west tower may be only slightly later, say c1300. The south aisle with a three bay arcade to the nave and one more to the chancel, and the porch are late medieval. In the nave north wall is a 16th century window with round-arched lights under a square head and label.

The screen is of an early type with cusped ogival arches rising to a square top. Above is a solid tympanum which in 1758 was repainted with the Royal Arms, the Commandments, Creed, and the Lord's Prayer. There are old communion rails, plain 16th century pews and 18th century box pews, a panelled pulpit with a tester and attached pews for the reader and clerk. The plain circular Norman font is said to have come from elsewhere. On the north and south walls are oval tablets with texts. There are several monuments to the Lock family, notably Walter, d1667, and David, d1786, and there is also a monument to Samuel Flament, d1755.

PAYHEMBURY *St Mary* ST 088019

The 14th century west tower has a west doorway with fleurons on the jambs and voussoirs. The outer portal of the south porch also has fleurons. One of the capitals of the piers of the north arcade is carved with the arms of Bourchier, Courtenay, Ferrers and Malherbe, whilst on the outside of one of the windows are arms of Thomas Chard, last abbot of Forde, proving a 16th century date for this part, although one window contains fragments of 15th century glass. The church was restored in 1895-7 by G.Fellowes Prynne. The octagonal font has quatrefoils on the sides. There are old bench ends with two tiers of tracery and there is an 18th century pulpit with a tester. There are framed Royal Arms of 1740. There are medallion portraits held up by cherubs of Dorothy Goswell, d1745 and Timothy Terry, d1736.

Monument at Pilton Church   *Poor box at Pinhoe Church*

PENNYCROSS   *St Pancras*   SX 472578

This, the parish church of the Plymouth suburb of Weston Peverell, is a much extended manorial chapel with a 14th century chancel lying on a hill-top site. The transepts and nave are of c1820 but were remodelled in 1870. A north extension to link up with the church hall was built in 1984-5. There is no tower, just a small bell-cote on the west gable.

PETERS MARLAND   *St Peter*   SS 478135

Only the west tower with low buttresses survived the rebuilding of 1868.

PETER TAVY   *St Peter*   SX 513777

The west tower of granite ashlar has set-back buttresses, although a stair-turret intrudes on the NW pair. The north aisle has an arcade of three bays to the nave and one to the chancel, and then extends further east to end flush with the chancel east wall. The windows are all 15th century, as are those on the south side, where there is a porch and a transept with later set-back buttresses grafted onto 12th or 13th century rubble walling. The transept arch is double chamfered like those of the arcade. The octagonal font has tracery in panels. The tower screen incorporates old bench ends with heads in profile. There is a monument to Thomas Pocock, d1722.

PETROCKSTOW   *St Petrock*   SS 514092

Features of interest left after the rebuilding of 1879 by J.F.Gould are the diagonally buttressed west tower, the three bay north arcade with double-chamfered arches on octagonal piers, the square Norman font with blank arcading and rosettes, the Jacobean font cover and pulpit, a few fragments of medieval stained glass, and brass tablets to Lady Rolle, d1591, and Sir John Rolle of Stevenstone, d1648.

PILTON   *St Mary*   SS 556342

This church originally served a Benedictine priory. The north aisle windows are set high up above the line of the former cloister north of it. This aisle has an arcade of unmoulded pointed arches probably of c1200. In a transeptal position east of the north aisle is a 13th century tower with blocked arches to the north and east and a narrow pointed arch with a rib vault to the chancel. The basement, now filled with the organ, was once vaulted, or was intended to be. The tower was repaired in 1696 and the top part rebuilt in 1845-50. This part is octagonal and it is clear that an octagonal spire was intended. The 15th century south aisle has an arcade of almost semi-circular arches on piers with leaf-capitals on the shafts. The chancel has an open-timber roof. The other parts have wagon roofs, the boarded one in the north aisle supposedly of 1639. Parts of an old screen have been used in the font cover. The late medieval stone pulpit has a panelled shaft and body. An iron hand holds an hourglass and there is a Jacobean tester. Across the nave and south aisle is a medieval screen, now lacking the cresting and coving. The south chapel is divided from the chancel by a screen with the initial R, referring to the Chichesters of Raleigh. There is an Elizabethan communion rail. There are kneeling figures of Sir Robert Chichester, d1627, and his wives, and a monument to Sir John Chichester, d1569. The many other tablets include one to Christopher Lethbridge, d1713.

PINHOE   *St Michael*

SX 955950

The chief items of interest are the poor box of c1700 with a small figure of a man in Queen Anne period costume, the medieval screen with four strips of scrollwork in the cornice, and the medieval wooden pulpit, a rather plain example. The chancel and south porch were rebuilt in 1879-80 but have some old masonry. The rest is late medieval and comprises a west tower with set-back buttresses, and a stair turret, and a nave and north aisle divided by an arcade with fleurons on the arches. The Norman font has two bands of decoration.

Pulpit at Pilton Church

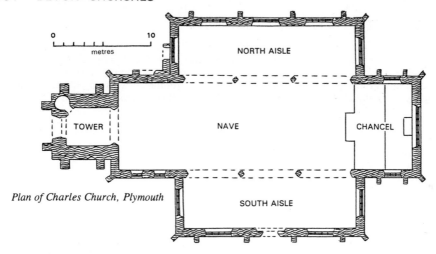

0   10
metres

NORTH AISLE

TOWER

NAVE

CHANCEL

Plan of Charles Church, Plymouth

SOUTH AISLE

PLYMOUTH   *Charles Church*   SX 482545

This is something of a rarity, an entirely new church begun in 1640 to serve a newly created parish. Delayed perhaps by the Civil War, work continued until 1658 and the dedication to King Charles the Martyr was assumed after the Restoration of 1660. The building is gothic in character with a wide nave and chancel flanked by wide north and south aisles stopping one bay short of both the west and east ends and having arcades of three very wide bays. The aisles have four-light windows and there is a wide entrance on the south but no porch. The east window is of six lights with Decorated style tracery. There is a west tower with set-back buttresses with bell-openings of three pointed lights under a round head. The pineapple finial must date from 1708, whilst the stone spire in replacement of a wooden one is of 1766. The church was restored in 1864, 1883 and 1889 but is now a preserved ruin within a roundabout on the ring-road after being gutted by bombing during World War II.

PLYMOUTH   *St Andrew*   SX 478544

Apart from two big vestries added either side of the south porch and a third beside the south chapel, this is essentially a 15th century church, impressive by its size (it is the largest parish church in SW England) but mostly rather plain as there are no battlements except on the tower, few buttresses, and the windows have been restored. In 1460 the merchant Thomas Yogge donated funds for building the huge tower with set-back buttresses, arches in the north and south walls, and pinnacles rising to 41m. There are records of the mason John Dew working on building the south aisle in 1481-2 and John Andrew was working on St John's aisle in 1487-8. The wide nave and equally wide aisles have arcades of six bays, and the chancel and its chapels have three bay arcades, the piers marking the position of the screen being more substantial than the others. There are north and south porches and two bay outer aisles, otherwise interpretable as transepts flanking the nave with east chapels flanking the western bays of the chancel chapels. The church was much damaged by World War II bombing and was given new roofs in 1949-57. No old furnishings survive but there are a number of monuments, the oldest being a 13th century female effigy, now rather defaced, kneeling figures of 1635 of John Sparke and his wife, a 17th century shrouded figure rising from a sarcophagus, and a bust by Chantrey of the Reverend Zachariah Mudge, d1769. See photo on page 166.

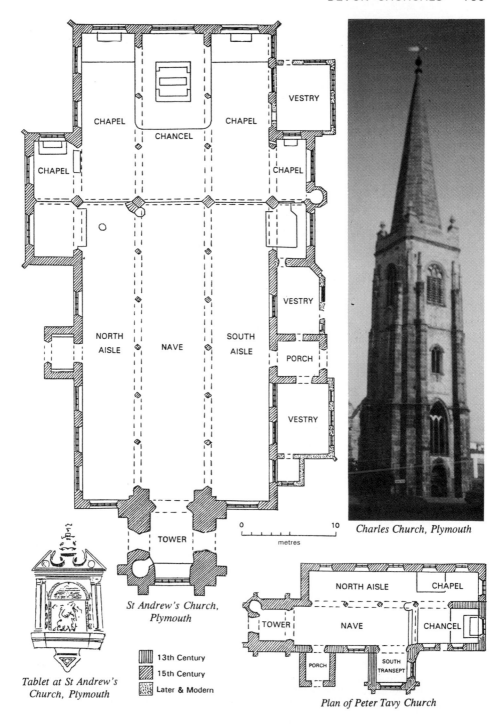

VESTRY

CHAPEL   CHANCEL   CHAPEL

CHAPEL   CHAPEL

VESTRY

NORTH   NAVE   SOUTH   PORCH
AISLE   AISLE

VESTRY

0   10

metres

TOWER

Charles Church, Plymouth

*St Andrew's Church,
Plymouth*

*Tablet at St Andrew's
Church, Plymouth*

||| 13th Century

/// 15th Century

::: Later & Modern

NORTH AISLE   CHAPEL

TOWER   NAVE   CHANCEL

PORCH   SOUTH
TRANSEPT

Plan of Peter Tavy Church

St Andrew's Church, Plymouth

PLYMPTON   *St Maurice*   SX 537564

This church stands just east of the castle site. The tower with set-back buttresses, a polygonal stair turret with a conical roof and large three-light bell-openings was under construction in the 1440s. The aisled nave and the two storey south porch are also of that period but were much restored in 1878, and re-roofed in 1905. Integrated with the second pier from the east on the south side are the steps and base of a medieval pulpit. The present pulpit is 17th century.

PLYMPTON   *St Mary*   SX 526557

This church originated as a chapel attached to the priory. The oldest parts are the chancel with a five light window with a six-pointed star in a circle at the top, and the outer north chapel, originally a detached building. Both are early 14th century with original piscina, and the chancel has sedilia as well. The granite ashlar west tower with set-back buttresses and large bell-openings and polygonal pinnacles, and the aisled nave with a tiny north porch and a two-storey south porch, plus the chancel chapels, and the octagonal font are all early 15th century, the arcades being of seven bays with the arches four-centred. The south side is all embattled with pinnacles and there are three niches on the porch facade with statues of the Trinity, and the Annunciation. Below the window is the crest of the Strode family. The porch has a lierne-vault with three ridge ribs and three transverse ribs and the springers are supported on angel corbels. Some time after 1452 an outer south aisle three bays long with a granite arcade was added to the east of the porch.

   In the outer north aisle is a medieval cross-slab and an effigy of Richard Strode, d1464, on a tomb chest with little figures of mourners. In the south chapel is a recess containing an effigy thought to be William Courtenay of Loughtor. There is also a wall monument with kneeling effigies of Sir William Strode, d1637, flanked by his two wives. There are also several interesting 19th century monuments.

Screen at Plymtree Church

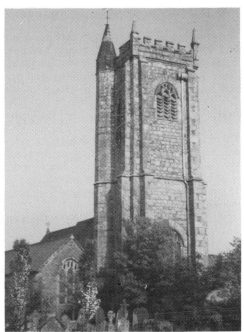

Plympton St Maurice Church

PLYMSTOCK   *St Mary & All Saints*   SX 517530

The church is essentially late medieval but must represent at least two phases for the four bay granite arcades differ from each other. The southern one has double-chamfered arches and octagonal piers with concave sides, whilst the northern one has moulded arches with piers of the usual Devon type with four shafts and hollows between them. The west tower has set-back buttresses reaching up to a parapet on a corbel table, above which rises an embattled stair-turret. The circular Norman font of sandstone has an upside down palmette frieze. The medieval screen was re-erected in the 19th century and lacks its coving. A chest has been made up from early 16th century carved panels probably from Germany and once part of a font cover. There are several monuments to the Harris family of Radford. One of the mid 17th century has kneeling figures set facing each other round a corner. Another has a small kneeling figure of John Harris, d1677.

PLYMTREE   *St John*   ST 052029

The nave has a blocked plain Norman north doorway. The chancel is also early but lacks datable features. Of the 15th century are the south aisle with large three-light windows nook-shafted on the inside, the diagonally buttressed west tower with a low stair-turret with a decorated top, and the octagonal font with quatrefoils. The fine screen with Bourchier and Stafford emblems was the gift of Isabel, widow of Humphrey Stafford, Earl of Devon, who was beheaded in 1470. The painted figures on the wainscoting are early 16th century. Of that period also are the bench ends with tracery which fill the whole nave. The altar rails and the panelling with a relief behind the altar are 17th century. The altar table and pulpit are 18th century.

POLTIMORE   *St Mary*   SX 966968

The west tower with a an original door and a semi-circular stair-turret is 14th century. The south arcade, the squints and most of the other features date from a rebuilding in 1879-84 by R.M.Fulford. There is a plain Norman font. One window in the chancel has a fragment of old glass discovered during the restoration of the medieval rood-screen. There are recumbent effigies of 1604 of Richard Bampfield, and his wife.

POUGHILL   *St Michael*   SS 856085

There is a green man on the west respond of the north arcade which is of three bays, plus a fourth bay with panelling with fleurons between the north chapel and chancel. The plain west tower and the wagon roofs are also late medieval, but the chancel was rebuilt in 1855-6. There are old tiles under the tower and box pews in the aisle. There is a monument to Gertrude Pyncombe, d1730.

POWDERHAM   *St Clement*   SX 973844

The diagonally buttressed west tower may be of the period of the foundation of the castle (some distance away) in the 1390s. The aisles with five bay arcades are later, the eastern pier capitals having the arms of Sir William Courtenay, d1485 and his wife. In the 1860s the chancel was extended by one bay, and the windows renewed. Of that period is most of the rood screen (but with a few old parts) and the upholstery of the Courtenay family pew (a rare survival) in the screened off east bay of the north aisle. There is an old door in the porch and one north window has fragments of original glass. The only pre-Victorian monument is an effigy of Elizabeth de Bohun, d1378, whose daughter married the third Earl of Devon.

PRINCETOWN   *St Michael*   SX 587737

The church is of 1813 by Daniel Alexander with alterations of 1898 and 1908. It contains an 18th century pulpit carved with evangelists from St Sidwell's Exeter.

PUDDINGTON   *St Thomas a Becket*   SS 833107

The choir stalls incorporate a 17th century oak bench. The rest was rebuilt in 1837, when a south porch and north aisle were added. The aisle was rebuilt in 1880.

Doorway at Pyworthy

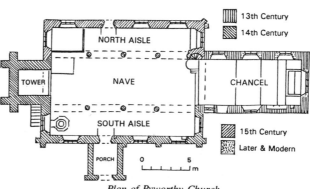

Plan of Pyworthy Church

Pyworthy Church

Rattery Church

PYWORTHY *St Swithun* SS 313029

This church differs from the norm for Devon in that late medieval work is confined to several windows in the south aisle and the rebuilding of the north aisle in ashlar above the older rubble lowest courses. The doorway there is 14th century and also of that period are the west tower with corner buttresses, the south aisle with a four bay arcade and clerestory and probably the south porch. The lower parts of the clerestory windows are boarded up as a consequence of the heightening of the aisle roof in the 15th century. The chancel is of c1300 with restored Y-tracery in the windows and original jambs to the priest's doorway. There is a plain octagonal font.

RACKENFORD *All Saints* SS 851183

The west tower with diagonal buttresses and a NE stair-turret has a west doorway with a renewed 14th century type window above. The rest is 15th century with an arcade of four bays with crude capitals between a nave and a north aisle which does not reach quite as far west. The south side and porch were rebuilt in 1827 and a restoration that began in 1877 has removed all features of interest except a large octagonal late medieval font with tracery motifs.

RATTERY *St Mary* SX 741616

This building commands wide views and is roughcast. The late 13th or 14th century west tower has low diagonal buttresses and battlements on a corbel-table. The narrow aisle have arcades with double-chamfered arches on octagonal granite piers and there are transepts. The chancel is presumably after 1426 when the then chancel was described as too small and dark for services. The south transept has a window with Y-tracery set into 15th century jambs. The screen was restored in 1911.

Rewe Church   *St Budeaux Church*

REVELSTOKE   *St Peter*   SX 564466

This building, since 1982 looked after by the Redundant Churches Fund, lies alone on a cliff above Stoke Bay. It was abandoned after the Barings of Membland built a new church at Noss Mayo in 1882. The nave is roofless but the chancel was reroofed in the 1960s and closed off by glazing. The south aisle has a three bay arcade and three-light windows without tracery. It retains a rafter roof with bosses. The small NW tower has a saddle-back top. The north transept has a 14th century window.

REWE   *St Mary*   SX 946993

The polygonal stair-turret only reaches halfway up the thin west tower, the top of which was rebuilt in 1914. The 15th century north aisle has an arcade with angels with shields on the capitals. The embattled north chapel or Wadham Chantry of c1500 is now filled with the organ, hiding a monument to Paul Draper, d1689. The chancel has late medieval windows but the cinquefoiled piscina is probably earlier. The nave south wall and porch were rebuilt in the 1860s. The seating of that period incorporates 32 old bench ends with tracery motifs and the arms of Sir Nicholas Wadham. There is an old screen and there is an almsbox dated 1632 on a fluted column. Monuments to the Tripp family in the chancel include one to Frances, d1794.

RINGMORE   *All Hallows*   SX 653460

This is a cruciform 13th century church with on the south side a low tower of c1300 with lancets, diagonal buttresses, battlements and a small spire. All the other windows are lancets with or without trefoiled heads, although some were restored in 1862-3. Patterned medieval paintings were then revealed on the chancel arch.

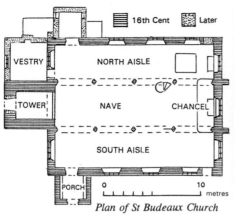

16th Cent   Later

VESTRY   NORTH AISLE

TOWER   NAVE   CHANCEL

SOUTH AISLE

PORCH   0   10   metres

Plan of St Budeaux Church

Ringmore Chapel

RINGMORE   *St Nicholas*   SX 924723

This 13th century chapel-of-ease lies by the Teign estuary west of Sheldon. Probably original are the vaulted porch, the tiny windows west of it and the Victorian north vestry, plus the west lancet and another of which there are traces in the south wall.

ROBOROUGH   *St Peter*   SS 577171

The north wall and the chancel were rebuilt during a heavy restoration of 1868. Old features are the south arcade with granite piers, the west tower with diagonal buttresses and pinnacles, and two slate tablets of 1648 and 1652 to two daughters of the Fortescue family.

ROCKBEARE   *St Mary*   SY 020953

The church contains 19th century monuments to the Porters of Rockbeare and was mostly rebuilt in 1887-9 by Hayward and Tair. Old features are the diagonally buttressed west tower of grey ashlar with a stair-turret and a fine west doorway with fleurons on the arch, the north aisle wall and arcade, the wagon roofs with bosses and the Elizabethan parapet of the west gallery.

ROSE ASH   *St Peter*   SS 788212

Only the west tower, the north arcade, the rood-screen, the chapel screens dated 1618 with arms of Anne of Denmark and Prince Henry, the communion rails of c1700, and a few memorials to the Southcombe family survived the restoration by Ashworth in 1874 followed by a rebuilding in 1882-92 by St Aubyn and Wadling.

ST BUDEAUX   *St Budeaux*   SX 454593

The west tower may be 13th or 14th century. The rest was rebuilt in 1563 as an aisled nave with four bay arcades with a short projecting sanctuary. The south aisle has one arched window between two with straight heads. No furnishings survived the restoration of 1876 by James Hine but there are monuments to John Fownes, d1669, Lewis Stanley, d1693, and Charles Fortescue, d1715, and a tomb chest of 1600 to Roger Budockshead and Sir William Gorges and their families.

ST GILES IN THE WOOD   *St Giles*   SS 534190

The outer walls and diagonally buttressed west tower survived the rebuilding of 1862-3 by John Hayward for the Hon. Mark Rolle. An organ chamber and vestry were added in 1879. The porch is set rather far east and has the outer portal facing east, a very unusual feature. One capital of the former arcades lies outside by the Se corner and part of an 18th century tablet is fixed to the outside of the tower. In a part of the south aisle now closed off by a glass screen is a semi-reclining effigy of Thomas Chafe of Odsett, c1630. The upper half of the brass of Alenora Pollard, d1430, has been restored. There is also a brass to Joanna Risdon, d1610 and there are several other brasses with just heraldry and inscriptions.

ST GILES ON THE HEATH   *St Giles*   SS 354007

The chancel retains one small 13th century window but was restored in 1868, when the south wall was rebuilt re-using the old windows and a low west tower added with a slated pyramidal spire. The five bay south arcade is 15th century, and there is a circular Norman font. Only the wainscot remains of the old screen. There are a few old bench ends with two blank cusped arches with roundels in which are a rose, fleur-de-lys and a frontal head. There are two 18th century slate wall monuments.

SALCOMBE   *Holy Trinity*   SX 740393

This church of 1843 by J.H.Ball has a chancel of 1889 by J.D.Sedding and lies in an elevated position above Batson Creek. It contains a late medieval octagonal font with 17th century ornamentation, probably a relic of the original chapel-of-ease to Malborough consecrated in 1395 on another site and rebuilt in 1801.

SALCOMBE REGIS   *St Mary and St Peter*   SY 148888

This church is rather different from what one normally finds in Devon. The only 15th century part is a diagonally buttressed west tower with a polygonal SE stair turret, and the only 16th century part is an unusual feature, a NW vestry projecting further west than the tower and set over a charnel house. Slight traces of a Norman priest's doorway survive in the chancel, which has windows of c1300, just lancets in the sidewalls but of three lights to the east. The arcades are of two bays, early 13th century with a circular pier on the north and perhaps late 13th century with a cruciform pier on the south. Both aisles have 13th century walling, that on the south having an original south doorway of two orders and a west lancet, plus two Victorian windows, whilst the north has 15th and 16th century windows, one of which has old glass. The lectern is probably 15th century. The tower screen and pulpit are 18th century. There is a tablet to Joanna Avant, d1695 with a multilingual inscription.

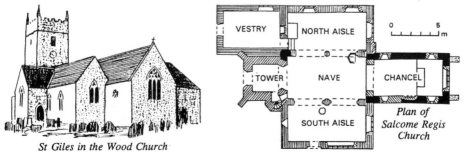

St Giles in the Wood Church

VESTRY	NORTH AISLE	
TOWER	NAVE	CHANCEL
SOUTH AISLE		

0   5 m

Plan of Salcombe Regis Church

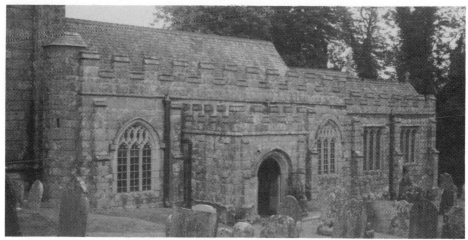

Sampford Courtenay Church

SAMPFORD COURTENAY   *St Andrew*   SS 633013

The church is essentially of the last years of the 15th century and has a wide nave with arcades of four bays plus one on the north and two early 16th century bays on the south. Four of the south piers have capitals with fleurons. The east window of five lights with panel tracery may be after 1549, when the Prayer Book Rebellion started in this village and the church is thought to have been damaged in the conflict. The west tower has set-back buttresses, big pinnacles, and a hoodmoulded west doorway with a four light window over it. There are pointed-arched 19th century windows on the embattled south show-side of granite with a porch with set-back buttresses and a stair turret at the west end of the aisle. The plain north windows may be 16th century. The low embattled building east of the chancel is of uncertain date and purpose. There are fine wagon roofs with bosses carved with motifs such as a wheel of rabbits and a sow and piglets, whilst there is a dragon on the northern wall-plate of the chancel. The pulpit is 18th century and communion ralls of that date now form part of the choir stalls. The scalloped font with canted sides is Norman. Several windows contain fragments of 15th and 16th century glass with shields, etc.

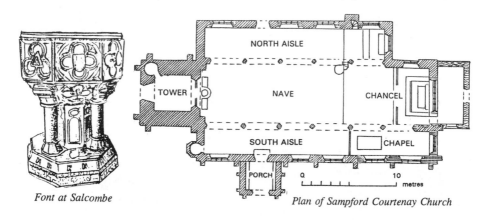

Font at Salcombe

Plan of Sampford Courtenay Church

SAMPFORD PEVERELL   *St Mary*   ST 030143

The church consecrated in 1318 had a mid 13th century nave and chancel with lancet windows in twos and threes with quatrefoils above, probably the work dedicated in 1259, and a newly built west tower with diagonal buttresses. There is a piscina with paired arches and in the north wall is a pair of trefoiled arches rebated for a door. The tower lost a shingle spire when rebuilt in 1815, whilst the nave north wall was rebuilt in 1861-4 by Ashworth. The south aisle was added in 1498 by Henry VII's mother, Lady Margaret Beaufort. It has quatrefoil panelling on the west gable, three light windows and an arcade with tall piers with capitals only on the shafts. The chamber with a chimney to the west is later. The south door is of the period of the aisle. The circular Norman font has bands of decoration at the top and bottom of the bowl and bottom of the pillar. There is a very damaged effigy of a cross-legged knight. A brass plate has a kneeling figure of Lady Margaret Poulett, d1602. There is a monument with putti heads and skulls to Margaret Collins, d1655.

SAMPFORD SPINEY   *St Mary*   SX 534725

The north transept has a tomb recess and window in the north wall and a piscina inn the east wall which clearly date it as 14th century. The arch towards the nave has a carved head on the west side. The nave north wall could be older and is now obscured by a Victorian vestry. The south aisle with a four bay arcade of granite. and the south porch and west tower with set-back buttresses are early 16th century. There is a niche on the tower south wall. The octagonal font with shields is probably of the same period. The sanctuary dates from the restoration of 1867.

SANDFORD   *St Swithun*   SS 828026

This was originally a chapel-of-ease to Crediton probably of 1523-4, when it was reopened with a licence for a burial ground. There are aisles of five bays, the eastern two originally divided off as chapel by a screen. One pier has an image niche and another has a carving of two fighting boys. There are ceiled wagon roofs in the aisles with carved wall-plates and bosses. The nave roof was raised and restored when a clerestory was added by Hayward in 1847-8. He also added the chancel and a new set of fittings. There are 16th century bench ends with early Renaissance ornamentation and profile heads, and a fine west gallery of 1657. There is a brass with a recumbent figure of Mary Dowrich, d1604.

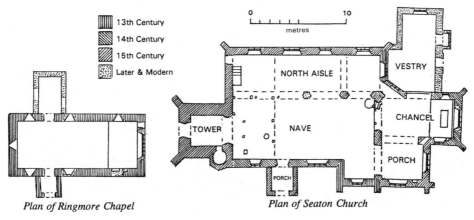

Plan of Ringmore Chapel   *Plan of Seaton Church*

SATTERLEIGH *St Peter* SS 668225

This is a small 15th century chapel with a weatherboarded bell-turret and no north windows. The screen has gone but a tympanum with inscriptions remains above where it was and there is a celure above this part. There are old bench ends with tracery, a mid 17th century pulpit, and an octagonal font with quatrefoils.

SEATON *St Gregory* SY 246905

The church lies east of the Axe some way inland. It has an odd layout with the chancel flush with the north arcade but much narrower than the nave so the interior looks lopsided. The nave was widened to the south some time before the 15th century west tower with diagonal buttresses was added. The east end of the north aisle was formerly a transept of c1300 with an east window with intersecting tracery and a wide squint through to the chancel. The 15th century south chapel also has a squint into the chancel. West of it is what remained of the south transept after the nave was widened into its space. The south porch and north aisle windows are late medieval. In 1817 the western half of the arcade was removed to make way for an extension of the west gallery. There are 19th century vestries north of the chancel.

SHAUGH PRIOR *St Edward* SX 544632

The four bay arcades look the same but if the Victorian south windows reproduce what was there before the south aisle may be of the end of 14th century, whilst the north aisle with a rood-loft stair projection is more likely to be 16th century. The chancel south window certainly looks 16th century. The late 15th century west tower has set-back buttresses and a central polygonal stair turret on the south side. The porch is vaulted and has an upper room reached by a NW turret staircase. In 1871 the late medieval font cover in the form of an octagonal lantern was discovered in a cow-shed and returned to the church after restoration. The steep conical top is surrounded by small figures. The church lies on the SW edge of Dartmoor.

Sampford Peverell Church

Shaugh Prior Church

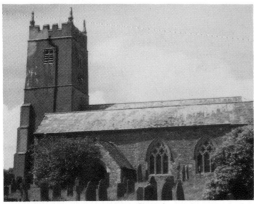

Shebbear Church

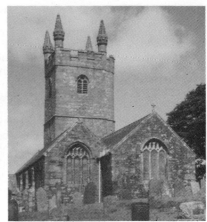

Sheepstor Church

SHEBBEAR   *St Michael*   SS 438093

The church is mostly 14th century although the windows and chancel arch have been renewed. It has a nave and chancel and a south aisle with a porch, the arcade being of four bays of double-chamfered arches on square piers with chamfered corners. There is a reset Norman south doorway with one order of colonettes but three orders of arch voussoirs decorated with beak-heads and chevrons. The only 15th century part is the south chapel with a two bay arcade towards the chancel. The chapel and the nave and chancel have old wagon roofs. The pulpit is Elizabethan and has crude figures in arched panels. There is a slate plate to William Rigsby, 1699, and a 14th century female effigy, possibly Lady Prendergast of Ludford.

SHEEPSTOR   *St Leonard*   SX 560677

The church is mostly late medieval with a west tower with polygonal pinnacles, a south aisle with a granite arcade of four bays, and a chancel and shallow north transept connected by a squint, but it was heavily restored in 1862 by Blachford for Sir Massey Lopes. It contains a small alabaster semi-reclining effigy of Elizabeth Elford, d1641 with her baby by her side and three kneeling daughters.

SHELDON   *St James*   ST 120086

In 1871 Hayward rebuilt the nave, chancel and south porch. Old are the embattled 15th century tower with a three-light west window and parts of the former screen reused in various furnishings.

SHERFORD   *St Martin*   SX 779444

The church is mostly late medieval but the pointed-trefoiled piscina in the chancel goes back to c1300. The third bay of the four bay arches of double chamfered arches on octagonal piers are higher, as if for transepts. The south side is embattled with a south porch and rood-loft stair turret. The north side has a doorway piercing a buttress and two windows with a five-point star in the tracery. The west tower has diagonal buttresses and a central stair-turret. The screen has been badly restored at the top. There are paintings on the wainscoting. The pulpit incorporates some medieval panelling. There is a monument to Elizabeth Reynell, d1662.

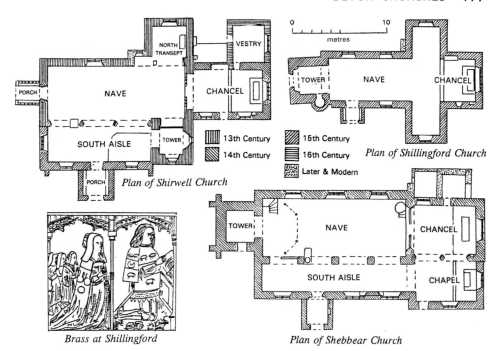

13th Century 15th Century
14th Century 16th Century
Later & Modern

Plan of Shillingford Church

Plan of Shirwell Church

Brass at Shillingford

Plan of Shebbear Church

SHILLINGFORD *St George* SX 904878

This is a small cruciform church lying alone in a field. Mostly probably 15th century, it was heavily restored in 1856 but has a roof with some old bosses, a few 16th century bench ends and stained glass shields, plus a west tower with a polygonal SE stair-turret and a west window with arms of Sir William Huddesfield, d1499, Attorney General under Edward IV, and his wife Katherine Courtenay. In the chancel is an Easter Sepulchre type monument to them with a brass depicting them kneeling with their children under ogival arches. The font also bears the Huddesfield Arms.

SHIRWELL *St Peter* SS 598374

The nave, the north transept and the south transeptal tower are probably all 13th century. The 14th century chancel has a plain pointed chancel arch and a piscina and contains an effigy of Blanche St Leger, d1483 on a tomb chest in a recess in the north wall, but its windows are doorway are all renewed. The tower has original lancets lower down but the belfry windows and pinnacles are 15th century. The crude arch leading west out of the tower suggests there was an early south aisle but the present 15th century one with a porch and an arcade of three bays. The middle merlon of the porch parapet has an inscription "This church was beautified in ye year of our Lord 1704" with the names of Sir Arthur Chichester and three others. The timber pier by the entrance to the north transept is of uncertain date. The west doorway is 14th century with an original door, and there is a 15th century timber porch beyond it, a very unusual feature in Devon. The NE vestry has an east window suggesting it was added c1500. The nave has a wagon roof with moulded ribs and bosses. The square Norman font has four arches on each side. There are monuments to Lady Ann Chichester, d1723, Frances Lugg, d1712, and Mary Stucley, d1705.

SHOBROOKE   *St Swithin*   SS 863011

The church stands by a farm with a holy well nearby. Reset in the south aisle added by Ashworth in 1879 is a Norman doorway with one order of columns with scalloped capitals and a hoodmould with a head at the top. Of the 15th century are the west tower with a panelled tower arch and the north arcade and the north wall, but the windows are of 1840 or 1879. There are two 17th century pews and glass of 1881.

SHUTE   *St Michael*   SY 254975

The 14th century crossing tower is narrower than the nave, chancel and transepts. As a result it has diagonal wings connecting it to the outer walls on the NE, NW and SW, and each of these are pierced by squints. The 15th century north chapel has a band of foliage on its arcade piers. It contains a monument with and standing effigy of Sir William Pole, Master of the Household under Queen Anne, d1741. There are several other monuments to the Poles, who lived in Shute Barton next door. The north aisle with a three bay arcade was added in 1811. A vestry was added beyond the north transept by Ashworth in 1869 and the roofs and windows then renewed. There is a font with quatrefoils and the chapel has old heraldic stained glass.

SIDBURY   *St Giles*   SY 139918

The chancel with clasping pilaster corner buttresses and one original small window on each side is Norman. Beneath it is a plain Saxon crypt 3m square which was filled in and its upper part removed when the chancel was built, and only discovered again in 1898. Another Saxon relic is the fragment of a 10th century cross with interlace built into the south transept west wall. Also Norman is the west tower with clasping and mid-wall pilaster buttresses and a pair of two-light bell-openings. The lowest stage is vaulted with two heavy diagonal ribs resting on lion mask corbels. The statues of a saint and bishop in niches on the west side were discovered in 1843, when the top was rebuilt by J.Hayward and a stone spire which had given problems for a while was then removed. The present spire and battlements are of 1884.

The three bay south arcade is of c1200, whilst the north arcade is slightly later, but there the eastern part with a clustered pier is a rebuilding of 1884. Beyond the aisles each side has a fourth bay of the late 13th century, when transepts were added. The transepts have each windows with an early type of bar tracery with three grouped lancets. There are four squints, one from each transept and one from each east corner of the nave. These are 14th century, when the chancel was remodelled with new windows. The wall paintings may date from that time. The outer walls of both aisles were rebuilt in the 15th century and the south side made into a show side with battlements and a two storey vaulted porch. The polygonal stair turret of the porch lies just round the SW corner from a similar one added to the tower. The octagonal font with quatrefoils is 15th century. The west gallery of 1620 was extended for the organ in 1754. There is a monument to John Stone, d1617.

SIDMOUTH   *St Nicholas & St Giles*   SY 126874

In 1859-60 William White rebuilt the church on the old plan, retaining the corner-buttressed 15th century west tower with a polygonal stair turret on the south side, and adding north and south porches, transepts and an aisled chancel. The stained glass is mostly of the 1860s but one 15th century shield showing the five wounds of Christ has been reset in the north chapel. In the south chapel is a monument to Mary Lisle of Northumberland, d1791. There are many 19th century memorials.

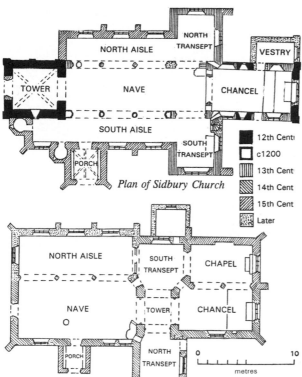

Plan of Sidbury Church

■	12th Cent
□	c1200
▥	13th Cent
▨	14th Cent
▧	15th Cent
▦	Later

Sidbury: tower vault corbel

Plan of Shute Church

0   10
metres

Shobrooke Church

Sidbury Church

Slapton Church   *South Brent Church*

SILVERTON   *St Mary*   SS 957028

The north aisle was erected with funds left by a rector who died in 1479, and the east respond of the north arcade has a rebus of a rector of 1519-31, so the church is mostly of that period, except that the chancel was mostly rebuilt in 1861-3 by John Ashworth. It has a medieval chancel arch. The west tower has diagonal buttresses and an octagonal NE stair-turret and the porch at the SW corner with a rib vault projects half in and half beyond the aisle. Three piers have image niches and there is an old wagon roof. The north chapel has an original parclose screen. The west gallery dates from 1734, there is an iron-clamped chest, and also a 17th century almsbox. Outside is the base of a late medieval churchyard cross.

SLAPTON   *St James*   SX 821450

The low west tower with a broach-spire is 13th or 14th century. It and the chancel with Decorated style windows must have existed when the church was dedicated in 1318. There are 15th century aisles and a two storey north porch with a stair projection on the west side. The screen was removed during World War II and has been poorly reassembled. The stem of the pulpit is medieval. The lofty ruined tower further north is a relic of a collegiate chantry founded in 1372 by Guy de Brien.

SOURTON   *St Thomas*   SX 536904

The 14th century chancel retains one south lancet. The nave and north aisle with a three bay arcade and the small tower with set-back buttresses are 15th century. The south porch looks like work of c1200 but may be 17th or 18th century. There are Royal Arms of Charles II but no other furnishings of interest.

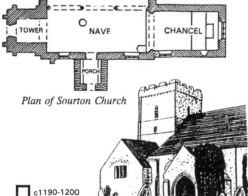

Plan of Slapton Church

Plan of Sourton Church

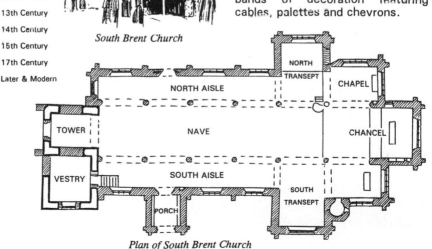

South Brent Church

□ c1190-1200
▥ 13th Century
▧ 14th Century
▨ 15th Century
▤ 17th Century
▦ Later & Modern

SOUTH BRENT   *St Petrock*

SX 696603

What was originally a Norman central tower now lies at the west end of the present late medieval church. It has blocked round-headed arches to north and south. The chamber south of it represents the former south transept although not much Norman masonry probably now remains in it. It contains an upper room reached from steps in the south aisle. The upper part of the tower is later, with battlements on a corbel table, probably 13th century. The dedication of three altars in 1436 may refer to the completion of the existing church, which has arcades of six bays of double-chamfered arches on tall octagonal granite piers. The aisles are not particularly wide, but there are transepts opening off the fifth bay. The sixth bay opens into chancel chapels possibly of slightly later date, with a polygonal stair-turret on the south side between the chapel and the transept. A restoration in 1870 saw the windows all renewed and all the old furnishings removed except for a circular Norman font with three bands of decoration featuring cables, palettes and chevrons.

Plan of South Brent Church

SOUTH HUISH   *St Andrew*   SX 694411

The old church was dismantled and left as a ruin after a new church was built at Galmpton, to which the font was taken, whilst the south arcade went to Dodbrooke. The south porch predates the 15th century aisle but has a 16th century outer entrance. The nave and chancel may be 13th century. The north transept is an addition, probably of the 14th century, and had a squint towards the chancel. The 15th century west tower has set-back buttresses and very modest bell-openings.

SOUTHLEIGH   *St Lawrence*   SY 205935

A south aisle as wide as the nave was added in 1827, the chancel was rebuilt in 1852-4, and there was a restoration of 1880 by Hayward. This has left a low west tower, a plain Norman south doorway, a 13th century north arcade with circular piers, a chancel arch of c1300, and a monument to Robert Drake, d1600.

SOUTH MILTON   *All Saints*   SX 698429

The south doorway has what looks like a 17th or 18th century arch set on Norman jambs. The circular font is certainly Norman, with a cable moulding, chevrons with faces, and a frieze with two animals and a woman falling back. The 15th century west tower has set-back buttresses and a central polygonal stair-turret on the south side. The 13th century south transept has a squint into the chancel. The south porch could be 13th century too. The north aisle with a five bay arcade and the north chapel with a single wider arch towards the chancel are of c1500, as are the chancel windows. The rood screen has painted figures in white clothes on the wainscoting, and there is a slightly later parclose screen.

Interior of South Milton Church

SOUTH MOLTON *St Mary Magdalene* SS 714260

The chancel is narrower and more thickly walled than the rest and probably 13th century. As a result the chancel arch has to be supported on big corbels, one of which is a human figure. Windows later inserted in the chancel have panelled jambs and corbels for statues on the each. The rest is a spacious all-embattled building with arcades of five bays with leaf-capitals, and transepts, that on the south having quatrefoils in the parapet. The aisles were widened in 1825-9 by C.Hedgeland and the only original window is behind the organ, whilst in 1864 C.E.Giles added a clerestory to the nave. The fine tower 32m high has set-back buttresses, battlements, tall pinnacles, a west doorway with fleurons with a four light window above, a niche on the south side with three heads above, and bell-openings with reticulated tracery. The octagonal font has a panelled shaft and cusped quatrefoils. Also late medieval is the octagonal stone pulpit with figures under canopies. There is a cartouche to Joan Bawden, d1709, and there are two late 17th century architectural tablets.

SOUTH POOL *St Nicholas & St Cyriacus* SX 777404

Although it has aisles and transepts, the church is dwarfed by the 15th century tower with set-back buttresses and a central polygonal stair turret. There is a porch at the west end of the south aisle. The window tracery and the piers and mounded arches of the arcades are of granite. There is a circular Norman font with arches to which columns and figures were probably originally added in paint. The splendid screen retains a coving only on the portions in the aisles. The wainscoting has early 16th century arabesques. A tomb chest in a recess serving as an Easter

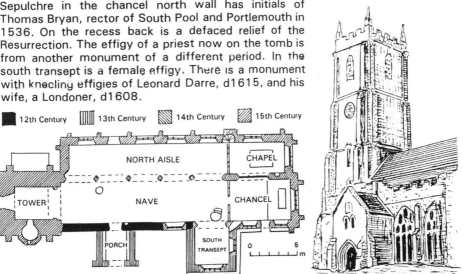

Plan of South Huish Old Church

Sepulchre in the chancel north wall has initials of Thomas Bryan, rector of South Pool and Portlemouth in 1536. On the recess back is a defaced relief of the Resurrection. The effigy of a priest now on the tomb is from another monument of a different period. In the south transept is a female effigy. There is a monument with kneeling effigies of Leonard Darre, d1615, and his wife, a Londoner, d1608.

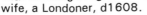
◼ 12th Century   ▥ 13th Century   ▨ 14th Century   ▧ 15th Century

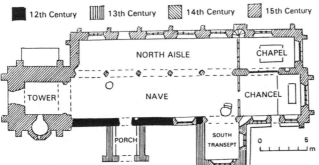

Plan of South Milton Church

South Molton Church

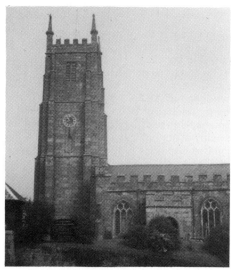

South Tawton Church

Stockland Church

SOUTH TAWTON   *St Andrew*   SX 653945

This is a substantial late medieval church mostly of granite and having an ashlar-faced west tower with set-back buttresses, battlements and obelisk pinnacles. The south side with a porch and rood-loft stair-turret is all embattled. The north aisle windows were renewed in 1881. The chancel is perhaps earlier than the rest. There are old wagon roofs, one boss having a sheila-na-gig. The early 18th century pulpit has inlaid figures of the Evangelists and foliage. The altar rails are partly of 1675. There is a recumbent effigy of John Wykes of North Wyke, d1591, and a monument of 1651 has kneeling effigies of Robert Burgoyne and his wife and family.

SOUTH ZEAL   *St Mary*   SX 651556

This small medieval chapel in the middle of the main street was used as a school from 1773 until restored in 1877. It is embattled with four corner obelisks, but these and the windows probably date from 1713, the date that appears on it.

SOWTON   *St Michael*   SY 976926

John Hayward rebuilt the church in 1844-5 except for the medieval north arcade.

SPREYTON   *St Michael*   SX 698977

An inscription on the wagon roof in the chancel has the names Henry le Maygne, Vicar, "a native of Normandy who caused me to be built A.D.1451" and "wrote all this with his own hand" and Robert of Rouen of Becdenne, Prior of Cowick and Richard Talbot, Lord of Spreyton, who "gave of their goods to my building". The whole church, of ashlar granite, may well be of that period, and less elaborate old wagon roofs remain in the nave and aisle. There are straight-headed windows with minimal tracery and a west tower with set-back buttresses. The octagonal font is Norman with primitive figures in relief on the pillar and panels on the bowl

STAVERTON   *St Paul de Leon*   SX 794640

The five bay arcades have some odd features and may be early but with some later rebuilding. They have moulded sandstone arches on granite octagonal piers with fleurons on the capitals. One pier on the north continues up above the capital. The chancel has a south window with star-shaped tracery, probably early 15th century. Also of about that time are the south chapel, the two storey porch, and the door to the vestry. The west tower with a polygonal stair turret is probably 14th century. The aisles have old roofs with bosses but the windows are of 1872-82 by Ewan Christian. The rood screen was much restored in the 1890s, the pier casings and loft dating from then. There is a brass to John Rowe, d1592, on the outside of the church. A monument of 1629 to the Worth family has the children above the parents, all of them kneeling. There are several monuments to the Gould family.

STOCKLAND   *St Michael*   ST 245046

The wide nave has a 14th century south doorway, and the shallow south transept has an east lancet of that date. The chancel features are 16th century. Of the 15th century are the west tower with set-back buttresses, and the embattled north and aisle and north chapel with a rood-loft stair-turret between them. The chapel has just one arch towards the chancel whilst the aisle has three wide arches and then two narrower ones at the west end, the respond there having the Courtenay arms. The tower doorway has a fruit and foliage scroll along the jambs and voussoirs and there are gargoyles and battlements with pierced quatrefoils. There are monuments to Amos Collard, d1747, and the Reverend William Keate, d1777.

STOCKLEIGH ENGLISH   *St Mary*   SS 851064

The west tower with small pinnacles, the aisleless nave, and the lower and narrower chancel arch are late medieval, but the chancel arch is of the restoration of 1878-83. The best of the monuments to the Bellows of Stockleigh Court is to William d1789.

STOCKLEIGH POMEROY   *St Mary*   SS 877037

The chancel was rebuilt in 1841 but retains lancets, including a group of three at the east end, from the building consecrated in 1201. The south side of the nave and the porch were rebuilt in 1861-3 by William White, but there is a reset Norman doorway. Of the 16th century are the north arcade with figures on the pier capitals and the bench ends with foliage, initials, heraldry, two-tier tracery and profiled heads in medallions. Other bench end panels have been used in the pulpit. Under the arch of the early tower are fragments of a 15th century rood screen.

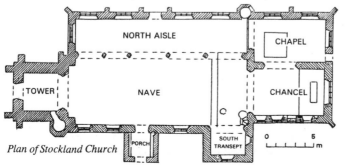

Plan of Stockland Church

Font at Stoke Canon

Stoke Damerel Church

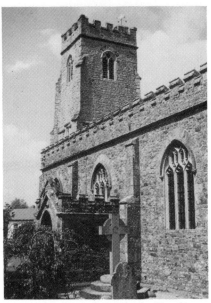

Stoke Canon Church

STOKE CANON   *St Mary Magdalene*   SX 939980

The church is of 1835 by John Mason except for the diagonally buttressed late medieval tower. Inside are a Jacobean pulpit and an interesting Norman font with four figures against the stem, four atlas figures at the corners with arms raised to carry the bowl, upon which are four beasts crouching down trying to bite off the heads of the atlas figures. Between the beasts are other motifs.

STOKE DAMEREL   *St Andrew*   SX 467563

Originally a village church, this structure was rebuilt in 1751 as a wide preaching box to serve the northern fringe of Devonport, except for the 15th century west tower with diagonal buttresses and pinnacles. The arcades have oak Tuscan columns on high bases and there are round headed windows. The building much altered in the 19th century and the chancel rebuilt in 1868. A Lady Chapel east of it was erected in 1902 as part of a plan to make the church a cathedral serving Devonport, but this was demolished in 1967. There is an old font. There are many 18th and 19th century memorials to men serving in the army and navy.

STOKE FLEMING   *St Peter*   SX 862484

The 15th century west tower has set-back buttresses and a polygonal stair-turret in the centre of the north side. The western bays of the arcades are 14th century with steeply-pointed red sandstone arches with double chamfers on octagonal piers with concave sides. The fourth pier is thought to be part of a 15th century rebuild with higher arches to take a rood-screen and has three steps in the diagonals between four main shafts. There are transepts beyond the fourth bay, possibly of 13th or 14th century date. The low chancel is closed off by a chancel arch. There is a female effigy of c1300. There is also a fine brass to John Corp and his grand-daughter Eleanor, d1391, who is shown shorter than him and set on a pedestal.

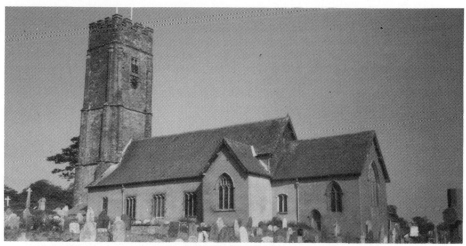

Stoke Fleming Church

STOKE GABRIEL   *St Mary & St Gabriel*   SX 849572

The tower is perhaps 14th century, being battered and having low buttresses and an unmoulded tower arch. The piers of the two arcades have leaf capitals. Those next to the screen, which has wainscot paintings indicating a date not later than 1450, have in addition flying angels with shields. The windows are wide and have simple tracery. The fine north doorway has a square outer frame. The medieval pulpit has a palm-like foot and nodding canopies. There are three medieval bench' ends, a few box pews and other seating incorporating 18th century panelling.

Interior of Stoke Gabriel Church

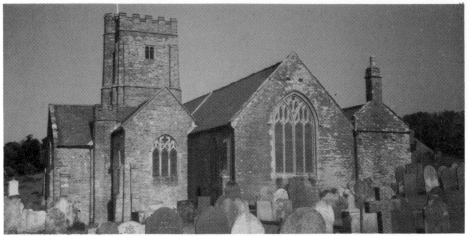

Stokenham Church

STOKEINTEIGNHEAD   *St Andrew*   SX 916705

The exterior is roughcast and the diagonally buttressed 15th century west tower with a stair-turret is whitewashed except for the battlements. The church has aisles and transepts with arcades of four bays with the northern piers having capitals with shield-holding angels and saints in ogival-headed niches between them. The chancel was rebuilt in 1865 but has a 14th century piscina and contains the earliest brass in Devon, that of the priest Thomas Taggell, d1375. The windows are mostly of 1894, but the roofs are old. The screen originally had a loft supported on a flat top instead of a coving. In the nave is a heart-shaped monument to Elizabeth Furlong, d1641. A tablet to the Graeme family says "nine of them suffered in their country's cause".

STOKENHAM   *St Michael*   SX 808428

The church is 15th century but was restored in 1874 and 1890 and the tower with set-back buttresses and a central polygonal stair-turret was rebuilt in 1636, that year appearing in cast iron figures on the west door. There are arcades of six bays with the arches almost semi-circular, and a chancel projecting beyond. The chancel contains a double piscina with crocketed ogival arches. A porch and transept lie on the south side. The screen has been restored and the wainscot paintings have been renewed. There is also a medieval parclose screen. There are tablets to John Somaster, d1681 and the Holdsmiths of Widdicombe, governors of Dartmouth Castle.

STOKE RIVERS   *St Bartholomew*   SS 634355   plan

The diagonally buttressed west tower with a SE stair-turret may be 15th century, but the rest is mostly 16th century, although older masonry probably remains in the nave and chancel. The chancel is said to have been lengthened in 1832, when most of the old woodwork was removed. The north windows are square-headed with three four-centred headed lights. The arcade of four bays has piers with crude block-like capitals. The pulpit has 16th century early Renaissance panels. The font cover with a finial is probably 17th century and there are old tiles nearby. There is panelling of the 18th century along the nave and aisle walls.

STOODLEIGH   *St Margaret*   SS 924188

The church was rebuilt in 1879-80 by Henry Woodyer for Thomas Carew Daniel of Stoodleigh Court. Old parts are the diagonally buttressed west tower with a polygonal NE stair-turret, the west two bays of the south arcade with leaf capitals on the piers, parts of the wagon roofs, and the reset panelled arch between the new chancel and south chapel. There is also a circular Norman font with two faces on the stem.

STOWFORD   *St John Baptist*   SX 433870

The west tower has alternating bands of red sandstone and granite. The south chapel is of two bays with a marked angle between the two in the outside south wall, as the east bay is parallel with the chancel, which inclines to the south, whilst the west bay is parallel with the rebuilt south aisle wall and the three bay arcade. The nave, aisle, and chapel all have medieval roofs. In 1874 Sir George Gilbert Scott added a north aisle and reset in it the original medieval north windows. Transferred into this new aisle are two monuments to the Harris family of Haine, one ordered in 1726 with standing figures of Christopher and his wife, and the other to John, d1770.

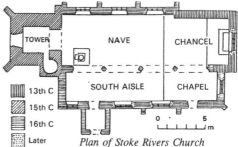

Plan of Stoke Rivers Church

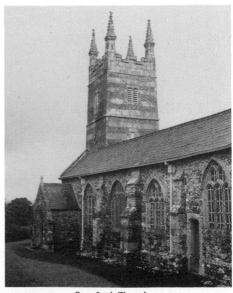

Stokeinteignhead Church   *Stowford Church*

Taddiport Chapel

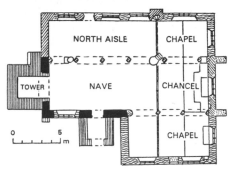

Plan of Sutcombe Church

STRETE *St Michael* SX 840471

This chapel-of-ease to Blackawton was rebuilt in 1836 by Joseph Lidstone except for the diagonally buttressed west tower.

SUTCOMBE *St Andrew*

SS 347117

Font cupboard at Swimbridge

The south doorway may be Norman and has an early porch in front of it. The three bay early 15th century arcade starts east of these. The north arcade has three narrow bays and two wider east bays and is probably later 15th century. The outer walls of both aisles look still later, with plain mullioned windows of three lights except for the arched window in the north chapel east wall. The west tower with an unmoulded tower arch and no west doorway may be 13th century. The granite octagonal font has simple motifs on it. Only the wainscoting survives of the screen. There are many bench ends with initials, heraldry, Flamboyant tracery and Renaissance motifs. The pulpit has Renaissance panels and there are old tiles, some larger than usual. The east window, although renewed, contains fragments of old glass. There are monuments of the 1760s to Jonathan Prideaux and Clement Davie.

SWIMBRIDGE   *St James*   SS 621300

The slim west tower with a battered plinth is probably 13th century but the lead-covered broach-spire may be later. The nave has aisles with three bay arcades, the piers on the north side having leaf capitals. The north aisle is thought to have been newly built in 1422 when John d'Abernon asked in his will be to buried within it, but the plain mullioned windows must be 16th or 17th century. The aisle walls were lowered and a dormer window in the nave roof removed during a restoration by J.L.Pearson in 1879-82. The chancel is flanked by chapels, that on the north having an arch with a head-corbel. The addition of a vestry has altered the original arrangement here with a wide squint. The south aisle and porch are embattled. The windows on that side are straight-headed with tracery. The oldest of the roofs is that in the chancel. The north chapel has a flat ceiling with bosses. The nave and aisles have wagon roofs with bosses. There is a very fine screen with leaf-decoration on the wainscoting and above it the nave and south aisle have celures with cross-ribs. The church was held by the Deans of Exeter Cathedral and this may account for the fine furnishings. In the 18th century the font was placed in a panelled casing with folding cupboard doors and a canopy above with a ribbed and starred ceiling, older woodwork being incorporated. The medieval pulpit has figures of saints under nodding ogee canopies in leaf-framed panels. There are old bench ends with tracery. There is a half-figure of Tristram Chichester, d1654. There are also tablets to Charles Cutliffe, d1670, and the lawyer John Rosier, d1658, with an interesting inscription.

SYDENHAM DAMEREL   *St Mary*   SX 409760

The church was rebuilt smaller (without the south aisle) after being destroyed by fire in 1957. Old features are the west tower with set-back buttresses and large polygonal pinnacles, the late medieval north windows, and the slate plate to John Richards, d1634.

TADDIPORT   *St Mary Magdalene*   SS 487187

This small chapel by Taddiport bridge served a leper hospital founded in 1344. In the 15th century a small tower was inserted into the west end of the chapel and the south doorway was then blocked and another opened out further east, now renewed. The north chapel without a arch dividing it off is probably 16th century, the period of the painted texts restored in 1971.

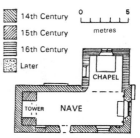

Taddiport Chapel; plan

TALATON   *St James*   SY 067998

The diagonally buttressed west tower is probably of the same period as the bell in contains which was given by Johanne de Beauchamp, d1435. The buttresses and stair turret have niches with statues of the Virgin and Child, the Evangelists and St Michael. The south aisle with a two bay arcade and an original south door is also 15th century. In 1859-60 Edward Ashworth added the north aisle, remodelled the porch, rebuilt the roofs using old bosses and provided a celure above the old screen. There are a few medieval bench ends. The monuments include those of John Leach, d1613, and Charles Harwood, d1718.

Tamerton Foliot Church

TAMERTON FOLIOT   *St Mary*   SX 471609

The west tower, the south aisle and porch are all of the end of the 15th century and there are five bay arcades, the northern one being slightly earlier. The aisle on that side was rebuilt wider in 1894-5. The nave has a wagon roof with bosses. The octagonal font has shields on the bowl and blank arches on the stem. The 17th century pulpit incorporates older linenfold panels. The mid 14th century effigies on a tomb chest are thought to be Sir Thomas Gorges and his wife. There are kneeling effigies of Sir John Coplestone and his wife Susannah made in 1617 and re-erected in 1894. Susannah Calmady, d1617, (but her monument is later) is depicted standing up in her burial shroud. There is also an effigy of the ten-year-old Coplestone Bampfylde, d1669, and there are several tablets to the Radcliffes of Warleigh.

Tavistock Church

TAVISTOCK   *St Eustace*   SX 482745

Of the church dedicated in 1318 there remain the base of the tower with large ribbed arches to north and south to allow processions to pass through (it also functions as a gateway to the abbey cemetery), an ogee-arched recess in the north aisle, and a small arch at the east end of that aisle. There are references to building work in 1352 and 1380 in money was given for building the Clothworkers Aisle in 1442, but most of the present church, apart from Victorian vestries and restoration, seems to be early 16th century. The large four-light windows have simple tracery and there are carved bosses on all the roofs. The outer south aisle has a ceiled roof with angels and its arcade has more decoration on the abaci of the piers. The octagonal font has shields in quatrefoils. The iron-board chest may be 14th century. There is much 19th century stained glass. On a tomb chest are recumbent effigies of John Fytz, d1590 with his wife and their son, d1605. On a tomb chest is a semi-reclining effigy of John Glanville, d1600 with his wife kneeling on the floor. There is also a monument of c1800 to the Carpenter family

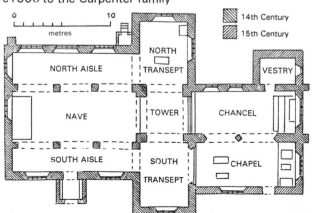

Plan of Tawstock Church

Tavistock Church

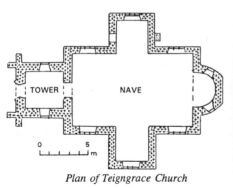

Plan of Teigngrace Church

Tawstock Church

TAWSTOCK   *St Peter*   SS 560300

Some masonry may remain of a 12th century church but the features of the present building are mostly 14th century. It has a tall central tower with transepts, an aisled nave of three bays with a south porch bearing a sundial of 1757, and a chancel, to which in the 15th century were added a south chapel with a two bay arcade and a two storey NE vestry still retaining a grille in its east window. The piers are just square blocks with slight chamfers with mouldings, the arches having a plain outer order and a inner order resting on corbels carved either as heads or with leaves. The east window has an octofoil above three cusped lights, and the chancel north windows have quatrefoils above cusped lights, whilst the transepts have three-light end windows with reticulation. In the 15th century the aisles were given new roofs at a higher level and battlements, plus new four-light windows. Squinches convert the square of the crossing into an octagon higher up and then further arches convert this to a smaller square for the tower superstructure. The nave, chancel and south chapel all have 15th century wagon roofs, and the porch has a wagon roof boarded with cross-ribs. The transept wagon roofs were plastered over in the 18th century.

Fine old screens close off the chancel and south chapel. The north transept contains an altar with panelling of c1500 and a manorial pew with rosettes on the ceiling and motifs including the knot emblem of the Bourchier family. This transept contains a gallery to connect the outside stair to the NW with the tower top. One of the bench ends has arms of Henry VIII and others are carved with monsters. The octagonal pulpit incorporates late medieval panelling and there is an hourglass stand in the form of an arm. The font cover incorporates medieval work and there are some old tiles. Two north windows have some fragments of 15th century stained glass.

The oldest monument is a fine wooden effigy of a 14th century female. In the south chapel are a six-poster type tomb with an effigy of Frances, Lady Fitzwarren, d1589, and kneeling effigies of Thomas Hinson, d1614, and his wife, and the 3rd Earl's steward William Shippon, d1633. There are also monuments to Henry Bourchier, 5th Earl of Bath, d1659, his wife Lady Rachel Fane, d1680, and Peter Gold, 1666. In the north transept is a tomb chest with a slate back plate with kneeling figures of Sir John Wrey, d1597, and his family, transferred here in 1924 from St Ive in Cornwall. There are also monuments to Lady Rolle, d1705, Sir Henry Northcote, d1729, and Ann Chilcot, d1758 and her husband Thomas, organist of Bath. In the chancel is an alabaster monument with recumbent effigies of William Bourchier, 3rd Earl of Bath, d1623, and his wife. There is also a kneeling figure of the Mary St John, d1631. In the south transept are monuments to Sir Bourchier Wrey, d1784, Ann, Lady Wrey, d1791 and various other members of the Wrey family.

TEDBURN ST MARY   *St Mary*

SX 817942

Of the 15th century are the diagonally buttressed west tower of ashlar with a polygonal SE stair-turret, and the south porch with four heads at the corners, possibly for intended vaulting. The south transept has a 13th century west lancet and a piscina and a 14th century ogee-headed recess. The north arcade has 14th century responds but the piers and tall arches are later. The chancel was rebuilt by John Ashworth in 1868. The nave and aisle have restored wagon roofs, and there are bench ends with tracery panels and shields. A brass has kneeling figures of Edward Gee and his wife Jane, d1613 above a long English and Latin verse.

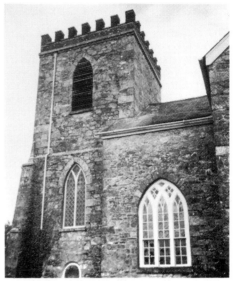

Teigngrace Church

TEIGNGRACE   *St Peter & St Paul*   SX 850739

The Templers of Stover House had this building rebuilt in 1786 as a cruciform structure with narrow transepts opening off a short but wide man body with an east apse with a straight east face outside and a west tower with battered corner buttresses, altogether quite a singular design. The apse has a pointed head and there is a shallow unlighted dome over the centre of the church. Monuments to the Templers include those of James, d1782, and his wife Mary, d1784, and Charles, d1786, the shipwreck scene illustrating the manner of his demise. Captain William, d1805, and his brother were also lost at sea. There is a late 18th century font.

TEIGNMOUTH   *St James*   SX 939732

A 13th century west tower of sandstone with lancet windows adjoins an octagonal church with a central lantern, thin windows and polygonal buttresses of 1817-21 by A.Patey, by one southern corner of which is a medieval grave slab. The reredos has medieval canopy work in the middle and the chest has figures of St Peter and St Paul from a pulpit of 1735.

The church of St Michael at East Teignmouth was rebuilt in 1823 and added to in 1875 and 1887. The old church had a tower with a round SW corner stair turret set between the nave and chancel, probably of 12th century date. Prior to rebuilding there was a long north transept, but no south transept (see inside front cover).

TEMPLETON   *St Margaret*

This is a single chamber with square-headed south windows of the 15th century and a low west tower perhaps of the 13th century. The roof, the porch and the top stage of the tower are of 1877. The octagonal font bowl stands on a Victorian stem and has a tall pyramidal 17th century cover. The choir stalls incorporate a few 17th century panels. There are a few fragments of old glass. There is a monument to Daniel Cudmore, d1679.

TETCOTT   *Holy Cross*   SX 332966

The church is reached through the outbuildings of the manor house. It has a west tower with cusped pinnacles, of red stone but with an occasional band of granite. The nave, narrower chancel and south transept are all 13th century. Of that date are the heads of two north windows, a reset lancet in the Victorian SE vestry, and a lancet with a cusped head beside the Victorian porch. There are old benches, some pew rails of c1700 in the south transept, and a circular Norman font with a top border of saltire crosses and corner faces and half rosettes on the base.

THELBRIDGE   *St David*   SS 788122

The church was much rebuilt in 1871-2 by Packham and Croote, but retains medieval masonry, a reset 15th century east window and a scalloped square Norman font.

THORNBURY   *St Peter*   SS 401085

The Norman south doorway has two orders of colonettes with spur bases and scalloped capitals. The small south transept must be early but its arch to the nave is Victorian, as are the chancel arch and the chancel windows. The windows on either side of the porch look part of the rebuilding of 1524 after a fire. The late 14th or early 15th century north chapel has a two bay arcade of double chamfered arches on an octagonal pier to the chancel and contains a mutilated monument with recumbent effigies and a relief of Humphrey Specot, d1590, and his wife Elizabeth. There is a short two bay north aisle of later in the 15th century. The low tower may be 14th century. The font has a 13th century bowl and the chancel seats contain material re-used from the former screen and bench ends.

Effigies in Thornbury Church

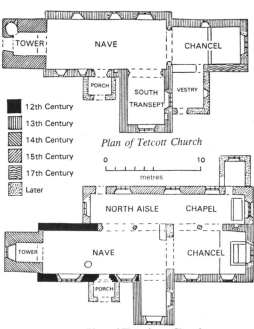

Plan of Tetcott Church

■	12th Century
▥	13th Century
▧	14th Century
▨	15th Century
≈	17th Century
▦	Later

Plan of Thornbury Church

Thornbury Church

Thorverton Church

THORVERTON   *St Thomas of Canterbury*   SS 924024

The aisles were heightened in 1834 to accommodate galleries and the north transept was added in 1864. The piers (also raised) have angels on the capitals. The west tower has set-back buttresses and a low stair turret. The south porch has blind arcading on the east and west walls and a vault with a central boss carved with the Holy Trinity. Other bosses have the four Fathers of the Church and the four Evangelists. There is a monument to Roger Tuckfield, d1683, and his wife, d1677.

THROWLEIGH   *St Mary*   SX 668908

This is a late medieval granite ashlar church on the side of Dartmoor. It has a nave and north aisle, a south porch, chancel and a west tower with set-back buttresses. The most interesting features are the Easter Sepulchre recess in the chancel north wall and the projecting priest's doorway with scrolls in the jambs and voussoirs and leaves on the spandrels, and a buttress rising above it. The font has quatrefoils on the bowl and a moulded pillar. The pulpit contains fragments from a former screen dated 1544. There are old wagon roofs, that in the chancel with bosses.

Vault boss in porch at Thorverton

THRUSHELTON   *St George*   SX 447876

This small church was formerly a chapel-of-ease to Marystow. The west tower with a rectangular NE stair-turret, the chancel and the south aisle with an arcade of two bays of double-chamfered arches on an octagonal pier are all 14th century. The nave north wall is probably older, although it contains 15th century windows and has a later plinth. The porch and south chapel are 15th century. There are old wagon roofs, those of the aisle and chapel being ceiled with bosses and carved wall-plates.

THURLESTONE   *All Saints*   SX 674429

The lofty 15th century west tower has set-back buttresses and a polygonal stair-turret in the centre of the south side rising above the main battlements. The 13th century chancel has three deeply splayed lancets and a double piscina with pointed trefoil-headed niches and a pierced pointed quatrefoil above as tracery. The south aisle has an arcade of double-chamfered arches, four-light windows without tracery, and an embattled two storey porch. The south chapel has a buttress which divides to allow a priest's doorway below. The altar here contains parts of the old screen. The three-light north windows were rebuilt in 1685. The circular Norman font has a palmette frieze, a cable moulding and chevrons. There are kneeling effigies of Rector Henry Luscombe, d1634, and Thomas Stephens, d1658, and his wife and family.

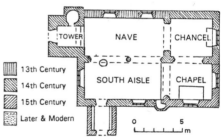

Plan of Thrushelton Church

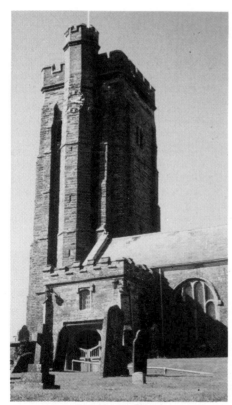

Thurlestone Church

Interior of Thrushelton Church

TIVERTON   *St George*

SS 955124

This building was begun c1714 for Dissenters, but was used as a warehouse until it was finally completed for use by Anglicans in 1727-33. Designed by London architect John James, it has rusticated quoins, segmental-headed lower windows and round headed upper windows lighting galleries on piers with Ionic columns above. The gallery levels were raised in 1842. There are north and south doors in the westernmost bay. The sanctuary projection is balanced by a west projection carrying a bell-turret. There is a segmental barrel vaulted ceiling with coffering on the part above the altar. reset on the west gallery of 1842 is a cartouche with the diocesan arms and a lion's head mask. The altar rails with twisted balusters are original.

St George's Church, Tiverton

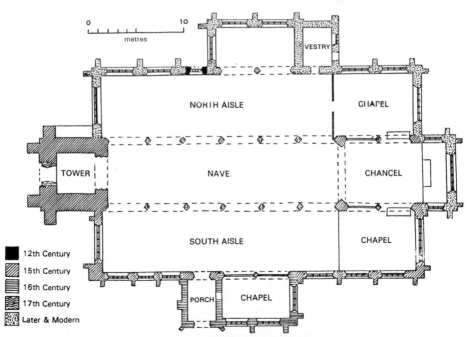

Plan of St Peter's Church Tiverton

TIVERTON   *St Peter*   SS 954128

The church lies beside the castle at the north end of the town. Towards the town it has an impressive show front with a sparkling white porch and south chapel of limewashed limestone projecting from an embattled sandstone south aisle. The porch and chapel were built by the merchant John Greenway in 1517, whose initials (I.G.) appear over the inner doorway along with kneeling effigies of himself and his wife on either side of the Assumption of the Virgin. The porch was rebuilt in 1825 and repaired in 1908 and the 1980s, but retains an original vault panelled with ogee reticulation with motifs such as eagles and fishes in the panels. Symbols of the source of Greenway's wealth, such as ships, are all over the chapel. It has double stepped and pierced battlements with heraldic panels below and a string course with scenes of the Passion of Christ. There is blank tracery around the four light windows. The chapel is divided from the aisle by a stone screen and has a fan-vault with pendants. Now fixed on the west wall are brasses of John, d1529, and his wife.

The tall west tower of sandstone has set-back buttresses and eight pinnacles. The west doorway is one of the few relics of much work done on the church in the early 17th century. On the north side of the church is a reset Norman doorway with chevrons on the jambs and voussoirs. The arcades of the chancel are 15th century but much of the rest of the church dates from the 1850s when Edward Ashworth rebuilt the outside of the chancel, the nave arcades, the chancel arch, renewed the windows, doubled the width of an early north aisle to match the width of the south aisle, and added a double transept on the north side to balance the Greenway chapel.

The furnishings and stained glass are mostly 19th century but there is a brass candelabra which was purchased in 1709. On the south side of the chancel is a tomb chest to John Waldron, d1579. Opposite it is a monument to George Slee, d1613. There are other monuments to Roger Giffard, d1603, Richard Newte, d1678, and John Newte, d1792.

TOPSHAM   *St Margaret*   SX 965884

The church lies beside the Exe. It is entirely of 1874-6 by Edward Ashworth except for a sandstone medieval tower on the south side. The best features inside are a circular Norman font with fluted chevrons and an animal with its head looking backwards and holding an apple in its mouth, and Duckworth monuments of c1820.

TORBRYAN   *Holy Trinity*   SX 820668

This all-late medieval church with its exterior all rendered has recently been taken over by the Redundant Churches Fund. It has a west tower with set-back buttresses and a central polygonal stair turret on the south side. The south buttresses have niches for figures set on head corbels. There are arcades of five bays with the arches more steeply pointed than is often the case in Devon, and then the chancel projects a further two bays. The north side has an embattled rood-loft staircase. The south side has large four-light windows and an embattled two storey porch projecting from the west bay. The porch has a fine fan-vault. The aisles have flat roofs set below lean-to ones, whilst the nave has a plastered wagon roof. The chancel chapels have east windows with star-tracery. There is a fine old screen across the whole church. It has painted saints in the wainscoting. Parts of the screen that once encased the piers have been used to form the pulpit. There are box pews with candleholders. Fragments of old glass remain in several windows, including saints and the arms of the de Bryan and Wolston families in the east window. There are several good ledger stones and there is a slate slab to William Peter, d1614, and his wife, d1600.

Torbryan Church

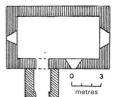

St Peter's Church, Tiverton

St Michael's Chapel, Torquay

TORQUAY   *St Mary*   SX 918660

In the church of 1856-61 by J.W.Hugall, rebuilt in 1952-6 after being damaged during World War II, is a Norman font with scenes of a man with a dog, a man with a sword falling over, a harpist, a boar and a dog, and a man on horseback.

TORQUAY   *St Michael*   SX 903652

This is a small vaulted chapel of c1300, now derelict. It has thick walls set on a rock north of the old village of Tormohun. A cliff drops dramatically below the SW corner. The floor is now the native rock but presumably this was covered with earth or wood originally. There is a small window in each wall except the north and a south porch.

TORQUAY   *St Saviour*   SX 909644

The former parish church of Tormohun is now a Greek Orthodox church dedicated to St Andrew. The battered west tower is 14th century. The rest is 15th century with ceiled wagon roofs, but the aisles were restored in 1849 and the chancel was extended in 1873-4. The western arch of the south arcade lies on a carved bust instead of a respond. On the back of the brass to Wilmot Cary, d1581, are fragments of two Flemish brasses of c1400. There is a tomb chest of Thomas Cary, d1567, an effigy of Thomas Ridgeway, d1604, and a monument to George Cary, d1758.

Totnes Church

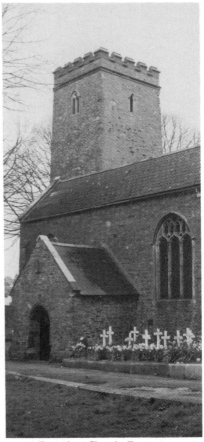

Tormohun Church, Torquay

TOTNES   *St Mary*   SX 802605

In 1445 the parishioners made an agreement with the priory for the construction of a new chancel for the parish church. The town was to pay for construction and the priory for subsequent upkeep. In order to made space for it the tower of the priory church had to be removed and a diagonal passage made between the two buildings. This still exists below the chancel NE corner, although it has long been blocked up and the priory church has vanished. The nave probably dates from the 1430s and has arcades of four bays up to the stone screen, and then one wider bay for the chancel chapel, St Leonard on the north side, and St George on the south side. The piers have a more complex section than usual and the arches are almost semicircular. The four-light windows also have almost semicircular heads. The aisles are embattled and the south side has pinnacles and a porch with a ceiling with ribs and bosses. The outer and inner doorways have decoration in the jambs, voussoirs and spandrels. The inner door of c1550 has Renaissance ornamentation. The nave and chancel have ceiled wagon roofs with bosses. The outer north aisle four bays long was added in 1824 and remodelled in 1869, and the main east window is of 1874 by the Scott family.

Screen at Totnes Church   *Interior of Totnes Church*

The tower was erected in the 1450s in imitation of that at Ashburton. It has set-back buttresses and a central polygonal stair turret on the south side. There are niches high up with in the central one a bearded mitred head and the inscription "I made this tore", which is supposed to refer to Bishop Lacy. The seated figures on either side are thought to be Prior Stoke and the Earl of Devon. The stone screen running across the width of the church and continued into parclose screens to divided off the chapels from the chancel dates from c1460. It has canopies for statues on the mullions and at the top ogival crocketed arches with leafy finials. The roof loft was removed during the restoration of 1867-74, and galleries disappeared at the same time. On the north side of the chancel one bay further east is an ornamental projection containing a rood-loft staircase. The stone screen must have been built one bay further west than was originally intended fifteen years earlier.

The octagonal font with richly cusped quatrefoils is 15th century. There is a pulpit with two tiers of blank arches. The brass candelabra was acquired in 1701. In the south chapel is a small tomb chest in an ogival-headed recess to Walter Smith, d1555. In the north aisle are kneeling effigies of Christopher Blackall, d1633, with his four wives Elizabeth, d1608, Penelope, d1616, Susanna, d1622, and Dorothea.

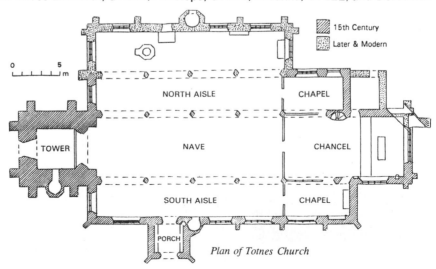

Plan of Totnes Church

Trentishoe Church

Trusham Church

TRENTISHOE   *St Peter*   SS 646486

This is a tiny church lying by a farm far from any village. There is a 16th century window on the south side. The slightly narrower chancel was built in 1861 and until then there was a tympanum between the nave and chancel. A tiny tower dating from 1638 is perched on a thickening of the west wall. The musicians' gallery has a hole in the parapet to allow space for the double bass. The porch is Victorian.

TRUSHAM   *St Michael*   SX 856822

The nave and chancel may represent the church dedicated in 1259, although no 'early features remain apart from a plain circular Norman font and a Norman pillar piscina in the form of a scalloped capital. The west tower and the north aisle with a three bay arcade with granite piers are both on a modest scale and late medieval. Only the main uprights of the screen appear to have survived the restorations of 1865 and 1890. An Easter Sepulchre recess in the chancel contains a brass and a painting of Hugh Staplehill, d1583, and his wife Sabrina and family. A wooden monument to John Stooke, d1697 and his wife is painted to simulate marble.

TWITCHEN   *St Peter*   SS 789305

The diagonally buttressed medieval west tower with a NE stair-turret and the nave and chancel of 1844 by Hayward are on different axes to each other, evidence the newer parts are on old footings. The circular Norman font has chevrons.

Ugborough Church

UFFCULME   *St Mary*   ST 069127

The three bay north arcade of double-chamfered arches on circular piers is 13th or 14th century. The south arcade and the arches further east are 15th century. In 1843 John Hayward rebuilt the chancel, and in 1847-9 he built a spire on the medieval west tower in place of a spire which fell in the early 18th century. At the same time he added an outer south aisle. The plastered roofs of the nave and north aisle are probably 18th century. The font of 1719 incorporates a panel probably of foreign workmanship showing the Ascension. The end sections of the fine screen are of 1847-9. The tower screen has been made up from parts from an organ gallery of 1629. There are monuments of c1650 and c1700 to the Walrond family, one having busts of a man, woman and boy and the other a reclined figure in armour and a wig.

UGBOROUGH   *St Peter*   SX 677556

The granite ashlar west tower 28m high has set-back buttresses and polygonal pinnacles corbelled out from a bell stage with three-light openings. The church has embattled aisles with 14th century arcades of six bays, then there are transepts and then chancel chapels of two bays of rather later date. There is a medieval vestry on the north side. The north aisle roof has bosses with heads, foliage, and a sow and piglets. Most of the palmettes on the chalice-shaped Norman font have been cut off. The nave section of the screen has been cut down to the wainscoting with painted panels of the 1520s, but the aisle sections are more complete. The figures include the Annunciation, the Assumption of the Virgin and the Martyrdom of St Sebastian. There is also an old parclose screen. The monuments include an early 16th century brass of a lady, a tablet to Thomas and John Kind, d1792 and 1795, and oval tablets in the chancel to members of the Fownes family who died in 1680, 1706 and 1712.

Ugborough Church

Uplowman Church

UPLOWMAN   *St Peter*   ST 014155

Of the 14th century are the embattled west tower and one capital from a former arcade in the porch. The rest of the church was rebuilt c1500 by Lady Margaret Beaufort. Of that period are the font with quatrefoils on the bowl and panelling on the stem, the south arcade and a broad tomb arch between the chancel and south chapel with heraldry and a bracket for a statue between the two east responds. However, Hayward rebuilt much of the church in 1863-6, and added a new chancel.

UPLYME   *St Peter & St Paul*   SY 325934

Apart from the diagonally buttressed west tower with a NE stair turret and the three bay north arcade, the church is mostly of 1829, the date of the north gallery, and 1875. The pulpit is Jacobean. Its tester now serves as a table in the vestry. Panelling and stalls in the chancel incorporate parts from the medieval rood screen.

UPOTTERY   *St Mary*   ST 202076

The presence of a Norman corbel table over the arch from the north chapel to the chancel is hard to explain unless there was a Norman chancel further east than the present one. The aisle, with a three bay arcade to the nave, and chapel were mostly rebuilt in 1875. The nave and chancel details look Victorian also, and there is a big organ-chamber-cum-vestry of 1897 on the south side of the chancel, but the diagonally buttressed west tower with a SE turret and fleurons on the doorway is 15th century, and so is the octagonal font with quatrefoil panels. One south window has fragments of old glass. There are several monuments to the Addington family, one of which, Viscount Sidmouth, a former Prime Minister, had much work carried out on the church in the 1820s. There is also a monument to John Hutchins, d1709.

UPTON HELLIONS *St Mary*

SS 843033

The nave and chancel are both Norman and there is an original south doorway with one order of colonettes with scalloped capitals, and a block-capital shaped font. The 16th century south aisle has a porch at the west end. Between the two is an opening in a quatrefoil, presumably a form of squint. The arcade has piers of a lozenge-shaped section with four shafts. There are ceiled wagon roofs, that in the aisle being more elaborate. There are old bench ends with foliage. One has a lion couchant. There are Royal Arms of painted plaster. There are kneeling effigies of Richard Reynell, d1631, and his wife, and also a monument to the Reverend James Carington, d1794.

UPTON PYNE *Our Lady*

SX 910978

The earliest part is the narrow double-chamfered 13th century chancel arch. The diagonally buttressed west tower has a statue of King David upon the stair turret, a figure of Christ over the west window, and the Evangelists on the corners of the parapet below the pinnacles. The east bay of the south arcade has angels on the capitals and leaves and shields on the jambs and voussoirs. This bay serves a chapel with a window with German glass dated 1630 and two tomb recesses, one of which has an effigy of Edmund Larder, d1521. The piers of the north arcade were replaced in 1833 but the capitals are medieval. The chancel was rebuilt by William White in 1874-5 and the organ chamber then added, but one window is 15th century. The west gallery has an 18th century balustrade.

Upton Pyne Church

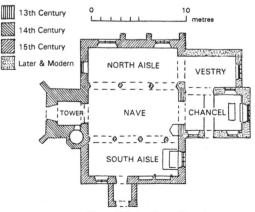

- ▥ 13th Century
- ▧ 14th Century
- ▨ 15th Century
- ▦ Later & Modern

0 · · · · · 10 metres

Plan of Upton Pyne Church

Washfield Church

Walkhampton Church

VENN OTTERY   *St Gregory*   SY 078912

The chief survivals of a rebuilding in 1882 by Packham and Croote are the low west tower with paired square-headed belfry windows and old bench ends with foliage.

VIRGINSTOW   *St Bridget*   SX 377927

The church was entirely rebuilt in 1851 by William Rundle for the Reverend Peter Cann, but it contains a Norman font with a recut cable moulding.

WALKHAMPTON   *St Mary*   SX 537702

The church lies high above the village on the side of Dartmoor with only one house for company. The 15th century granite ashlar tower has diagonal buttresses which at the bell stage are replaced by the polygonal supports of the large crocketed pinnacles. The tower arch has large head-corbels. Of the same period are the south porch and the north aisle with three-light windows with pointed-headed lights. The south aisle added east of the porch has later-looking round-arched lights to the windows but the arcades are similar. A squint from the north transept formerly has a free-standing corner column. There is an octagonal 15th century font with shields.

WARKLEIGH   *St John Evangelist*   SS 643228

The church lies alone except for a farmhouse. The diagonally buttressed west tower has pinnacles. There is a south aisle with a three bay arcade plus a fourth bay between the chancel rebuilt in 1850 and the south chapel, with a squint also between the two. The chapel has larger windows than the rest of the church. Underneath the medieval roof is a 19th century one, to which the old bosses have been fixed. The tower arch screen contains parts of old bench ends with Renaissance foliage and profile heads in medallions. A rare treasure is the tiny late medieval Pyx Case used for taking the Blessed Sacrament for administration to the sick.

WASHFIELD   *St Mary*   SS 935155

There is panelling on the arch of the diagonally buttressed west tower with a NE stair-turret. The north arcade is of three bays plus a fourth arch with leaf capitals on the piers from the chancel a north chapel. The south side was rebuilt in 1875 to designs by the rector, the Reverend W.Lloyd Jones, with a new vestry and organ chamber, but the south doorway is 14th century. The square font has two sides with six blank arches, whilst the other sides have chevrons. The screen of 1624 has Corinthian columns and is crowned by the Royal Arms of James I. The monuments include a brass inscription and shield to Alice Steynings, d1605, a brass with kneeling figures of Henry Worth, d1606, and his wife, plus a tablet to Henry Worth, d1630.

WASHFORD PYNE   *St Peter*   SS 812119

The base of the tower is old. The rest was rebuilt in 1882-4 by R.M.Fulford.

WEARE GIFFARD   *Holy Trinity*   SS 467221

There are concave-sided capitals on the piers of the five bay arcade of the south aisle. The 15th century windows have tracery with the lights linked by round-headed arches. The south chapel east window has the outer four lights ogee-headed with a quatrefoil above, whilst the centre light continues up to the window head. The chancel roof has collars on arched braces, kingposts and traceried spandrels, an unusual type in Devon but probably another work by the designer of the roof of the hall of the manor house. The south aisle has a wagon roof as usual. The south door with vertical panels is medieval. The Norman font has scallops under the bowl. There is a 15th century wall painting showing St Sebastian being martyred by archers. In the south aisle are remains of a 15th century Jesse window. Other windows have fragments of old glass. Of c1300 are the effigies of a cross-legged knight and lady. A wall-monument of 1638 has kneeling figures of four generations of the Fortescue family, and one of the bench ends bears their initials, indicating a date after 1510.

Welcombe Church

WELCOMBE   *St Nectan*   SS 228184

The west tower bears the date 1731 but is likely to be late medieval, whilst the south porch has a sundial dated 1735. The church itself is cruciform, the transepts being later additions, but without any early features. The screen is probably early 14th century and has wainscoting incorporating old bench ends. The decorated wall-plate and bosses on the central part of the wagon roof suggests it was originally further west, so that the transepts would have opened off the chancel. The pulpit has 16th century early Renaissance panels and the lectern is Jacobean.

WEMBURY   *St Werburgh*   SX 518485

The church is mostly late medieval with four bay arcades, a south aisle and porch with old wagon roofs with bosses, and a diagonally buttressed west tower with a square-headed west doorway and a stair-turret rising above the main battlements. A large monument has a semi-reclining effigy of Sir John Hele, d1608 with his wife lying recumbent below and in front of him. There is also another large monument with a small kneeling effigy of Lady Narborough, d1678, one of the Calmadys of Langdon.

WEMBWORTHY   *St Michael*   SS 663099

Rebuilding of the nave and south aisle in 1840 and the chancel in 1869 has left parts of the original ceiled wagon roofs, the tower of 1626 at the west end of the aisle with Royal Arms of 1770 over its doorway, pieces of 15th century glass in one east window, and monuments to Mary Bury, d1651, and Lawrence Clotworthy, d1655.

WEST ALVINGTON *All Saints*

SX 723439

The trefoil-headed piscina dates the chancel as 14th century. The rest is late medieval with six bay arcades, the south aisle embattled with a two storey porch containing a fireplace, and a west tower with set-back buttresses and big polygonal pinnacles. The leaf decoration on the panels of the octagonal font looks 17th century. Only the part of the rood-screen crossing the aisle is original. The screen closing off the south chapel from the chancel has Flamboyant tracery forms. In the chancel north wall is an Easter Sepulchre tomb in a recess originally with brasses on the back. There is a big monument with coupled columns to one of the Bastard family, d1703.

WEST ANSTEY *St Petrock*

SS 853275

The tub shaped font with saltire crosses and palmette decoration is Norman and the nave and narrower chancel reflect a Norman plan, even though the present walls are perhaps 14th century, the likely age of the piscina. The diagonally buttressed west tower, the south doorway and porch and the north aisle are all late medieval but the windows are of William White's restoration of 1887 except for one west of the porch. There are leaf capitals on the arcade piers. There are a few old bench ends and one window in the chancel has fragments of old glass.

West Alvington Church

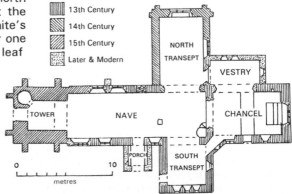

Plan of West Down Church

West Ogwell Church

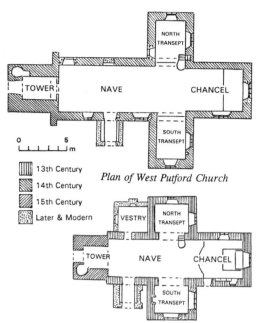

13th Century
14th Century
15th Century
Later & Modern

Plan of West Putford Church

Plan of West Ogwell Church

WEST BUCKLAND   *St Peter*   SS 657314

The church was entirely rebuilt in 1860 by R.D.Gould except for the west tower with four diagonal buttresses and the octagonal font with quatrefoils, both 15th century.

WEST DOWN   *St Calixtus*   SS 516421

The nave, south transept and chancel are all probably 13th century. The transept has a plain pointed arch to the nave, three renewed south lancets, and a squint to the chancel. The nave retains one possibly old window on the south side. The chancel has one south lancet, three renewed ones in the east wall, and a blocked priest's doorway. It was repaired in 1675, and restored in 1841, whilst the floor level was raised in 1872. The 14th century north transept is larger than its counterpart and is entered by under a heavy double-hollow-chamfered arch. It has an open wagon roof of trefoil section and a north window with reticulated tracery. The oak effigy of a man in lawyer's robes is assumed to be Sir John Stowford, Chief Justice of the Common Pleas. The cinquefoil-cusped piscina was transferred to the chancel north wall when a small chapel was added in the angle between the two. The west tower looks late medieval but the top at least was rebuilt in 1711-12. A font has been formed from a Norman scalloped capital probably with the decoration hacked off.

WESTLEIGH   *St Peter*   SS 473286

The renewed chancel windows are of c1300, and the south doorway and porch are 14th century. Of the 15th century are the north aisle and the west tower with clasping angle buttresses and a polygonal stair turret on the south side. There are old tiles and several monuments to the Cleveland family of Tapeley, the most notable being that of John, d1763.

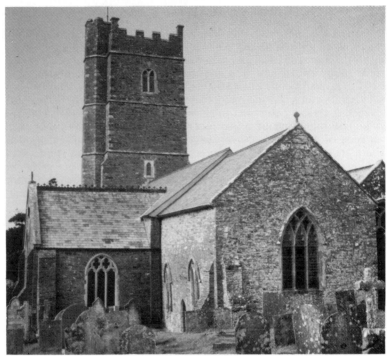

Westleigh Church

WEST OGWELL *Dedication Unknown* SX 819701

This church has been in the care of the Redundant Churches Fund since 1982. It is a small cruciform building of c1300. Of that date are the sedilia with trefoiled heads, the east windows of the north transept and chancel with cusped intersected tracery and the chancel north window with Y-tracery. The west tower is perhaps of c1400 with an older window with intersected tracery reset in it. There are two 15th century windows in the south transept, although that facing east has re-used carved heads on the rere-arch, similar to those on the chancel windows. The fireplace here must have been for a former family pew. The NW vestry and the south porch are 19th century. There is a 17th century pulpit, and the altar rails are of c1800.

WEST PUTFORD *St Stephen* SS 359157

This is a cruciform 14th century church with original windows in the nave west of the Victorian porch and in the transepts, where the three-light east windows have intersecting tracery. However the north transept north window has a window of c1400 and the ogival-headed piscina in the south transept may be of that period, so perhaps they and the tower are later additions. The tower top with round-arched belfry windows is in any case 16th century but rebuilt in 1883. There are old tiles and a few old benches. The pulpit and communion rails with twisted balusters are 18th century. The south door is medieval although it is dated 1620. There are Royal Arms dated 1714. There are many slate ledger stones of the 17th and 18th centuries. The oval font with a cable moulding between the bowl and shaft is Norman.

WEST WOOLFARDISWORTHY   *All Hallows*   SS 333211

There is a Norman south doorway with one order of colonettes with beakheads and chevrons on the arches and the font on five shafts of blue stone is also Norman. The south transept and chancel are perhaps 13th century, although the priest's doorway could be of almost any date and the transept has suffered from the restoration of 1872. The north aisle of c1500 has an arcade of five wide bays with granite piers with capitals only on the main shafts and decorated abaci. The 15th century west tower has clasping corner buttresses and a central polygonal stair turret on the south side. The rebuilding of 1648 recorded on an inscription was perhaps when the cornices of the plastered-over wagon roofs were put up and the NE vestry added. There are many old benches carved with heraldry, initials, saints, the instruments of the Passion and a rare image of Christ crucified. There is a semi-reclining effigy of Richard Cole, d1614, and there are also monuments to Richard Hammett, d1766, and his wife Elizabeth, d1787, John Robbins, d1784, and John Whitlock, d1752.

WEST WORLINGTON   *St Mary*   SS 770127

The church is reached through an arch under the former church house. It has a short 13th or 14th century west tower with a crooked shingled spire. The late medieval south aisle has a three bay arcade with angels and leaves on the pier capitals. Both the aisle and the south porch have original wagon roofs. The chancel was much restored in 1881 and the rest repaired in 1905-13. There are some 16th century bench ends with tracery and an old screen between the chancel and south chapel.

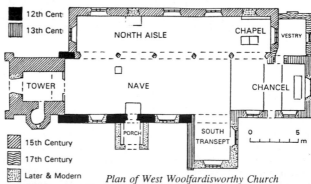

■ 12th Cent
▦ 13th Cent
▨ 15th Century
〰 17th Century
⋯ Later & Modern

NORTH AISLE   CHAPEL   VESTRY

TOWER   NAVE   CHANCEL

PORCH   SOUTH TRANSEPT

0   5 m

Plan of West Woolfardisworthy Church

West Worlington Church   *Effigies in Whitchurch Church*

Monument at Whitchurch Church

Tomb in West Woolfardisworthy Church

WHIMPLE *St Mary* SY 044972

The church was heavily restored by John Hayward in 1845, and a south aisle added with an arcade matching the existing north arcade. Other old features are the low ashlar-faced west tower with stunted pinnacles and eight early 16th century painted panels of the former rood-screen.

WHITCHURCH *St Andrew* SX 494728

There is a plain Norman south doorway, east of which is a trefoil-headed stoup. Of c1300 is the chancel with one cinque-foiled window and an Easter Sepulchre recess on the north side, now containing a slate plate to Pashaw Allyn, d1626. The chancel inclines to the south and has an east end of 1879 by John Hayward although the east window with intersecting tracery looks reused original work. Both north and south chapels, and also the south porch, were then rebuilt. The granite south transept (the rest is of slate) has a squint into the chancel. The 15th century north aisle has a rood-loft stair projection in the outer wall and an arcade of four bays with moulded arches on tall piers. The set-back buttresses on the 14th century west tower with a NE stair-turret appear to be additions of the 15th century, when the top stage with diagonal buttresses was added. The plain octagonal font has shields in panels. There are monuments to Francis Pengelly, d1722, and Mary Pengelly, d1797.

WHITESTONE *St Catherine* SX 882934

The features are 15th and 19th century, the chancel having been rebuilt in 1866-8 by R.M.Fulford, but the plan form is older with a nave and chancel separated by a chancel arch, a north aisle with a two bay arcade with an octagonal pier, and a north chapel with a single arch to the chancel. There is also a diagonally-buttressed west tower with a polygonal stair-turret. The west screen was created in 1915 out of a west gallery dated 1621 with shields. The chapel screen is also early 17th century. Only the stem of the pulpit is medieval. Two windows have fragments of old glass.

Interior of Widecome-in-the-Moor Church

WIDECOME-IN-THE-MOOR   *St Pancras*   SX 719768

This is a long and low church on the side of Dartmoor with arcades of six bays of double-chamfered arches on octagonal piers. There are transepts, a south porch and a lofty granite ashlar tower with set-back buttresses, polygonal pinnacles and three-light bell-openings. The roofs of the three west bays are higher than the rest, presumably the result of rebuilding in phases. Only the wainscoting with early 16th century painted saints survives of the rood-screen. Four painted boards dated 1786 under the tower have verses describing a thunderstorm of 1638.

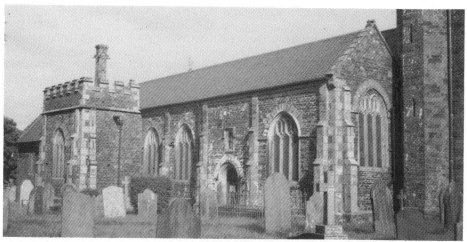

Winkleigh Church

WIDWORTHY   *St Cuthbert*   SY 214994

This is a small church with a nave with a 13th century south doorway and a narrower chancel with a 14th century cinquefoil-headed piscina. The transepts may be of c1400, that the on the south having an ogee-headed piscina and the northern one having diagonal buttresses. Each is entered from the nave by an arch on responds with fleurons. There is a west tower with diagonal buttresses. The porch and NE vestry are Victorian. There is a fine effigy of a knight of c1400, and a tablet to Alice Isack, d1685, plus several monuments to the Marwoods: James, d1767, Sarah, d1787, and a joint effort to Robert, d1783, Sarah, d1797, and James, d1811.

WILLAND   *St Mary*   ST 037104

There is heraldry and foliage on the capitals of the north arcade piers, and the south porch has a decorated top and inscription. The screen of c1400 has a later straight cresting with a vine scroll. The small plain tower is probably rather earlier.

WINKLEIGH   *All Saints*   SS 633081

A head built into the south wall is probably Norman. The chancel is early 14th century, or rather was until a heavy restoration by R.D.Gould in 1871-3, when the wagon roofs of the nave and aisle were repaired and new fittings provided. The north side is a show front with an embattled north transept and the 15th century north aisle having buttresses between the large windows. The south transept or Gidleigh chapel was not added until the 17th century. The tower has buttresses low down and a top with cusped pinnacles. The north arcade of granite is of five bays, plus a sixth to the north chapel with a more elaborate moulding like that on the chancel arch and the north transept arch. The aisle west window has stained glass of angels with shields. The quatrefoil shaped font has panelling on the stem.

Widecombe Church

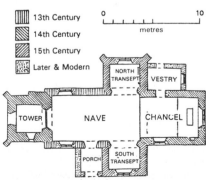

Plan of Widworthy Church

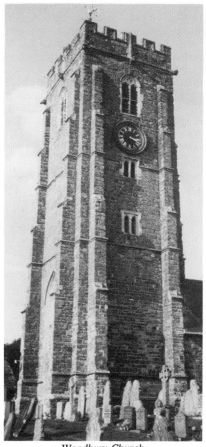

Woodbury Church

Witheridge Church

WITHERIDGE   *St John Baptist*   SS 804146

The chancel has one 13th century south window but the east window is of 1877. The north and south aisles are 15th century with tall arcades of four bays. The south chapel has a squint to the chancel and a south window with a canopied niche. The south doorway has fleurons on the jambs and an image niche above. The octagonal font with quatrefoils and the pulpit with figures in narrow panels under nodding-ogee canopies are also late medieval, as is the west tower with set-back buttresses, although its upper parts with round headed windows and obelisk pinnacles date from a rebuilding of 1841, when the nave and priest's doorway were embattled.

WITHYCOMBE RALEIGH   *St John*   SY 028834

The church lies beyond the north end of the village and was a chapel-of-ease to East Budleigh. It was neglected after a new chapel further south was built in 1720, and only the west tower with orange diagonal buttresses and a panelled tower arch and the north aisle survived demolition in 1788. The rest was rebuilt in 1925.

Wolborough Church

Withycombe Raleigh Church

WOLBOROUGH   *St Mary*   SX 854704

This is the parish church of the southern half of Newton Abbot, lying on a hill SW of the town. The west tower is 13th or 14th century. There are north and south aisles with arcades of six bays, the piers having octagonal main shafts with concave sides, the south aisle being known to date from 1516. The very shallow north and south transeptal chapels are huge five light plain mullioned windows probably of 1710. The south porch has a fireplace and a doorway with leaves in the spandrels and fleurons on the jambs and lintel. It contains fragments of an alabaster panel showing the Resurrection. The circular Norman font has palmette decoration. There are painted figures on the wainscoting of the rood screen and also on the screens closing off the transeptal chapels. The late 15th century brass eagle lectern was probably made in East Anglia. A few window tops have bits of old stained glass. In the south chapel is a canopied table tomb of William Balcall, d1516. There are recumbent effigies of Sir Richard Reynell and his wife on a monument made in 1634.

WOODBURY   *St Swithin*   SY 019873

The tall west tower with a tier of two-light windows and a foliage scroll on the jambs and arch of the west doorway could be of the period of the consecration of 1409. The north aisle with arcade piers of a more complex section than usual is later, not being completed until the 1530s. The panelled arch between the chancel and north chapel has a squint and was probably intended as a canopy for a monument to Richard Haydon, d1533, whose arms appear on a capital. The tower arch is also panelled. There are old wagon roofs in the chancel and south porch. The north windows and much of the chancel date from the restoration ongoing from the 1840s until the 1890s. The late medieval font is octagonal with quatrefoils and rib patterns on the stem. The screen is old but much restored. The Elizabethan communion rails and font rails are said to have come from a church in Exeter. The nave and aisle have 18th century panelling. The pulpit was made in 1635 by a local man, Thomas Crutchard. The trumpeting angel from the tester of 1777 is now fixed on the organ screen. There are old stall ends in the chancel and old bench ends in the nave. The south transept east window contains fragments of 16th century glass inserted there in 1963. On a tomb chest are recumbent effigies of an Elizabethan couple probably of the Prideaux family.

Yarcombe Church

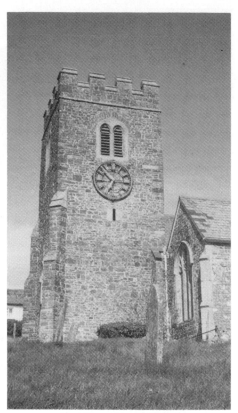

Zeal Monachorum Church

WOODLAND *St John* SX 791688

This is a small church with a three bay north arcade of almost semicircular arches and a battered west tower with a central polygonal stair-turret and low pinnacles. Also 15th century are the octagonal granite font and some stained glass in the east window tracery showing the Four Doctors of the Church. A brass to Thomas Culling, d1670 features cherub's heads.

WOODLEIGH *St Mary* SX 738489

The church has transepts but no aisles and is probably late 13th or 14th century, although no early features remain other than an octagonal font of c1200 with two pointed blank arches on each side. The west tower has renewed battlements on a corbel table. One window in the south transept is dated 1647. In the chancel is an Easter Sepulchre type tomb chest of Rector Thomas Smith, died c1526.

WOOLFARDISWORTHY *St Mary* SS 820086

The church was mostly rebuilt in 1845 by Hayward. The tower is medieval and the chancel retains a restored medieval wagon roof with a richly moulded wall-plate.

YARCOME   *St John*   ST 246082

The chancel was rebuilt in 1890-1 but otherwise this is a late medieval church with the nave fully aisled although the transepts at the east end of it could contain older work. The transept arches have angel corbels. Both transepts have squints to the chancel, that on the north being wide, and the south transept has traces of a long-blocked up east window and a set of Royal Arms of much later date. The roofs of various type are all old. The octagonal font has quatrefoils and shields.

YARNSCOMBE   *St Andrew*   SS 561236

A plain pointed arch leads from the Norman nave into the 13th century north transeptal tower. The chancel is probably 14th century, having an east window and piscina of that date. The south aisle with a four bay granite arcade and a porch and rood-loft stair projection is late medieval, and at that time the tower was given diagonal buttresses with pinnacles and a polygonal stair-turret on the west side. The octagonal font with quatrefoils and tracery and the ceiled wagon roofs are also of that period. The east window of the aisle has a fragment of original stained glass and there are some old tiles. The chancel has an early 16th century Easter Sepulchre recess in the north wall in which is a slab with an inscription to John Cockworthy and his wife. There is another recess in the aisle. There are many good ledger stones and also a monument to John Pollard, d1667, with frontal heads in roundels.

YEALMPTON   *St Bartholomew*   SX 578518

The church was rebuilt by William Butterfield in 1849-50 and a west tower added in 1914-5 by Charles King. The church contains a Norman font with a wavy pattern on it. An inscription to one of the Coplestones has on the reverse part of a Flemish brass of c1400. There is a tomb chest to Mary Copplestone, d1630. Other monuments include Edward Polloxfen, d1710, Polloxfen Bastard, d1732, Edmund and Balwin Pollexfen Bastard, both d1773, several other Bastards, and Thomas Veale, d1780. In the churchyard is a 6th or 7th century inscribed stone with the word Toreus.

ZEAL MONACHORUM   *St Peter*   SS 720040

The north transept has one restored window of 14th century type although the masonry is probably older. The west tower and the south aisle with a four bay arcade and the south porch all have diagonal buttresses and could be late 14th century. Several windows and the NE vestry are Victorian, and the tub-shaped font with chevrons and cable mouldings is Norman.

MANORIAL CHAPELS

AYSHFORD - 15th century, restored after secular use in 1847. Wagon roof. Tomb of Henry Ayshford, d1666, aged 1.
BICKLEIGH - Thatched Norman chapel with tufa south doorway. Wagon roof and nave windows 15th century.
MARISTOW - Present chapel of 1871 by St Aubyn. Parts from older chapel reused in a nearby folly.

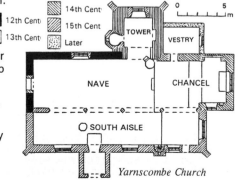

14th Cent
12th Cent
15th Cent
13th Cent
Later

TOWER   VESTRY
NAVE   CHANCEL
SOUTH AISLE

Yarnscombe Church

LIST OF LATER ANGLICAN CHURCHES

ALPHINGTON - St James - By Butterfield, 1849-51 and 1879-83.
APPLEDORE - St Mary - 1838 by J.Williams, tower & west end 1909 by John Smith.
ASHILL - St Stephen - 1882 by R.M.Fulford. Combined with schoolroom.
AVONWICK - St James - 1878 by R.M.Fulford. Combined with schoolroom.
BARNSTAPLE - St John Baptist - 1883 by G.R.Abbott, replacing chapel of 1820.
BARNSTAPLE - Holy Trinity - Tower, 1843-5, rest rebuilt by William White, 1867.
BEER - St Michael - 1876-7 by Hayward & Son for patron Mark Rolle.
BERE ALSTON - Holy Trinity - 1848.
BLACKBOROUGH - All Saints - 1838 by James Knowles for the 4th Earl of Egremont.
BOVEY TRACEY - St John - 1853 by R.C.Carpenter for Canon Charles Courtenay.
BRADFIELD - All Saints - 1875 by Hayward.
BROOKING - St Barnabas - 1850-5.
BUDLEIGH SALTERTON - St Peter - 1891-3 by G.F.Prynne. Replaced chapel of 1811.
CHARDSTOCK - All Saints - 1840, enlarged in 1890.
CHEVITHORNE - St Thomas - 1843 by Benjamin Ferrey for Rev William Rayer.
CHITTLEHAMHOLT - St John Baptist - 1838 by John Gould for Lord Rolle.
CHUDLEIGH KNIGHTON - St Paul - 1841-2 by Scott & Moffatt.
COLLATON ST MARY - 1864-6 by J.W.Rowell. SW tower of sandstone.
COLYFORD - St Michael - 1888-9 by R.M.Fulford.
COUNTESS WEAR - St Luke - 1837-8 by Henry Lloyd. Chancel 1895 by Harbottle.
COVE - St John Baptist - 1855 by Edward Ashworth, replacing medieval church.
COWLEY - St Leonard - 1867-8 by Rhode Hawkins.
CREDITON HAMLETS - St Luke - 1835.
CROYDE - St Mary - Small single chamber of 1874 by roadside.
DARTMOUTH - St Barnabas - 1831 with east end of 1884. Now antique store.
DEVONPORT - St Barnabas - By J.P.St Aubyn, c1880.
EXETER - All Saints - 1861-2 by Edward Ashworth. At Whipton.
EXETER - Emmanuel - 1896-7 by Harold Brakspear. SE tower never built.
EXETER - St Mark - 1934-7 by Earnest F Hooper. Red brick.
EXETER - St Matthew - 1881-90 by Fulford & Harvey. Cruciform. Incomplete tower.
EXETER - St Michael - 1865-8 by Rhode Hawkins.
EXMOUTH - Holy Trinity - 1905-7 by G.H.Fellowes Prynne, on site of chapel of 1824.
EXMOUTH - All Saints - 1896-7. Apsed SE Lady Chapel. Tower added 1907.
EXWICK - St Andrew - 1841-2 by John Hayward
HARBERTONFORD - St Peter - 1859 by J.Nottidge. Cruciform with canted apse.
HARTLAND - St John - 1837-9. Clock of 1622 from former town hall on site.
HERNER - St James - Built for the Chichester family in the 1880s.
HOCKWORTHY - St Simon & St Jude - Tower 1848. Rest rebuilt 1864 by Greenway.
HOLLOCOMBE - St Michael & All Angels - 1890-1 by Edward Keenor. Now a house.
HONITON - St Paul - 1835-8 by Charles Fowler on site of chapel-of-ease.
HORRABRIDGE - St John Baptist - 1893 by G.F.Pryne on site of church of 1835.
ILFRACOMBE - St Peter - 1902-3 by G.Fellowes Prynne. Arts & Crafts details.
ILFRACOMBE - St Philip & St James - 1856 by Hayward. NE tower with spire.
IVYBRIDGE - St John - 1882 by Hine & Odgers. North aisle added 1887.
LANDSCOVE - St Matthew - 1849-51 by J.L.Pearson. SE tower with broach spire.
LEE - St Matthew - Chapel-of-ease of 1833, restored by Hayward in 1860.
LOWER BRIXHAM - All Saints - 1819-24 by Lidstone. Rebuilt 1885, 1892, 1900-6.
LOWER HOOE - St John - 1854 by William White.
LYNMOUTH - St John Baptist - 1869-70 by E.Dolby. Enlarged 1908. Tower 1921.
NEWTON ABBOT - St Luke - 1936 by Arthur Martin. Very unusual plan-form.
NEWTON ABBOT - St Michael & All Angels - 1910. Red brick.
NEWTON ABBOT - St Paul - 1859-61 by J.W.Rowell. Cruciform with canted apse.
NORTH BRENTOR - Christ Church - 1856 by Richard Gosling.
NOSS MAYO - St Peter - 1882 by J.P.St Aubyn on site of chapel-of-ease.
OLDRIDGE - Chapal of 1841-3 by John Medley on site of chapel rebuilt in 1789.
PAIGNTON - Christ Church - 1886-8 by E.Gabriel & W.G.Couldrey. Cruciform.
PAIGNTON - St Andrew - 1892-7 by Fulford, Tait & Harvey. West end 1929-30.
PAIGNTON - St George - 1939 by E.Maufe, nave 1962, sacristy 1965.

PAIGNTON - St Paul - 1939 by N.F.Cachemaille Day. NE tower. Cruciform.
PETTON - Neo-Norman chapel of 1846-8 by Gideon Boyce.
PLYMOUTH - Ascension - 1956 by Potter & Hare. Porch tower.
PLYMOUTH - Emmanuel - 1870 by W.H.Read. Extended 1881 by Hine & Odgers.
PLYMOUTH - Holy Spirit - 1960. In Clittaford Rd, Southway.
PLYMOUTH - St Aidan - 1953. Red brick. Old font found in local creek.
PLYMOUTH - St Augustine - 1898-1904 by C.King. Restored after war damage.
PLYMOUTH - Bartholomew - 1958 by A.C.Luxton. In Tavistock Rd.
PLYMOUTH - St Boniface - 1911 by Caroe. In Victoria Rd, St Budeaux.
PLYMOUTH - St Chad - 1955-6 by A.C.Luxton. At Whitleigh Green.
PLYMOUTH - St James The Less - 1958. Red Brick. In Ham Drive, Ham.
PLYMOUTH - St John Evangelist - 1851-5 by Benjamin Ferrey. At Sutton-on-Plym.
PLYMOUTH - St Jude - 1875-6 - by James Hine. By Beaumont Rd & Tothill Rd.
PLYMOUTH - St Luke - 1828 by J.H.Ball. Now a store for the library.
PLYMOUTH - St Mary - 1911 by T.R.Kitsell. Incomplete. At Laira.
PLYMOUTH - St Mary & St Mary Magdalene - 1899 and 1910. Since 1988 a hall.
PLYMOUTH - St Matthias - 1887 by Hine & Odgers. At North Hill.
PLYMOUTH - St Michael - 1843-5 by Benjamin Ferrey. Albert Rd, Morice Town.
PLYMOUTH - St Paul - 1963 by Pearn & Procter. Torridge Rd, Efford.
PLYMOUTH - St Peter - Chancel 1849-50. Nave 1880-2. Large tower of 1906.
PLYMOUTH - St Philip - 1912-13 by N.Alton Blazeley. At Weston Mill.
PLYMOUTH - St Simon - 1903-5 by Harbottle Reed. West front of 1956.
PLYMOUTH - St Thomas - 1907 by Hine, Odgers & May. Royal Navy Ave, Keyham.
ROMANSLEIGH - St Rumon - Rebuilt by Ashworth in 1868. Tower added 1887.
ROUSDON - St Pancras - 1872. Now used by the school as a store.
SAUNTON - St Anne - 1897 by F.J Commin. Chancel; nave never built.
SHEEPWASH - St Lawrence - 1879-80 by J.F.Gould. Tower 1889. Medieval font.
SIDFORD - St Peter - 1867-73 by C.F.Edwards.
SIDMOUTH - All Saints - 1837 by J.H.Taylor. Cruciform.
SIDMOUTH - St Francis - 1929 by W.D.Caroe. West end later.
SOWTON - St Michael - 1844-5 by Harward for the Garratts. Good furnishings.
SPARKWELL - All Saints - Chancel 1904 by Sedding. Older nave and transept.
STARCROSS - St Paul- 1826, remodelled 1854 by David Mackintosh.
STONEHOUSE - St Paul - 1830-1 by Foulston. Chancel 1890 by Hine & Odgers.
TEIGNMOUTH - St Michael - rebuilt 1823 and 1875. Tower 1887-9. S. Chapel 1925.
TEIGNMOUTH - St Peter - 1893-1902 by E.H.Sedding. Arts & Crafts decoration.
TIPTON ST JOHN - St John 1839-40 by John Hayward for the Coleridge family.
TORQUAY - All Saints - 1865-7 by Butterfield. East end and tower 1872-4.
TORQUAY - All Saints - 1883 by J.L.Pearson. Transepts. Polygonal apse.
TORQUAY - Christ Church - 1868 by Habershon, Brock & Webb. SW porch tower.
TORQUAY - Holy Trinity - 1894-6 by J.Watson. NW tower with spire.
TORQUAY - St John Baptist - 1897 by E.H.Harbottle. Nave remodelled 1924.
TORQUAY - St John Evangelist - 1861-73 by G.E.Street, replacing chapel of 1822.
TORQUAY - St Luke - 1863 by Arthur Blomfield. Gabled north aisle. NE turret.
TORQUAY - St Mary - 1856-7 by Anthony Salvin. Converted to a theatre in 1986.
TORQUAY - St Martin - 1938 by N.Cachemaille Day. Neo-Norman.
TORQUAY - St Mary Magdalene - 1843-9 by Salvin. In Union St, Upton.
TORQUAY - St Matthew - 1895-1904 by Nicholson & Corlette.
TORQUAY - St Mathias - 1858 by Salvin, south side 1865, east end 1882-5.
WEST HILL - St Michael - 1845-6 by Wollaston. West extension 1978.
WESTWARD HO! - Holy Trinity - 1867 by W.C.Oliver.
WESTWOOD - St Paul - 1873 by Ashworth.
WITHLEIGH - St Catherine - Small chapel of 1846 by Hayward.
WOODBURY - Christ Church - By William Phillips, opened 1861. Later additions
WOODBURY SALTERTON - Holy Trinity - 1843-4 perhaps by Haywood.
WOOLACOMBE - St Sabinus - 1910 by W.D.Caroe. North aisle added 1950s.
YELVERTON - St Paul - 1910-14 by Nicholson & Corlette. NE tower.
YEOFORD - Holy Trinity - 1891 - Small red brick chapel of 1891.

GLOSSARY OF ARCHITECTURAL TERMS

Abacus	- A flat slab on top of a capital.
Ashlar	- Masonry of blocks with even faces and square edges.
Baroque	- A whimsical and odd form of the Classical architectural style.
Beakhead	- Decorative motif of bird or beast heads, often biting a roll moulding.
Broaches	- Sloping half pyramids adapting an octagonal spire to a square tower.
Cartouche	- A tablet with an ornate frame, usually enclosing an inscription.
Celure	- A panelled or very ornate part of a wagon roof over a screen or altar.
Chancel	- The eastern part of a church used by the clergy.
Chevron Ornament	- A Norman ornament with continuous Vs forming a zig-zag.
Clerestory	- An upper storey pierced by windows lighting the floor below.
Collar Beam	- A tie-beam used higher up near the apex of the roof.
Corbel Table	- A row of corbels supporting the eaves of a roof.
Crossing Tower	- A tower built on four arches in the middle of a cruciform church.
Cruciform Church	- A cross-shaped church with transepts forming the arms of the cross.
Cusp	- A projecting point between the foils of a foiled Gothic arch.
Dado	- The decorative covering of the lower part of a wall or screen.
Decorated	- The architecture style in vogue in England c1300-1380.
Easter Sepulchre	- A recess in a chancel which received an effigy of Christ at Easter.
Elizabethan	- Of the time of Queen Elizabeth I (1558-1603).
Fan Vault	- Vault with fan-like patterns. In fashion from c1440 to 1530.
Flamboyant	- The latest phase of French Gothic, with ogival arches in the tracery.
Fleuron	- A decorative carved flower or leaf.
Foil	- A lobe formed by the cusping of a circle or arch.
Four Centred Arch	- A low, flattish arch with each curve drawn from two compass points.
Gargoyle	- A water spout shaped like an animal or human head below a parapet.
Green Man	- A figure with foliage or fruit coming from the mouth and-or hair, etc.
Head Stops	- Heads of humans or beasts forming the ends of a hoodmould.
Hoodmould	- A projecting moulding above a lintel or arch to throw off water.
Jacobean	- Of the time of King James I (1603-25).
Jamb	- The side of a doorway, window, or other opening.
Lancet	- A long and comparatively narrow window with a pointed head.
Light	- A compartment of a window.
Lintel	- A horizontal stone or beam spanning an opening.
Merlon	- An upstanding part of a crenellated parapet. The indents are crenels.
Miserichord	- Bracket underneath hinged choir stall seat to support standing person.
Mullion	- A vertical member dividing the lights of a window.
Nave	- The part of a church in which the congregation sits or stands.
Norman	- A division of English Romanesque architecture from 1066 to 1200.
Ogival Arch	- Arch of oriental origin with both convex and concave curves.
Parclose Screen	- A screen closing off a chapel from the rest of a church.
Pediment	- Low-pitched gable used in classical and neo-classical architecture.
Perpendicular	- The architectural style in vogue in England c1380-1540.
Pilaster	- Flat buttress or pier attached to a wall.
Piscina	- A stone basin used for rinsing out holy vessels after a mass.
Plinth	- The projecting base of a wall.
Quoins	- Dressed stones at the corners of a building.
Rere-Arch	- An arch on the inside face of a window embrasure or doorway.
Reredos	- Structure behind and above an altar forming a backdrop to it.
Respond	- A half pier or column bonded into a wall and carrying an arch.
Reticulation	- Tracery with a net-like appearence. Current c1330-70.
Rood Screen	- A screen with a crucifix mounted on it between a nave and chancel.
Sedilia	- Seats for clergy (usually three) in the south wall of a chancel.
Sheila-Na-Gig	- A female fertility symbol with the legs wide open to show the vulva.
Spandrel	- The surface between two arches or between an arch and a corner.
Squint	- Opening allowing the main altar to be seen from a subsiderary one.
Tester	- A sounding board above a 17th or 18th century pulpit.
Tie-Beam	- A beam connecting the slopes of a roof at or near its foot.
Tracery	- Intersecting ribwork in the upper part of a later Gothic window.
Transom	- A horizontal member dividing the lights of a window.
Tympanum	- The space between the lintel of a doorway and the arch above it.
Venetian Window	- Window with square headed lights on either side of an arched light.
Victorian	- Of the time of Queen Victoria (1837-1901).
Voussoir	- A wedge shaped stone forming part of an arch.
Wall Plate	- A timber laid longitudinally along the top of a wall.